Critical Communication Studies

Communication and Society

General Editor: James Curran

Critical Communication Studies

Communication, History and Theory in America

Hanno Hardt

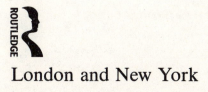

London and New York

First published 1992
by Routledge
11 New Fetter Lane, London EC4P 4EE

Simultaneously published in the USA and Canada
by Routledge
a division of Routledge, Chapman and Hall, Inc.
29 West 35th Street, New York, NY 10001

Typeset in 10/12pt Times by
Falcon Typographic Art Ltd, Edinburgh & London
Printed in Great Britain by
T. J. Press (Padstow) Ltd, Padstow, Cornwall

British Library Cataloguing in Publication Data
Hardt, Hanno
   Critical communication studies: communication, history
   and theory in America. – (Communication and society).
   1. Communication
   I. Title II. Series
   302.2

Library of Congress Cataloging in Publication Data
Hardt, Hanno.
   Critical communication studies: essays on
   communication, history, and theory / Hanno Hardt.
   p. cm. – (Communication and society)
   Includes bibliographical references and index.
   1. Communication – Research – United States. 2.
   Critical theory. 3. Pragmatism. 4. Communication and
culture.
   I. Series: Communication and society (Routledge (Firm))
   P91.3.H37 1992
   302.2—dc20   91 – 16892

ISBN 0–415–06819–3
ISBN 0–415–07137–2 (pbk)

With love
to Nicole, Katreen, and Nina
– and to the memory of Mimi and Apa

Contents

Preface and acknowledgments

> The process of transcendence is as much an incorporation as it is a rejection.
>
> Georg Wilhelm Friedrich Hegel

In recent years communication and media studies in the United States have come under the influence of a body of British literature identified with the intellectual traditions of Richard Hoggart, Raymond Williams and the University of Birmingham Centre for Contemporary Cultural Studies, notably under the leadership of Stuart Hall. Indeed, the writings of the British Cultural Studies group constitute a significant contribution to the field of communication research, representing the most decisive theoretical break in the field of communication and media studies in the United States that has captured the attention of scholarly journals since the domination of traditional sociology a generation ago.

The fascination with new ideas, particularly the continuing challenge of Marxism, the appeal of a European renaissance in the study of culture and society, particularly enhanced by its immediate accessibility as an English language text, and a heightened sense of criticism concerning current definitions of society as basic presuppositions for the use of British Cultural Studies in the realm of communication scholarship in the United States, offer the context for this book.

A major problem of American thought continues to be the question of molding its European heritage to fit the specific needs of American culture. The American encounter with British Cultural Studies is a contemporary development in the intellectual tradition of recreating social theories as an exercise in cultural exploitation. In this case, the development of communication studies represents a convenient vehicle for progressive ideas, including some reformist notions about the field that are rooted in Pragmatism and early American sociology. Theoretical change, on the other hand, constitutes a response to existing theories as determinants of such historical processes and provides insight into the conditions of American communication research. Thus, existing theories of (mass) communication have not only played an important role in the creation of the historical reality of media and society, but their role and function in the definition of democracy, the exercise of political power and the process of everyday life continue to help shape research agendas.

This book explores the development of communication research as a problem of adapting and integrating theoretical constructs as they emerge from a continuing intellectual exchange of social and political ideas located within the specific historical context of American social theories and the renewed challenge of a Marxist perspective. In this context, the book focuses upon the idea of the "critical" as it emerged from the literature of mass communication research in the United States, informed by Pragmatism and the practice of a positivistic social science, more recently expressed elsewhere under the influence of Marxism, particularly by Critical Theory and Cultural Studies. Thus, the term "critical" refers to the rise of social criticism as it emerged from the nineteenth century with the advancement of science and the effects of industrialization. Although frequently linked to socialism and Marx's critique of political economy, social criticism as a scientific approach to solving social problems should be considered in the social and cultural context of different theories which have as their determinate goal the improvement of society. Similarly, the idea of culture should be broadly interpreted to refer to the social context of human existence. As a result, the study of culture has been a concern of many disciplines, including the field of communication studies.

It is widely recognized that the idea of communication represents a shared interest in a social phenomenon that has long occupied a variety of disciplines. American social scientists have been particularly committed to such a study of communication, expressed most recently through an exploration of the processes of ideological representations and struggle with and within the media. They have emphasized the relationship between media, power, and the maintenance of social order. Lately, media sociology has revealed a need for an alternative explanation of media and communication in society that stresses the importance of culture and cultural expressions. Although it has focused on the example of British Cultural Studies as such an appropriate alternative, there had been earlier encounters with a critical, cultural tradition in the American social sciences.

This book is the result of a number of efforts to formulate a historical perspective on critical communication research in the United States. As such, it does not claim to be a comprehensive intellectual history of communication and media studies, but rather an invitation to contemplate the need for such a history. Although various attempts have been made to reconstruct the path of communication science and research in the United States, much is left to be done. The book represents my own effort to help construct a sense of understanding the course of ideas about the centrality of communication in social thought. These ideas emerged from the social and political culture of the United States as a developing country that moved within a few generations from social and political experiments in colonization, urban expansion and industrialization to world leadership in democratic practices. During this time questions of communication and the role of the media became a practical concern of those realizing the power of language and the capabilities of information technologies to transcend cultural and political boundaries. Culture as the arena for political and commercial discourse remains the context for the study of communication, and provides the rationale for the growth of social scientific research interests.

The book focuses on the emergence of a notion of critique that is inherent in the idea of democracy and can be defined as thinking about freedom and responsibility and the contribution that intellectual pursuits can make to the welfare of society. Academic intellectuals, in particular, have a tendency to distance themselves in their own projects and critiques from the conditions of everyday life. This book is an attempt to argue for the proximity of critical communication studies to social and political reality and its potential to contribute to the welfare of society. In doing so, I am suggesting that the notion of praxis become a major consideration in any study of communication.

The book moves through what I consider distinct periods in the history of communication studies in an effort to identify and define the rise of a "critical" perspective by concentrating on representative and significant issues concerning communication and society. For this reason, the reader will find that references to the work of individuals, or the position of research organizations, appear as part of my argument; I felt no obligation to name or list others, perhaps equally important for the development of the field, assuming that many communication theorists or researchers can be identified with specific individual leaders and their agenda-setting role in the field. Thus, I have ignored the obsession to identify "father" figures among communication researchers; I want to suggest, instead, that influences were far more widespread or diverse than can be subsumed under what I would consider a directed and self-serving definition of fraternal leadership. The emergence of communication studies in the United States is too complex to permit such a simple reduction. For one reason, the field has always been fragmented or dissected to reflect specialization which bestowed power and influence. The result has been an aggregate of information about producers, channels and consumers which created a field of communication studies without communication. Second, in order to reintroduce the notion of communication, it becomes necessary to rely on a variety of established considerations of language, symbols and culture. The book also tries to address these issues as they pertain to a critical understanding of society.

At the same time, no attempt has been made to recreate the complexity and variety of philosophical positions, like Pragmatism or Marxism, in their different versions; rather, the focus of my discussion has remained on how historically determined theoretical positions have reflected on questions of communication, media and culture.

The book describes some of the intellectual and professional forces that shaped interests about communication and formed alliances in the pursuit of specific research goals. But the history of communication research is also part of the cultural history of the United States; thus, the direction of communication studies, its ideological habitat, and its theoretical and practical challenges, can only be explained in the interaction of political, social and economic environments with their specific demands on the field for information, and the climate of the educational system, which encourages certain ways of looking at the world.

This book is not about a particular concern with the past, but reflects the encounter with a literature of communication theory that continues to affect our thinking. I believe that notions about communication and its development through various disciplines, as well as the formulation of a critique of society through the perspective of communication, are expressions of an ideological position that rests in the relation between the intellectual practice of communication theorists and history. Such a narrative is hardly linear, and an author faces the dilemma of describing complex, multi-layered conditions or developments in a language that cannot accommodate such complexity. As a result, there is some necessary repetition of the discussion of events or ideas as the study of communication and media moved through various stages of refocusing on issues of society or culture.

The book also attempts to address the question of history and theory, albeit indirectly. There is a need to come to terms with the role of history in the definition of the field, as well as in the study of communication and media. Definitions of terms, areas of scholarly interest, dominations of theories or models of communication can be understood only in their historical substance. They are the products and expressions of historical conditions. It is in this context that the notion of "critical" emerges from the pertinent literature and gains meaning in the discourse of the field. Likewise, theoretical discourse still maintains the status of a marginal activity in communication and media studies for reasons that lie in the historical role of social theories in a practice-oriented environment.

The book addresses the consequences of particular ways of doing communication research for the field; that is, the impact of definitions of communication and delimitations of the field on the process of learning. It is addressed to what C. Wright Mills once called the "feudal structure" of graduate education. The classical tradition of the social sciences, in which communication research rests, is rarely acknowledged, while attitudes about communication studies are entrenched and students move in a closed system of definitions and opportunities towards degrees and promotions. Furthermore, a critique of communication research that remains within its historical boundaries also remains within its system of values and signals its own inability to overcome the status quo. Although changes have occurred in recent years, and it may have become fashionable to introduce courses in "critical" communication to the curriculum, the quality of the commitment to these developments remains unclear.

The book identifies an emerging field of study that had been cut off from the vibrant and controversial discussions of culture in the United States by its location at the margins of a larger discipline and in the realm of specific professional concerns. The result has been the rise of communication research as a technical field whose methodological capabilities attracted the interest of specialists in culture and politics, for instance, while it was unable to advance theoretical explanations in support of its own cause. In addition, the professional nature of graduate programs has led to specializations and careers in the application of sophisticated methodologies; it obscured the cultural or political vision and redirected the field away from the challenges of theory and history.

The book is not intended to provide a discussion of the relationship between theories and the social structure of the United States; much needs to be done to explain in some detail the historical circumstances of such a relationship. This would include an analysis of the educational system and the ways in which social theory, and more specifically communication and media theory, have been presented, preserved, reinforced or challenged in the university environment. Such a project would involve a study of those who reproduce the dominant paradigm of communication research and their specific intellectual, political and economic dependencies within contemporary society. It would also require the identification of dissent and the location of various alternative positions on the margins of academic institutions, including those individual voices whose passionate and intelligent response to the organization of communication research in university environments remains confined to professional meetings and personal conversations.

The segmentation of intellectual space is a major problem in modern society; it is also obvious in communication studies, which is one of the prime examples of the development of academic interests into manageable and controllable areas of intellectual activity. The book reflects the results of these organizational schemes for a field whose very mission must be the integration of a number of disciplines and areas of intellectual endeavor under considerations like culture or society.

Contemporary communication research suffers from the mechanistic orientation of its practitioners, who should not be excused from sharing in the social and political realities of media studies. They are reluctant participants in the convergence of the field with a number of disciplines. Communication research is the product of a social-scientific culture which is limited by its own language; this book intends to show that the future of communication research belongs to a generation of scholars whose professional interests and intellectual inclinations have moved them beyond technical expertise and disciplinary boundaries to considerations of culture and politics and the role of communication in the definitions of society that benefit from multiple explanations of reality.

Traditional communication research rejected the partisan nature of knowledge and settled for the pursuit of concrete truths. Thus, the book is also about the potential of negation and resistance to forms of understanding communication research in the tradition of empirical sociology and all its features of an atheoretical, ossified system of delivering functional communication in the interest of dominant social and economic powers. There is intellectual richness and originality in considerations of culture that have been marginalized but maintain the possibility of rising against the dominant paradigm of communication research.

The field of communication studies needs a vision of theory as an instructive and useful instrument in a search for conditions which allow individuals to live a truly human existence. I hope that this book offers some insights into the long struggle towards this goal.

A word about terminology: throughout the book communication research, communication studies, (mass) communication research, or communication and media studies (or research) are used interchangeably. The usage of these terms was preferred to others, like communications, mass communication(s), or mass media, which are widespread in the literature. My reasons for selecting this terminology are partly historical, since communication and communication research appeared first in the literature, and partly because I share a dislike for the use of "mass" communication, which arose from concerns about propaganda and public opinion and deemphasizes the involvement of the subject in the process of communication.

The concepts of Pragmatism, Critical Theory and Cultural Studies appear in capitalized form to indicate their specific philosophical or theoretical meaning; thus Critical Theory refers to the Frankfurt School and Cultural Studies indicates the work that emerged from the Birmingham Centre.

Since the book is the result of my long-standing research interest in issues related to the history and theory of the field, parts have appeared elsewhere during the last few years. They include "British Cultural Studies and the Return of the 'Critical' in American Mass

Communication Research: Accommodation or Radical Change?" in *Journal of Communication Inquiry*, 10 (2) (Summer 1986), 117–25, and, as an expanded version, in "The Return of the 'Critical' and the Challenge of Radical Dissent: Critical Theory, Cultural Studies and American Mass Communication Research," in *Communication Yearbook* 12 (1989), 550–600; other parts also appeared in "Between Pragmatism and Marxism," *Critical Studies in Mass Communication* 6 (4) (December 1989), 421–6, in "Paul F. Lazarsfeld: Communication Research as Critical Research," in *Paul F. Lazarsfeld*, edited by Wolfgang R. Langenbucher, Munich: Verlag Ölschläger, 1990, 243–57, in "The Conscience of Society: Leo Lowenthal and Communication Research," *Journal of Communication* 41 (3) (Summer 1991), in press, and in "Alternative Visions of Democracy: Theories of Culture and Communication in the United States," in *Communication and Democracy*, edited by Slavko Splichal and Janet Wasko, Norwood, NJ: Ablex, 1991 (in press).

And finally, this book is the reflection of an intellectual and cultural perspective that is rooted in the personal and professional experience of living and working in the United States and Europe, and of a particular interest in the migration of ideas that began with my work on the influence of German scholarship on early American sociology.

Specifically, I want to acknowledge a number of institutions and individuals, whose material assistance, professional assurance or ideological solidarity have provided the context for my work over the last two decades. They include the University of Iowa and its School of Journalism and Mass Communication, the Institut für Publizistik at the Universität Münster, Germany, and Edvard Kardelj University and its Faculty of Sociology, Political Science and Journalism in Ljubljana, Yugoslavia; Winfried B. Lerg at Münster, Wolfgang Langenbucher at the Institut für Publizistik, Universität Wien, Austria, and Slavko Splichal at Ljubljana. I want to thank my colleagues, in particular James Curran at Goldsmiths' College, London, who has supported this project throughout its final stages, Ed McLuskie, whose intellectual interest has been a source of constant encouragement, Robert Craig, who has always generously shared his ideas, Kuan-Hsing Chen, David Tetzlaff, and Don McComb, among the recent editors of the *Journal of Communication Inquiry*, whose explorations of communication and media helped reinforce my own work, Beverly James, who provided a critical reading of the manuscript, and graduate students in my seminars throughout the years, whose intellectual curiosity has been a constant challenge and stimulation. I am indebted to their wisdom and patience. I would also like to thank my colleagues at Iowa, Kathryn Cirksena, who responded to a portion of chapter 5, Bonnie Brennen, who read the completed manuscript with great care, Molly O'Brien, who was my research assistant during the final phase of this project, and Maynard Cuppy, whose technical assistance has made my life much easier over the years. Last, not least, I owe much to Vida Zei, whose reading of various versions of the manuscript during the spring of 1990 helped more to sustain my efforts than she would be willing to admit.

Iowa City, November 1990   Hanno Hardt

Chapter 1

On defining the issues
Communication, history and theory

> A history of the past is worthless except as a documented way
> of talking about the future.
>
> Kenneth Burke

The literature of communication research in the United States is
rich in accumulated insights into the workings of communication
and the role and function of the media. It also reflects the
dominance of a strong and persistent social science tradition
that has survived various theoretical challenges during the last
sixty years.

Recently a number of historical accounts have appeared to help
document the development of the field and, in some cases, to
celebrate the accomplishments of a generation of communication
researchers. Such a need to trace the course of communication
research throughout its rise to independence and credibility within
a behavioral science tradition may be the inevitable sign of
age, the expression of a moment of certainty when truths arise
from expert self-reflection to produce a retrospective vision of
social-scientific discoveries that have helped define the meanings
of communication in modern society. This desire for a sense of
history caters to the need for recognition, but it also reifies and
reproduces the reality of communication research and challenges
the imagination.

An interest in historical explanations of the field, however, may
also serve to reinforce dominant expressions of theory and reassure
research practices at a time of change, when self-doubt, mixed with
the challenge of competing theories, threatens the foundations
of dominant articulations of communication research and their
traditional domain.

In either case, reflections on the contribution of communication
research to society, or realizations of intellectual challenges and the
prospects that the measured calm of a paradigm dialogue may erupt
into a paradigm struggle, constitute attempts to define the status of

the field. They are also evidence that communication research benefits from the general search for social and political explanations of society and continues to be part of an interdisciplinary theoretical debate.

The efforts of communication research throughout this century were rarely accompanied by self-reflection or directed by a self-conscious analysis of its own history, except for periodic reviews of the position of the field when the number of research perspectives, making claims on the centrality of communication in their pursuit of knowledge, increased the need for recognizing past accomplishments of the field; or more recently, when direct attacks on the authority of a traditional social science approach and its underlying philosophical premises persisted within the communication research establishment. Thus, a major effort to "rethink communication" from within the field was launched in the 1980s, beginning with a special issue of the *Journal of Communication* that dealt with the "ferment in the field" (1983), to the recent publication of position statements and research perspectives (Brenda Dervin *et al.*, 1989).

Dervin and her fellow editors noted the pluralistic challenges to traditional notions of the field, acknowledging widespread dissatisfaction with the state of communication inquiry; it is particularly interesting, however, that they wondered about technical-administrative aspects of organizing the field in the face of diverse ideological and intellectual expressions about communication by raising questions about constituting "a scholarly community," constructing "a coherent educational curriculum," establishing "disciplinary standards of evaluation," or developing "a coherent understanding of the knowledge of the field and our own place within it" (1989: II, 27). Their overtly administrative concerns seem to confirm the idea that the problem of theorizing about communication has always coexisted with attempts by academic units or professional organizations to harness theoretical and practical concerns.

Since the editors present their eclectic selections as reflections of communication studies (1989: I, 17), they invite some conclusions about the type and range of conceptions occupying the field. Indeed, the neglect of areas like political economy or feminist studies, in particular the emphasis on "cultural" studies, and the reliance on external expertise for the definition of its status within the social sciences, especially in the case of Rosengren, Giddens and Hall, help solidify an evolving definition of communication and offer, at least implicitly, descriptions of its exact intellectual boundaries.

More importantly, these deliberations reflect the dilemma of a field whose search for a theoretical grounding proceeds without an adequate understanding of its own intellectual history as a significant source of knowledge about its position among and within various disciplines. They had been initiated by a perceived need for critical insights into the relationship between communication studies and social theory and remain part of an ongoing process of legitimizing communication research and its relevance to contemporary analyses of culture. Although Anthony Giddens's conclusion about the centrality of communication studies "to what social theory is about and to what social science is about" (1989: I, 65) must have been viewed by communication research interests as a welcome reassurance of its status, it contributed little to an understanding of the field.

But it is equally plausible that the invitation to rethink communication reflects the tendencies of organized pressures to exhibit intellectual uniformity rather than to encourage an intellectual enterprise to experience a variety of paradigmatic choices; as Carolyn Marvin has pointed out, one cannot avoid such institutional moves toward "the elimination of intellectual variety, and perhaps vitality," and she concluded that "orthodoxy is no index of intellectual progress" (1989: II, 188). Therefore, the sense of closure as described by the type of questions concerning the intellectual, administrative and educational unity of the field as a community may be an indication of an anxiety to proceed, perhaps for political reasons, with a search for unifying principles. In any event, this approach is a strong reminder of the scientific desire during much earlier periods in the history of the social sciences to discover laws of human nature and find reassurance in the predictability of social practice. The practicality of such technical uniformity has been reinforced in a quite different fashion by Robert Craig's return to the original notion of philosophy as the foundation of all sciences. By locating communication as a practical art in a practical context at the center of any movement toward a unifying paradigm (1989: I, 118), he offered a "new" practical discipline of communication that related the contributions of empiricism, Critical Theory and hermeneutics.

Nevertheless, the quest for social knowledge and the prospects of rediscovering the subject have always been stronger than the unifying efforts of an organizational or territorial logic that characterizes the struggle for academic power.

At the same time, there also emerged an appreciation of the need to theorize and the need to tolerate other perspectives; that is to say, to recognize that communication research is aligned with a variety of substantive areas and disciplines from which it gains legitimacy and, ultimately, the strength to prevail politically over others. After all, the current practice of communication research has changed very little, as Craig has pointed out (1989: 1, 105), while new ideas employ different strategies to establish their own orthodoxies elsewhere.

Most importantly, throughout this period of rethinking communication, there have been scant references to the pivotal role of history and historical analysis. As a result, interpretations of the course of communication studies have exhausted themselves in definitional issues of disciplinary or intellectual boundaries or questions of periodicity while ignoring conceptual or analytical approaches to the history of communication research within the larger realm of social theory and history.

In general, the result of historical inquiry into the field has been fragmentary, mostly episodical or autobiographical in its accounts of the dominant empirical perspectives of communication research and contributes more to the reinforcement of specific theoretical positions than to answers about communication research in the context of social theories.[1]

The sporadic appearance of these historical assessments, however, offers answers which may provide the key to understanding what communication research is, the reasons for it, and its claims of being an autonomous science. In fact, it can be argued that communication research, like sociology and history, for instance, studies people and institutions in specific cultural, political and economic environments and under conditions of change; that its reasons for existence are buried in its history within academic disciplines and their relationship to the political and economic demands of society; and that its ambition to be recognized as an autonomous discipline has failed because of the ambiguity of its own claim to theory.

The identity of communication research as an integrated field of inquiry rests on the recognition of socio-historical interests in the study of communication, despite the initial impact of an American social science tradition that underestimated and ignored the significance of its historical dimension, and in light of developing notions of historical sociology or social history that carry the promise of a common terrain of study and common theoretical problems. In this sense, communication research shares the history and the problems of sociology, in particular, including its failure to understand and appreciate the need for historical analysis.

The prevalent nature of American communication research has been empirical, ahistorical and unreflective, recent criticism in journals and professional organizations notwithstanding. Its proximity to Pragmatism has provided a philosophical context for the celebration of instrumental values and the practicality of human action that reflects the utilitarian nature of liberal-pluralism. In this context, communication research has operated with a functional definition of the individual that emerged from the requirements of a technologically driven society in which cultural attitudes, that is, the potential of literary or historical explanations of social existence, gave way to the demands of industrial growth and technological superiority. Under these circumstances, historical analysis turns into a search for evidence that locates communication research in the path of scientific knowledge and on the side of social progress.

This approach to history reflects the success of the social sciences and the performance of communication research, in particular, in helping to produce a social climate that has resulted in a general lack of historical consciousness in society at large. Consequently, the understanding of the relationship between past and future and the need to act upon the present conditions of existence, that is, the dialectic between historical consciousness and ahistorical practice, has been upset. The loss of history was replaced by an obsession with facts and events to maintain a sense of direction, and communication research as an applied social science focused on the contemporariness of social or political problems. But by failing to look inward, communication research also failed to move forward.

The absence of history in communication research reflects a general condition of society. It coincides with the decline of dominant systems, beginning with the demise of grand social theories and concluding with the fall of great political powers. They are being replaced by a series of competing interests representing theoretical or political compromises or variations of dominant systems. Thus, the waning eras of functionalism and Marxism are characterized by the primacy of methodological and epistemological issues, while the death of communism is celebrated by an aging Western capitalism. It has provoked a search for new alliances among old constituencies and for new villains in an illusionary struggle for world domination. These recent developments are reminiscent of Alvin Gouldner's observations about the demise of transitional systems of power a few years ago when he remarked that

> The dying are entitled to a moment of insight and self-recognition. The old moneyed class in the West may discover that its deepest historical affinity with the political elite in the East is that both were transitional classes. In the East, the Vanguard Party was the communist equivalent of the Protestant Reformation; once having paved the way for the New Class, it (like Protestantism) becomes a hollow ideological shell.
>
> (1979: 93)

Twenty years later, the world has recognized the transitional nature of social and political theories and their exponents.

More specifically, the regime of Parsonian social theory has lost its exclusive influence on social thought because of its insistence on reducing social life to the idea of functions and equilibria. It operated in an ahistorical context and has been increasingly delegitimized by concrete social and political events in the United States and elsewhere. But most importantly perhaps, in the context of communication, "functionalist theories have lacked adequate accounts of human action," according to Giddens, who claimed that "human agents appear in Parsons's scheme . . . as 'cultural dopes,' not as actors who are highly knowledgeable (discursively and tacitly) about the institutions they produce and reproduce in and through their actions" (1981: 18).

In contrast, Giddens has proposed a theory of structuration which acknowledges the "duality of structure," by which he meant that "structured properties of social systems are simultaneously the *medium and outcome of social acts*" and suggested that "all social action consists of social practices, situated in time–space, and organized in a skilled and knowledgeable fashion by human agents" (1981: 19). Implicit in the notion of time–space as a constitutive element of social systems is the idea of history as an integral part of social theory. Efforts to recast functionalism, on the other hand, have not been able to restore the traditional grip of Parsons's functionalism on the social sciences.

Similarly, contemporary Marxism has embarked on the long march through history, from Marx and Hegel to Critical Theory and French structuralism. Its power has resided in a capacity for self-criticism and the seemingly endless creative energy of an intellectual commitment to reconstituting Marxism in different historical moments. Although attacked, reduced in its claims, and significantly altered by contemporary theorists, its revolutionizing utopian spirit has survived in an ambiguous and delimiting way and emerges sporadically in an urgent plea to respond to the real conditions of society. Marxism remains committed to providing intellectual leadership, it is imbedded in practice and encourages innovative and interdisciplinary analysis, particularly when it preserves its political dimension and considers a conception of human practice that realizes the active, practical relations among human actors and between human actors and their material environment.

Consequently, a series of theoretical perspectives, including hermeneutics, phenomenology and structuralism, has begun to replace the great theories, vying for the attention of scholars returning to the safety of old orthodoxies or trying to attract others who had turned completely away from the reconstruction of social theory. The resurgence of Marxism during the last decades, reflecting the extraordinary intellectual diversity of Western Marxism after the Second World War, marks an essential contribution to the encouragement of social theory in general.

Communication research moved from social or cultural concerns to predominantly social-scientific practices, particularly since the nineteenth century, replacing the earlier work of the Chicago School. Lately, however, communication research has been confronted with the emerging centrality of culture and cultural practice in contemporary theoretical discourse, including the requirements of historical understanding. Indeed, the idea of communication constitutes a point of contact between ideologically distinct approaches to the study of society on a terrain whose boundaries for explicating Marxist and non-Marxist theories often remain blurred in the definitions of critical and phenomenological approaches to communication.

By succumbing to a scientific approach the identity of communication research merged into the dominant structure of society, where it was absorbed in the reproduction of power and the maintenance of the economic system, and in the language of domination, and lost its ability to recognize its own history. Yet, recalling history remains a necessary condition for mapping a course of action; it is the key to identity and understanding.

The fate of communication research in the United States may well rest in its ability to recover its sense of history. This means that a discussion of the path of communication research must move beyond its reconstructed biography on to the contemporary terrain of theoretical discourse where the historical perspective dominates social theory and theorizing affects the use of history. The inability to recognize the relationship between history and theory and to consider the historical under the methodological pressures of the prevalent social-scientific mode of inquiry has seriously reduced the role of communication research to catering to the currents of contemporary priorities.

On the other hand, the "discovery" of history, not as a particular discipline but as a method of inquiry by a number of other academic fields of study, including literary studies and feminism, and the recovery of the notion of culture as the appropriate environment for the study of human actors, have already led to a different kind of scholarship that invents, borrows and returns ideas about communication without much respect for the sanctity of a particular field of social research or for the pressures of uniformity and performance within a given paradigm. It amounts to a rediscovery of the centrality of communication as a philosophical/theoretical concept within the context of thinking about the complexity of the social.

Thus, communication research may disappear completely, absorbed by a series of cultural or political and economic interests in the relationship between human subjects and society, whose ideas of Cultural Studies embrace questions of communication and who rely on communication research purely for topical references or methodological expertise. There is also the possibility, however, that the dominant perspective of communication research will adapt to the evolving conditions of multi-disciplinary analyses of the social environment by yielding to alternative definitions or visions of studying society with the result of changing the field forever. In either case, the boundaries of communication research are shifting to accommodate the diverse sites of communication in the study of culture and society.

The terrain of communication research is vast, encompassing the concerns of historians of civilization and theorists of society, who have always been drawn to the idea of language and communication as basic elements in the definition of humanity and in the construction of cultures. The notion of communication involves the use and application of the means of communication, ranging from the utilization of language to the production and reproduction of social realities through media. Raymond Williams once offered an appropriate reminder of the centrality of communication in the study of societies when he suggested that a "definition of language is always, implicitly or explicitly, a definition of human beings in the world" (1977: 21). It was also an appeal to consider the cultural dimensions of communication, which stretch beyond traditional boundaries of scholarly disciplines and become a new territory of cultural inquiry. In fact, the identification of communication research with the directions of specific academic disciplines, like sociology or psychology, is a product of a historical process that must be open to interpretation and reevaluation as these disciplinary boundaries are beginning to shift with the recognition of different theoretical and methodological needs.

A historical understanding of communication as human practice and as a means of production is also a prerequisite for an informed critique of the contemporary conditions of society, particularly when it is necessary to transcend the current stage of social and economic practice and to propose concrete steps toward a democratic system of communication.

Indeed, the ultimate goal of historical and theoretical insights into communication and society must be to help formulate a political agenda; these times require a type of communication research that addresses the definite conditions of social existence, including the need for change, and the potential contributions to building a better society. The preparation for alternative ways of looking at communication in society rests on a version of communication research that is able to conceive of differences and that appeals to the imagination which is rooted in historical consciousness. That is to say, the notion of change contains elements of remembrance and desire and an understanding of contemporary conditions that relies on reacting to images of the past and prospects of the future. Heidegger stressed the idea that history is not synonymous with the past; for the past is precisely what is no longer happening. And much less is history the merely contemporary, which never happens, but merely "passes," comes and goes by. History as happening is an acting and being acted upon which pass through the present, which are determined from out of the future, and which take over the past. It is precisely the present that vanishes in happening.

(1961: 36)

Such a view of history places the human subject at the center, identified and bound by the temporal determination of existence; it reflects Dilthey's influence on Heidegger, but is also reminiscent of Marxist writings that share a commitment to the concrete conditions of social practice. Dilthey talked about the individual as a historical being, for instance, "determined by his place in time and space and his position in the interaction of cultural systems and communities" (1962: 79). Its contemporary importance is reflected in the work of Anthony Giddens who has insisted that "social theory *must acknowledge, as it has not done previously, time–space intersections as essentially involved in all social existence*" (1979: 54).

In this context theory reveals itself as being historical; it is a social critique that is historical itself in its articulation of the relation between social practices and history. Social theory and theorizing depend on the specific historical conditions of social theorists in their dialogical contexts. Consequently, an understanding of history becomes a subjective, culturally privileged experience; Mikhail Bakhtin once said that there

is no first and last discourse, and dialogical context knows no limits (it disappears into an unlimited past and in our unlimited future). Even past meanings, that is those that have arisen in the dialogue of past centuries, can never be stable (completed once and for all, finished), they always change (renewing themselves) in the course of the dialogue's subsequent development, and yet to come,

and he insisted that "every meaning will celebrate its rebirth" (Todorov, 1984: 110). Bakhtin offered a humanistic outlook on the study of culture in which the human actor in his historicity becomes the center for understanding the realities of individual experience.

Horkheimer has also talked about the relatedness of history to time which resides "in the continuous alteration of the theoretician's existential judgment on society, for this judgment is conditioned by its conscious relation to the historical practice of society" (1972: 234). Such historical practice involves the experience and expression of culture, it engages human actors in their relations to social, political and economic institutions and provides a rationale for ways of doing and being. Thus, history is more than the reconstruction of the past; it is the experience of its effects and an articulation of such a confrontation with the past. There is, then, a relatedness of history to theory that is constituted in the relationship between theorists and their cultural environment. Theories are the product of historical practice within a cultural setting; they emerge from such environments as contemporary explanations of society.

Communication research in the United States is the result of a historical process that involved a particular societal setting in which explanations of communication met expectations of experiences with social or political conditions. In this sense, an understanding of communication coincided with notions of democracy and community and fitted into the ideas of a liberal-pluralist society in which the functional definition of individuals and their relationship with each other and society prevailed. In fact, the longevity of the dominant interests in communication research were guaranteed by the stability of political and economic conditions and the support of commercial interests in social research. They were engaged in the support of a status quo that provided a comfortable location among applied social sciences and helped reinforce a rationale for dominant communication research practices.

However, periods of stability are also periods of transformation and competition for domination and control. The development of communication research reflects such moments of adjustment to specific social and political conditions throughout modern times.

Thus, theories of communication that supported the notions of participation and democracy gave way to one-sided considerations of uses and effects in an atmosphere of warfare and commercial struggle. For instance, the vision of the tranquillity of communities organized around the idea of communication, the rise of a Great Society out of the plains of America, and the egalitarian nature of communication that conferred status on its participants and their intellectual abilities to join in the democratic experience reflected the idealism of an age that saw the rise of science and industry as a liberating force. The growth and prosperity of a rapidly changing society found theoretical confirmation in the neo-Darwinism of the 1920s and the functionalism of the 1930s, and shaped ideas about communication that emphasized the integration of individuals in the process of labor and consumption.

During this period communication research shifted from considering communication in terms of relationships, or notions of sharing and community, to questions of power and analyses of control and manipulation. Consequently, the idea of communication as a creative, intellectual process involving individuals and their social and cultural contributions to society was replaced by the notion of audiences, that is, by the passive and irresistibly open-minded condition of people whose understanding of participation was reduced to responding to the needs of an industrialized society.

Such views of the individual as object evolved with the spread of distrust and hatred and feelings of insecurity, caused by wars, economic instability and ideological isolation that have prevailed through most of this century. These conditions appeared with the beginning of the First World War and continued after the success of the Soviet Union, when the need for territorial claims was gradually replaced by ideological demands on the hearts and minds of people.

The development of communication research occurred under conditions of social and political upheavals; it coincided with the growth of the United States as an industrial superpower and benefitted from the domestic and foreign consequences of such changes. The production and dissemination of ideologically charged messages in the form of commercial advertising or political propaganda became a major concern; it was supported by industry and successive governments and reproduced in educational systems in the guise of patriotism. The fact that nationalism remains an effective if not overpowering force in the United States is the result of a strong homogenizing industrial culture.

Communication research as an applied social science participated in the creation of a social and political environment that was defined more frequently by references to its accessibility through formal channels of information than by its inherent cultural diversity. This perspective produced studies of messages and effects that privileged producers; it also reflected the presence of functionalism which, according to Giddens, accords "a priority to the object over the subject, or in some sense, to structure over action" (1979: 50).

In fact, communication research prospered in an entrepreneurial atmosphere in which the sense of culture and learning was redefined to fit the conditions of commerce. Over time this meant that the idea of education and the support of institutions of higher learning as sources of enlightenment were abandoned for notions of socialization and technical training to accommodate the rising demands for commercial relevancy. In the realm of the American ideal, the success of democracy relied on the generosity of those in control of economic power, for whom culture became a business and participation a financial investment. The emphasis on producing mass entertainment, rather than on the creation of art or on the potential enrichment of society through the encouragement of cultural diversity, yielded to commercial considerations and left the definition and support of creative activities to private enterprise or patronage. Paradoxically, even the accomplishment of a cultural avant-garde remains identified with its economic success, that is, its exploitation by the machinery of mass culture.

The commodification of society has also extended deeply into communication research, where dominant practitioners not only came to depend on the inevitable cycle of supply and demand, but also found their political strength in it. Indeed, university-level departments of journalism, communication and mass communication studies continue to respond to the need for expertise with professional programs that satisfy industrial clients and maintain a strong political base within academic circles. The voices of dissent were drowned in a chorus of approval some time ago when communication research won acceptance and respectability in the marketplace.

Communication research has supported the politics of modernization by submitting to an ideology of progress that was reminiscent of the Pragmatism of the 1920s, except that its goal became to strengthen the bureaucracies of power at the expense of the notion of participation as individual practice. The new technologies of communication, with their potential for saturating society, also produced new knowledge about the consequences of communication. They resulted in new forms and structures of a public discourse that was conducted through a commercial media system and supported by a culture industry that helped create needs and promote consumption. Conversations of culture, on the other hand, which are diverse, creative and individualistic in their historical existence, were significantly affected, if not reduced or discouraged by the politics of mass production.

The rise of communication research as a major social-scientific concern was aided by the demands of the marketplace and supported by the tradition of American functionalism. It was guided by the developments in sociology and psychology, in particular, and by the strong myth of "father" figures whose presence and stature in other disciplines also affected the definition of communication, including the understanding of theory and methodology; their activities and the force of the subsequent myth-making directed the field toward utilitarian considerations. David Manning White's earlier suggestion that "a science can progress, can be 'great,' even if there are no 'great' men in it" (1964: 546) supports the conclusion that the force of once-established conventions continued to direct the ways of thinking about communication beyond the initial phases of a new social-scientific perspective of communication research.

Specifically, the prevailing interests in American communication research drew on a social science environment that produced functionalism as a major theoretical position and its practitioners who dominated the field, including the study of communication. In fact, functionalism was "virtually coextensive with theory," according to Hawthorn, who felt that it "served to constitute a professional value" among American sociologists (1976: 214). It was a perspective imbued with optimism reminiscent of American Pragmatism, based on the belief in the perpetuity of the social system and the capacity to overcome instabilities or disorders. Communication as a social process could play a major role in the maintenance of the social system, and communication research, with its potential for generating knowledge about the relationship between people and political or economic structures in society, rose in importance, politically and academically.

The functionalism of communication research originated with the work of Paul Lazarsfeld, Robert Merton and Charles Wright, in particular, who contributed to a working definition of functional analysis in search of the specifications of communication and media consequences. The presence of functional analysis in the field of mass communication studies has been discussed by Roger Brown, who talked about "something of a vogue for the use of Merton's paradigm," noting that it was "somewhat mechanically" followed (1970: 55), and Gerald Kline, who concluded that the "major *leitmotiv* of communication research has been functionalist from the beginning" (1972: 26), although more recently Sari Thomas has argued that "functionalism has had virtually no place in mainstream communication theory and research" (1989: II, 376). Returning to original sources of functionalist thought, she insisted that uses and gratification approaches, in particular, have violated the traditional components, consisting of culturalism, conservationalism and relationalism, by not analyzing the phenomena "in the context of social integration and maintenance" (1989: II, 387–8).

Nevertheless, in his earlier review of functional analysis, Wright provided a number of examples of the widespread use of a functional perspective and suggested that it showed the "intellectual attractiveness and viability of a theoretical orientation coming into its time"; and he concluded that as "mass communication research enters the last quarter of the twentieth century, functional analysis appears live and well" (1975: 198). Although various modifications were introduced throughout the next decade, particularly in the form of what McQuail has called "individual functionalism" (1987: 72), which emerged primarily as "uses and gratification" research, there have been no major reconsiderations of the functionalist position; thus, contemporary analyses of communication and media and discussions of mass communication theory in the more recent introductory literature still proceed on the basis of a well-preserved structural functional paradigm (DeFleur and Ball-Rokeach, 1989: 125).

The preoccupation with a functional perspective grew out of the response to a Western utilitarian culture that Alvin Gouldner described as placing

> a great stress upon winning or losing, upon success or failure as such, rather than upon the character of the intention that shapes a person's course of action or upon the conformity of his intention with a preestablished rule or model of propriety.
> (1970: 65)

Notions of outcomes or effects become central concerns in a society in which the value of individuals or objects is related to their potential uses, which leads to attempts to determine the nature or extent of their consequences. The success of such activities, however, rests on knowledge as an "all-purpose utility in middle class society," according to Gouldner, who also suggested that in a "utilitarian culture knowledge and science are shaped by strongly instrumental conceptions" (1970: 69). In such a society cultural values become "desirable but dispensable graces" (1970: 75), contributing to the definitional problem of uselessness that affects the interpretation of social communication and cultural practice.

Instead, communication is defined in terms of effectiveness or efficiency, concentrating on the functions of messages or on the abilities of individuals or groups to process information, rather than in terms of individual intentions, cultural identity, or historical moments and problems of freedom and equality, for instance. In fact, these latter perspectives address the need to explore the conditions under which consequences become functional, that is, the specific conditions of culture.

The aftermath of the Second World War, with its readjustments to a peacetime economy, increasing social unrest and external threats of political instability, provided the societal context for a functionalist approach to the creation of a system inventory. It was based on Wright's definition of mass communication as "a special kind of social communication involving distinct operating conditions, primary among which are the nature of the audience, of the communication experience, and of the communicator" (1975: 5). He proposed a series of basic research questions that continued to dominate the field of (mass) communication research with alternating emphases between social and individual concerns, in particular (1975: 11).

Thus, communication research developed in a utilitarian atmosphere of a social science that focused on order and preferred the context of real social issues, pushing aside the complexity of theoretical problems for the business of investigating empirical phenomena ranging from communication behavior to media structures. It represented the "social science of a utilitarian culture" which, according to Gouldner, "always tends towards a theoryless empiricism, in which the conceptualization of problems is secondary and energies are instead given over to questions of measurement, research or experimental design, sampling or instrumentation" (1970: 82). Communication research was part of such a utilitarian culture in which the specter of facing a conceptual vacuum was successfully avoided by the mounting presence of industrial interests. It responded successfully to what Gouldner has called "the common-sense concerns and practical interests of clients, sponsors and research funders," which makes sociology and, by extension, communication research useful to them (1970: 82). The result was a type of problem orientation that concentrated on the notion of applicability as defined by the ideological context. It was also reflected in George Gerbner's implied ethics which called on "Students of communication" not to "shrink from defining their field where the problems of communication are, rather than where solutions might be easiest to find" (1962: 103).

In this context, communication research served to provide knowledge about the use of messages and media for purposes of maintaining control and stability of political or economic systems. As a participant in the world of commerce and industry communication research supported a fundamental belief in the survival of the social system and the role of the media to make a significant contribution to the maintenance and strength of society. It joined a conservative tradition and catered to the interests of those dedicated to preserving the status quo rather than to the desires of others who sought the opportunity to build on the conditions of social change.

Nevertheless, under increasing moments of instability at home and abroad and questions about its adequacy as a social theory of the postwar period, functionalism in the United States reacted to the potential of social change, and began to adopt a language of evolutionism that was based upon the acknowledgement of innovation and the need for adaptive capacities, which Parsons described as "prerequisites for socio-cultural development" (1964: 356); they included technology, kinship, language and religion which, according to Parsons, are the minimum requirements to "mark a society as truly human" (1964: 342). According to Gouldner, the problems of dealing with social change contributed to an increasing crisis of functionalism and an intellectual challenge which eventually led to a convergence with Marxism during the 1960s (1970: 369).

Despite a rising critique of functionalism, however, including the attacks of C. Wright Mills on "grand theory" and "abstracted empiricism" (1959), alternative interests in communication research with different theoretical propositions remained largely unsuccessful.

For instance, initial concerns about the role of communication in society had evolved from symbolic interactionism, which represents a major contribution to American social theory. It emerged from the work of George Herbert Mead and concentrated on the primacy of the acting subject. The reconceptualization of individuals in their relationship with groups stressed the notion of interaction and symbolic behavior, moving from earlier physical conceptions of society as an aggregate of individuals to the idea of shared meanings and language as a means of communication that united people. It was the concept of interaction that occupied the attention of contemporary sociologists and helped shape research agendas. In fact, the relationship between the individual and the social group provided an essential element in the rise of communication research, where questions of the way in which individuals interacted or associated with their respective environments through language and media institutions, in particular, were initially raised. Symbolic interactionism was a theoretical development that suited American conditions, not unlike functionalism, and, as Shaskolsky argued, could only have happened in the United States. He concluded that

> symbolic interaction theory is a worthy attempt to create a unique philosophical rationale for the finer aspects of American society – for what is known at the more colloquial level as the American way of life, characterized as it is by respect for the individual and a belief in gradual change to meet society's fluctuating needs.

(1970: 20)

Elsewhere, Giddens suggested "a partial accommodation between symbolic interactionism and functionalism in American sociology: the former is held to be a 'micro-sociology,' dealing with small-scale 'interpersonal' relations, while more embracing 'macro-sociological' tasks are left to the latter" (1979: 50).

Within more recent developments, the return to everyday life and the activities of ordinary people have been the focus of dramaturgical sociology and ethnomethodology, which are also contemporary reminders of the potential of symbolic interactionism. Both recover the acting human subject, although the dramaturgical approach by Erving Goffman destroys notions of cultural hierarchy, because it operates in an ahistorical atmosphere of encounters and dictates strategies of survival in a world through impression management. The result is a commodification of human relationships. The ethnomethodology of Harold Garfinkel is equally divorced from history and cultural environments and attempts to uncover the tacit rules or conventions that seem to hold together personal relationships, groups and, ultimately, society.

However, the dominant interests in communication research remained committed to the theoretical promise of functionalism under the influence of Parsons and Harvard sociology and the work of Merton and others, partly because it focused on social structures and society, and partly because it offered strong methodological leadership, particularly under Lazarsfeld and his work at Columbia University. Last not least, a significant number of communication researchers, who dominated communication research for the next forty years, were trained in the tradition of functionalism, although their understanding of its theoretical terminology and its implications has been disputed (Brown, 1970; Thomas, 1989). As a result, the methodological and theoretical dimensions of communication research came to be defined by a group of individuals whose scholarship was influenced by functionalism. Similarly, Delia's observation – that a "particular set of individual and professional interests that gave rise to the field's initial organization served to narrow it in important ways and to create unseen internal tensions that would shape the field's later history" (1987: 69) – addressed the issue of preferential theoretical treatments of communication in society.

Interactionism, on the other hand, continued to suffer from theoretical weaknesses; it did not come to grips with the concept of the self and the unconscious. According to Meltzer and others, it displayed methodological problems and ignored the influence of social organizations (1975: 92–3). Also, its practitioners in the field of communication research remained outside the mainstream, constituting a historical footnote to the development of the "field," which means outside the major thrust of communication research that was engaged in the practice of a "communication science."

Mainstream communication research moved virtually unscathed by major internal controversies or external encounters with the consequences of social or political developments through its first forty years, even though what began as an attack on the orthodoxy of social theory in the 1930s became orthodoxy by the 1970s. Underlying this development is the idea that a perfect theoretical explanation needs no change, particularly in a near-perfect environment. It is a reflection of the history of social and political thought in the United States, for which liberalism offered a perfect explanation of the American condition. Unlike the experiences of engaged and fragmented social and political thoughts in Europe, the idea of liberalism in the United States was never seriously challenged or overthrown by other perspectives like socialism, for instance. This makes the introduction of Marxist thought, or speculations about social democratic practices, particularly difficult. In fact, liberalism in the United States furnishes what amounts to a permanently installed theoretical environment in which social or political change is considered in terms of adjustments to technological advancement rather than in terms of the actual demise of its theoretical propositions.

For instance, the received history of the American press is grounded in the interests and allegiances of its authors; thus, middle-class values permeate the series of comprehensive press histories published during this century. They reflect a shared bias toward history as the story of institutions and their leaders at the expense of recognizing the definite conditions of production and consumption that involve newsworkers and readers in their concrete relations to the material world. Instead, there is frequent, if not unanimous, admiration of the success of free enterprise and entrepreneurial ingenuity that ultimately led to the establishment of "great" newspapers and to the evolution of newspaper chains and group ownership of the media. Because the writing of press histories has been an exercise in producing evidence for the success of the First Amendment and the democratic system, the historical narrative concentrates on the rise of the press as a major political institution in American society. In addition, press historians delivered the "facts" for presenting the American press as the prototype of a "free" media system in support of the role of the United States in world affairs. This history placed considerable emphasis upon the ideas of freedom of expression, free flow of information and the values of a free press system as essential elements of an exportable ideology. Few questions were raised about the specific functions of American newsworkers and their freedom of expression within the workplace, yet American press history reinforces the notion that content is a major determinant of a definition of a free and democratic press. Indeed, press historians rely heavily on the description of newspaper content to argue their points about the state of the press. Content as product and therefore as part of the free enterprise system becomes the story of entrepreneurs and their success (or failure) as peddlers of objective and truthful accounts of the day's events. The production of information, the process of indoctrination of journalists and their exploitation as cheap labor, are part of a barely visible foundation of American journalism history. Newsworkers remain anonymous, although recognized elements of the production process; they are trivialized as subjects and marginalized as a group or class of workers with professional or quasi-professional aspirations.

In such an atmosphere of historical reflection on media and society, communication research has operated with an understanding of change as methodological improvement that relates to the American experience with (technical) perfection and to the belief in a perpetual state of progress. And it is caught, like the objects of its investigations, in the sphere of consumption under conditions of exploitation and the false comforts of conformity.

At the same time, a critique of the ideological foundations of communication research amounted to speaking from outside the boundaries of the theoretical environment (and therefore often from outside the United States) and from a position of a future state of theoretical discourse that remained unimaginable, perhaps untrustworthy and certainly ideologically unacceptable as an alternative. As a result, alienation has become one of the consequences of maintaining different, if not to say foreign, values with respect to formulating oppositional theories of society.

Nevertheless, the influence of alternative visions, including Marxist perspectives on culture and communication, and increasing doubts about its own progress – theoretically, in terms of the concrete results of a generation of social research, and socially, in terms of its impact on policymaking and the betterment of society – resulted in what has been referred to by the *Journal of Communication* as the "ferment in the field" (1983). It suggested the possibility of a dialogue and allowed for an exchange of ideas which, in retrospect, provides an appropriate Goffmanesque example of impression management rather than a substantive debate among several different theoretical positions. In fact, notions of compromise or friendly accommodation in the spirit of common interests clouded the potential for the emergence of real differences and radical changes on this occasion.

Instead, most recently, the boundaries of communication research began to shift when academic interests that were traditionally identified with speech or interpersonal communication moved on to the terrain of social communication and were joined by others whose intellectual curiosity about culture seemed to be met by the potential of communication research as a source of analysis. The result was encouraging in that the dominant perspective of communication research had to rethink its theoretical foundations. It was confronted by alternative explanations of communication from a tradition of cultural studies that survived the heyday of positivism in communication research, and from a variety of Marxist positions that have emerged from encounters with European social theories.

These developments are also a reminder of the tradition of diversity in communication research. They form a collective history which reflects the struggle for the domination of a field of social research that had the potential of producing socially and politically relevant knowledge. They paralleled the rise of the modern social science establishment and consequently resulted in the triumph of a "communication science" whose foundations rested on a belief in the potential of methodologies to yield answers to questions about communication and society that would satisfy the curiosity of the theoretically inclined. Indeed, the preoccupation with methodological issues reflected the illusion that a manipulation of facts would eventually lead to theory. But, as Gareth Stedman Jones has remarked about the relationship between fact and theory in history, "those who tried to create theory out of facts, never understood that it was only theory that could constitute them as facts in the first place" (1972: 113). The focus of communication research was the "social" component of an inquiry that succeeded with the perfection of survey techniques and the subsequent rise of public opinion polls as measurements of participation in the social and political life of the United States. In the meantime, however, the search for an answer to Simmel's question of how society is possible had shifted to include questions about the quality of existence and concentrated on the potential for (political) change.

In this context, communication research began to recognize the importance of culture, that is, the need for a definition of society that centers on the presence of groups and individuals and their participation in the conditions of existence. Such a view requires historical reflection and calls upon theoretical constructs that recognize the importance of history and allow for the possibility of radical change. It appeals to a new approach to communication research that involves the recognition of the historical nature of theorizing and writing about communication and media; this view also encourages an intellectual pursuit that is committed to overcoming appeals to accommodate the orthodoxy of theoretical positions that remain aligned with a traditional liberal-pluralist perspective of communication in society.

The recognition of its own historical circumstances will lead to an understanding of the importance of history in the sociological analysis of communication and media phenomena. In fact, several years ago, C. Wright Mills suggested that "All sociology worthy of the name is 'historical sociology'," and he quoted Paul Sweezy's observation that sociology is an attempt "to write 'the present as history'" (1959: 162–3). A few years later, Anthony Giddens perceived such a unity when he concluded that as "a minimal claim it can be said that what history is, or should be, cannot be analyzed in separation from what the social sciences are, or should be." And he continued that there "simply are no logical or even methodological distinctions between social sciences and history – appropriately conceived" (1979: 230). And still another theorist, Walter G. Runciman, regarded sociology "as psychology plus social history" (1983: 32). Social history, however, is also the attempt to overcome the stereotypical formulation that sociology deals with the general and history with the unique; it is concerned with concepts of social structure and change in society which draw on sociological knowledge.

Contemporary communication research encounters an intellectual environment that has witnessed the convergence of history and social theory, partly because of a shifting interest toward a practice of historical sociology, and partly because of the influence of Marxist thought. Its relationship to culture as a viable context for the study of communication, that is, the importance of social, political and economic determinants in an analysis and interpretation of communication and media, approximate the concerns of social history.

In this context Berger and Luckmann built on the insights of the role of knowledge in the relationship between individuals and society and argued that the "dialectic between social reality and individual existence" be brought to bear upon the theoretical orientation of the social science (1966: 187). The authors rejected functionalist explanations in the social sciences as "theoretical legerdemain" and warned that a "purely structural sociology is endemically in danger of reifying social phenomena" (1966: 186). Their call for a sociology that recognizes and acts upon its position as a "humanistic discipline" is based on the appreciation of society as an ongoing historical process and the need to be "in a continuous conversation with both history and philosophy or lose its proper object of inquiry" (1966: 189).

Their contributions to the theoretical discourse in American sociology are based on the works of Husserl and Mead, in particular, and focus on the concept of understanding; they also reveal the compatibility of Marxist and Meadian ideas about the dialectic between society and the subject. In fact, Berger and Luckmann represented a return to the subject, they stressed the mapping of experienced reality and its production as knowledge in everyday life, while also calling attention to the problematic of intersubjectivity, interaction and intercommunication. Their sociology of knowledge is an attempt to locate the human actor in the objective and subjective reality of society, emphasizing the structural aspects of existence in the concreteness of social contexts and interests. It is also indebted to the contributions of Alfred Schutz, who called attention to the fact that

> all typifications of common-sense thinking are themselves integral elements of the concrete historical socio-cultural *Lebenswelt* within which they prevail as taken for granted and as socially approved. Their structure determines among other things the social distribution of knowledge and its relativity and relevance to the concrete social environment of a concrete group in a concrete historical situation. Here are the legitimate problems of relativism, historicism, and of the so-called sociology of knowledge.
>
> (1962: 149)

However, the theoretical weakness of Berger and Luckmann's sociology of knowledge approach, which is also indebted to Marxism – and that of interpretive sociology in general – lies in the failure to consider the economic and political dimensions of social reality, the need to relate the production and reproduction of the material life to the social production of meanings and knowledge, and therefore, to address the question of power and ideological struggle.

Although issues of communication related to language as the social medium of consciousness, for instance, are central concerns of these sociological endeavors, communication research has yet to claim its position in the formulation of a theoretical perspective that builds on the strength of a sociology of knowledge and takes advantage of the insights of interpretive sociology. It requires a commitment to the "social" in its everyday practices and relies on the strength of historical explanation; thus, it posits a challenge to the dominant practices of communication research that have tended to take social reality for granted.

An approach to historical analysis that centers on a social world, constituted by meanings and the production of knowledge in everyday life, is also reminiscent of methodological suggestions that are based on a materialist conception of history formulated by Marx in opposition to German idealist philosophy. Specifically, in their frequently quoted passage from *The German Ideology* Marx and Engels explained that they "set out from real, active men, and on the basis of their real life-process" and demonstrated "the development of the ideological reflexes and echoes of this life-process." They continued that

> phantoms formed in the human brain are also, necessarily, sublimates of their material life-process, which is empirically verifiable and bound to material premises. Morality, religion, metaphysics, all the rest of ideology and their corresponding forms of consciousness, thus no longer retain the semblance of independence. They have no history, no development; but men, developing their material production, and their material inter-course, alter, along with this their real existence, their thinking and the products of their thinking. Life is not determined by consciousness, but consciousness by life. In the first method of approach the starting point is consciousness, taken as the living individual; in the second it is the real living individuals themselves, as they are in actual life, and consciousness is considered solely as *their* consciousness.
>
> (1947: 14–15)

Their statement is an empowerment of "actual life" and provides an agenda for the analysis of the reality of social life; it reflects the search for answers about the definition of human subjects in their particular cultural relations with themselves and with their environments. It is also a clear articulation of an understanding of history as either starting from consciousness and missing real life, or as starting from real life and encountering ideological consciousness.

The development of historical sociology or social history, for that matter, offers an opportunity for communication research to explore the significance of communication in creating individuals through social relations and in producing knowledge, because both are determined by the historical circumstances of society. Indeed, questions of language and education, media and social groups, or gender and ethnicity, in the formation of individual consciousness constitute major areas of social and historical inquiry that affect a number of academic disciplines.

Such a broad vision characterizes the rise of social history as a distinct approach to an understanding of social life. For instance, when Eric J. Hobsbawm held that social history "can never be another specialization like economic or any other hyphenated histories because its subject matter cannot be isolated" (1971: 24), he suggested that social history typically embraces the whole experience of people and tries to include groups or classes of individuals not associated with elite establishments. In fact, according to Stearns, it

> rests on some distinctive assumptions of what the past consists of and how changes should be examined, most notably in its insistence on the importance of a history that embraces the officially powerless as well as the powerful and in stressing a presentation of the past and of change in terms of shifts in patterns of behavior and outlook, rather than a narrative of events.
>
> (1985: 322)

Such perspectives are based on theories of modernization or change and attempt to broaden the topical spectrum to include aspects or details of collective experiences which, together, may provide insights into the workings of contemporary society, particularly with respect to changing values and attitudes that prevail in specific subcultures.

For instance, Paul Baran's concept of economic surplus "is patently fundamental to any historian of the development of societies," according to Hobsbawm, who concluded that it is also "more objective and quantifiable, but also more primary" than the *Gemeinschaft-Gesellschaft* dichotomy (1971: 28). Historical inquiries into collective consciousness, cultural expressions, or patterns or uses of communication, utilizing sociological categories of analysis like age, gender or ethnicity, promise to provide some understanding of political and cultural changes among subcultures in the United States.

But the proximity to economics and sociology, which suggests the possibility of theoretical and methodological influences on social history, is also defined by intellectual or ideological predispositions of American historians. According to Henretta, they "have silently imbibed a pragmatic philosophical perspective from their culture. They accept the primacy of sense perception and attempt to establish the 'facts' in a 'spirit of neutral, passive detachment'" (1979: 1307).

Thus, Pragmatism, which encouraged the authority of the factual and led to a phenomenological perspective on human knowledge, and functionalism with its conceptual scheme that relied on notions of interdependence, order and stability, offered theoretical approaches to a historical inquiry into the social or cultural realities of the United States that proved to be more home-grown than the "foreign" demands of Marxism with its political dimension and its analytical view of class and power. Consequently, the reluctance to practice an engaged Marxist history has resulted in a flight into topical or methodological questions that reveal the apolitical nature of social history, despite the fact that Marxism offers a coherent theory of social change that is grounded in the historical and committed to a consideration of the totality of the cultural, political and economic experiences. Such a theory also acknowledges the presence of the individual in specific existential conditions and provides explanations of social relationships through notions of domination and class.

Instead, anthropological methodologies, combined with considerable doubt about the appropriateness of utilizing traditional, quantitative social research, seem to emerge as appropriate, and even desirable, approaches to the analysis of cultural practices. Although the uses of anthropological means of description and interpretation, in particular under the influence of the writings of Clifford Geertz, have yielded specificity and appreciation of detailed reportage, they have not led to resolving the issues of class and power. Indeed, there is an approximation between social history and cultural approaches to communication research that rests on the use and application of descriptive and interpretive methodologies.

However, the uses of anthropological means of analysis *per se* will not guarantee a decisive change from previous notions of history that exclude problems of political power or, for that matter, class struggle. Similarly, communication research that avoids considerations of power relations will deny the political reality of communication and media in the United States. In their critique of contemporary social history, Fox-Genovese and Genovese insist that the overriding importance of the political dimension of social history should be understood in the larger sense of "political," namely the formulation and implementation of class authority, with a full understanding that a true hegemony entails far more police power and defines itself within the customary limits established by the lower classes, but, nonetheless, cannot ultimately be severed from political processes in general and the use of force in particular – as the history of revolutions testifies.

(1976–7: 215–16)

The introduction of social and political concerns, the broad cultural approach to the study of individuals and society, considerations of gender and ethnicity, as well as the sustained impact of Marxism on social inquiry, resulted in the rise of the New Historicism as a cultural practice, particularly during the 1980s. The relationship between Marxism and history was emphasized in philosophical analyses of historical materialism, particularly by the reaction to the consequences of Althusserian Marxism, whose conception of history as "a process without a subject" reduced the notion of human agency to structure. In response to Edward Thompson's attack on Althusser's historiography, Perry Anderson suggested that "theory is now history, with a seriousness and severity it never was in the past; as history is equally theory, in all its exigency, in a way that is typically evaded before" (1983: 26).

The New Historicism is an expression of topics or attitudes, rather than a doctrinaire exploration of human agency. It is also a process of distrusting old positions, crossing academic disciplines and demonstrating the relatedness of culture and history, according to H. Aram Veeser, who described the New Historicism as setting aside

the potted history of ideas, the Marxist *grand recit*, the theory of economic stages, the lock-picking analysis *à clef*, and the study of authorial influence. By discarding what they view as monologic and myopic historiography, by demonstrating that social and cultural events commingle [*sic*] messily, by rigorously exposing the innumerable trade-offs, the competing bids and exchanges of culture, New Historicists can make a valid claim to have established new ways of studying history and a new awareness of how history and culture define each other.

(1989: xiii)

The New Historicism is a condition of contemporary intellectual existence, a carnival of ideas where competing theories draw attention to the complexity of problems that have been associated with locating the subject in the social, political and economic processes of society. Fox-Genovese has called it "A bastard child of a history that resembles anthropological 'thick description' and of a literary theory in search of its own possible significance" within a broad framework of cultural studies (1989: 213). It is, at least in its US version, also a reminder of the development of progressive history, not so much in its execution of a specific world view, but in its attempt to reflect the breadth of the concern and the depth of the issues that involve making sense of contemporary conditions.

Finally, there is a turning to the idea of a critical approach that will mean the end of communication research as it has been constituted and the beginning of a creative break, which will appeal to those intellectual interests in communication research that have recognized and supported a cultural studies perspective, with its built-in bias toward the historical and its connectedness with the theoretical; it will also accommodate the newly discovered Marxist perspectives as they became available in the United States particularly through Critical Theory and the British Cultural Studies tradition. Such a break will also support ways of rethinking communication in terms of the potential of feminist theories, particularly those that insist on the presence of the political dimension and the significance of analyzing the relationship of power and gender. The efforts of literary studies or social history, for instance, to benefit from a knowledge of communicative practices will help relocate communication research from a dominant position in an empirical social science tradition to a much broader context of humanistic studies. Such a context will insist on the reconceptualization of the subject as an active participant in the societal environment.

Underlying the theoretical propositions of Pragmatism and Marxism is the notion of progress, that is, a sense of the future, and therefore a way of life. Their differences are played out in their relationship to the realities of everyday existence. Pragmatism reflected on the rise of technology and industrialization, Marxism on the failures of bourgeois society to address the need for equality and freedom. Both created visions of utopia which established a sense of direction and guided people through most of the twentieth century, and yet there is a feeling of abandonment amidst the noise of inauthentic communication. Theories of society, and therefore theories of history, which address the concrete conditions of society, recognize the real needs of people, meet the growing expectations of praxis, and promote values and ethical norms, are the foundation of radical democratization.

The discourse of theory and history is not a consuming intellectual passion of a marginalized academic clique, but a cultural practice that characterizes the conduct of contemporary social inquiry; this includes those practitioners in the field of communication research who have begun to realize the potential of bridging disciplinary boundaries and of raising the question of communication in society in the context of an analysis of culture. After all, Raymond Williams suggested some time ago that

> the study of communication is a convergence, or attempted convergence, of people who were trained, initially, in very different fields: in history and philosophy, in literary and cultural studies, in sociology, technology and psychology. What all these people have in common, ultimately, is a field of interest.
>
> (1981: 11)

Such a cultural practice must begin with an understanding of the historical conditions of communication research, that is, its determination by the cultural, political and economic environment that was reflected in the theoretical discourse of Pragmatism, the conditions of empirical social research, and the emerging critique from alternative theoretical approaches that arose from the postwar experiences of Marxist criticism in Western Europe.

Chapter 2

On discovering communication
Pragmatism and the pursuit of social criticism

Philosophy is inherently criticism.

John Dewey

The history of communication theory and research in the United States has been guided by notions of democracy and the impact of technology on the nature of communication. It emerged from philosophical considerations and sociological practices that were enamored with the progress of science, but also embraced humanistic and literary interests in language, symbols and communication. Throughout this development, the idea of the critical, stimulated by the advancement of knowledge and provoked by the social and political consequences of social change, has persisted as an example of intellectual responsibility and moral leadership, beginning with the rise of American Pragmatism. Since then, the importance of communication in an emerging theory of society has been a major consideration in a continuing dialogue with Pragmatism and other competing social theories. Most recently, the European influence of Marxist and non-Marxist interpretations of mass culture have gained a considerable hearing in the United States. They are a reminder that throughout the intellectual history of the United States there has been a continuous influence of European thought, particularly British and Continental philosophy, upon the development of the American mind. In fact, Pragmatism as an American philosophy provides a vivid example of such influence. Thayer concluded his assessment of Pragmatism with the observation that "the conglomerate manifestations of the American mind . . . are the result of local adaptations, graftings, and crossings of the older loyalties and ideas that migrated from Europe" (1973: 228–9).

This was also the time when popular reform journalism stretched the possibilities of media use in the interest of public information, and ideas about community rose from decentralized notions of family to occupy a major place in the emerging theories of society. The closing of the frontier was also the beginning of a new era of different relationships between the individual and the industrial and commercial environment. The fears and aspirations of American society were reflected in the works of Henry George, Edward Bellamy and Henry Demarest Lloyd, whose best-selling books (*Progress and Poverty*, n.d.; *Looking Backward*, 1888; and *Wealth Against Commonwealth*, 1894, respectively) addressed the conditions of a changing society. They were utopian reformers, whose influence was acknowledged by many progressives, "who responded enthusiastically to their moral message if not always to their programme for building the good society" (Thomas, 1983: 354).

These ideas also had an impact on the theoretical discourse at the beginning of this century which was engaged in a critique of the existing philosophical tradition, when old orthodoxies were replaced by a dominant classical-religious perspective with a reformist-scientific position. These were the years of inspired interpretation and reasoned presentation of scientific evidence about the state of society. William Ogburn, who observed the tradition of social inquiry during the first thirty years of this century, found that

> much writing in social science, both in articles and in books, is still an undifferentiated mixture of attempts to persuade, to entertain, to interpret meanings, to be literary, to discuss ideas, and to express one's beliefs and prejudices, as well as to draw reliable conclusions from data. But a volume of writing known as social science research, which is concerned only with presenting the new knowledge and the method whereby it was discovered from data, has become very large in amount.
>
> (1964: 214)

The turn toward an empirical perspective, with all of the ramifications of a specific view of the world, was also the beginning of an American approach to the social and political environment. It remained a strong influence on the ideological position of American social scientists and their cultural biases as members of an intellectual community of inquirers and formulators of the American dream. The social sciences, more than any other branch of knowledge, then, contributed to the design and perpetuation of political and cultural beliefs, based upon faith in renewal and economic rewards. Communication and media studies share this tradition and carry the burden of scientific explanation and persuasion, particularly after the importance of communication in society has become an accepted premise for the study of culture and politics.

In fact, communication research has been profoundly influenced by the history of social thought in the United States; consequently, a study of the social-scientific exploration of modern society must consider the idea of communication as part of a struggle over positioning the social within human relationships and practices. This process provides the historical context for understanding the emergence of communication research.

In this spirit, Pragmatism becomes a thoroughly American attempt to adapt to the conditions of modern life. It was a break with the absolutism which had dominated academic thought and an attempt to produce a philosophical context for social-scientific inquiries into the twentieth century with the aid of a "biological imagination," and an emphasis on "human efforts," "collective action" and "meliorism," according to the contemporary observations of Ralph Barton Perry (1916). He concluded that Pragmatism views life as an "affair of forced adaptation to an indifferent and, at best, reluctantly plastic environment" while knowledge rises "from the exigencies of life, and the exigencies of life are real, perilous, and doubtful." Since "*Civilization*, not the totality of nature, nor any higher synthetic harmony, is the work of God," knowledge and the desire and "hope of better things . . . may conquer nature and subdue the insurrection of evil" (1916: 268).

Perry identified Pragmatism with collective action and power and suggested that it developed a theory of society, which

> attaches less significance to the direct relation between man and a dynastic God, and more to that relation to his fellows which may make a man a servant of collective life and lead him to a new conception of God as a leader of common cause.

Perry felt that Pragmatism "speaks for the spirit of making better," and he concluded that "It is the philosophy of impetuous youth, of Protestantism, of democracy, of secular progress – that blend of naiveté, vigor, and adventurous courage which proposes to possess the future, despite the present and the past" (1916: 268).

Pragmatism also offered the opportunity for a critique of society. It became a social philosophy that challenged traditions of thought and experience in its pursuit of truth and the conditions of a moral life. Its encouragement of criticism was based on the adoption of a social-scientific perspective. In this sense, critique was to be understood as flowing from expert deliberations, providing guidance through knowledge for an informed public. The goal was the support of an American democratic tradition that rested on the moral potential of human nature and was built on faith in social stability. But Pragmatism also recognized the inevitability of change and the need to adjust; in the resulting attempt to redefine the reality of liberal-pluralism, social criticism emerged as a form of self-discovery.

These observations capture the spirit and appeal of Pragmatism at a time of social upheaval, when migration and immigration created an industrialized, urban culture, while the potential of technological development conquered the minds of new and old Americans and, ultimately, defined the meaning of modern warfare with the outbreak of the First World War.

From the beginning of the movement American Pragmatists sought a reconciliation between morals and science (James), argued for the adoption of a scientific practice based upon the primacy of the community of inquirers (Peirce), suggested the importance of ethical processes in the discussion of social interests (Dewey), and based an understanding of the practical character of thought and reality upon a behavioral interpretation of the mind (Mead). But the underlying appeal of Pragmatism as a new foundation of social and scientific knowledge rested in Dewey's observation that Pragmatism

> presents itself as an extension of historical empiricism but with this fundamental difference, that it does not insist upon ante-cedent phenomena but consequent phenomena; not upon the precedents but upon the possibilities of action. And this change in point of view is almost revolutionary in its consequences.
>
> (1931: 24)

The idea of communication as a central element in a theory of society was produced by such "adaptations and crossings"; when it surfaced in the literature of the social sciences, it also reflected a philosophical movement which struggled against Cartesianism in modern philosophy to develop a new position in which the social became "*the* inclusive philosophic category" (Bernstein, 1967: 133). This conceptualization also anticipated the significance of action as an aspect of communication research which would need specific consideration and, eventually, justify the development of the field. Furthermore, these views reflected the optimism of a young society with its deep-seated belief in its own future, the potential for social action and the use of knowledge for the social good.

Pragmatism as an approach to the study of society also appealed to a new sense of culture that had emerged from the industrial revolution and the considerations of democracy as an American experience. That is to say, American Pragmatism intended to explore the conditions and meanings under which people interact as enterprising, moral individuals who share the possibility of change or improvement. The confrontation of traditional values and aspirations of a rural community with the consequences of technology and the commercialization of an urban society provided the context for the development of an American culture. In the wake of major social and economic changes in America due to industrialization, urbanization and education, social thought concentrated on the problems of value and change, tradition and innovation. The emerging spirit of survival, that is, the success of adapting to technological solutions, in turn, symbolized the exemplary strength of America for Europeans in their struggle for a democratic way of life after the experience of the First World War.

The nature of communication and questions of language are age-old philosophical issues; American Pragmatism, as a philosophical tradition, also recognized the centrality of communication to a social-philosophical explanation of American society. In fact, the significance of the telegraph, railroads, highways and rivers as means of transportation, and the spread of schools and newspapers as institutional sources of knowledge and experience provide the historical background for a theoretical discourse about the place of communication in modern society. Subsequently, a generation of philosophers, including Peirce, James, Dewey and Mead, in particular, offered visions of communication that were bound together by equally strong ideas about the role of individuals in society, the importance of community as shared experience and the possibilities of a democratic way of life supported by the new insights of a social science. At the same time, considerations of the process of communication raised moral issues about participation in the acquisition of knowledge and the use of symbolic power, including the means of communication.

Philosophical inquiries into the nature of language have ranged from the magical power of words to the authority of the symbolic environment and the role of communication in the emergence of the individual in modern culture. Alfred North Whitehead once spoke of language as "the civilization of expression in the social systems which use it" (1968: 34). At the end of the nineteenth century this civilization had become a major theoretical concern in American scholarship. With the work of Charles Peirce, the symbolic nature of the individual and the qualities of human discourse became necessary conditions of a theory of society. In his search for a method of clarifying ideas, Peirce offered a biologically oriented theory of inquiry, and contemplated the importance of signs as public or social instruments of communication. He was, however, as Hartshorne and Weiss concluded in their introduction to his collected works, "Never indeed a leader of movements," but "an originator of ideas" (1931: iii).

In fact, his considerable interest in questions of language and his theory of signs (semiotics) inspired the work of his contemporaries and continues to be recognized as a major contribution to the study of communication and culture. Specifically, his notion that everything is a sign as long as it is capable of being understood as standing for something else created a new way of understanding communication and human interaction in which the individual assumed a central position *vis-à-vis* words, that is, in the process of expression and interpretation. When Peirce proposed that "Man makes the word, and the word means nothing which the man has not made it mean, and that only to some man" (1934: 188), he also suggested that individuals and words "reciprocally educate each other; each increase of a man's information involves and is involved by, a corresponding increase of a word's information" (1934: 189). There is no escape from language, since language is being, or, as Peirce confirmed, "my language is the sum total of myself; for the man is the thought" (1934: 189). His theory also implies that individuals are always in touch with themselves and with others through language, suggesting the social implications of his work. Hugh Dalziel Duncan observed that "When one reasons, Peirce said, it is the critical self that one is trying to persuade, and all thought becomes a sign and such significations compose the nature of language." He also suggested that Peirce,

like other pragmatists, "rooted his theory in the purely formal properties of language as well as in its social context"
(1969: 201).

But his semiotic analysis is not only an acknowledgment
of the importance of language, it is also a confirmation that
scientific (and social) knowledge does not evolve from subjective
feelings, as truths cannot be decided a priori by individuals, they
must be tested and confirmed by a community of investigators. Peirce asserted that "the very origin of the conception
of reality . . . essentially involves the notion of a COMMUNITY,
without definite limits, and capable of a definite increase of
knowledge" (1934: 186–7). Since such a process of cooperative inquiry, that is, moving from doubt to belief, proceeds
indefinitely, knowledge can never be absolute. Consequently,
the proof of the real lies not only in the removal of doubt
within the realm of the community, but inquiry also empowers
the community. Peirce argued that "The opinion which is fated
to be ultimately agreed to by all who investigate, is what we
mean by the truth, and the object represented in this opinion
is the real" (1934: 268). In this sense, the truth is determined
by the decision of the community, while the identity of the
individual emerges from the "*consistency* of what he does and
thinks," because "his separate existence is manifested only by
ignorance and error." The individual apart from others "is only
a negation," because, according to Peirce, thought "has only
a potential existence, dependent on the future thought of the
community" (1934: 189).

Peirce's considerations of thought, belief, truth and reality were
questions of language and communication, expressed in terms of
signs, sign relations, and signification, related to the existence of
a cultural context and insistent upon the shared experience of the
community.

> What is important for Peirce is that signs are socially stand-
> ardized ways in which one thing (a thought, word, gesture, or
> object as *sign*) refers *us* (a community) to something else (the
> interpretant, the significant effect or translation of the sign,
> being itself another sign).
>
> (Thayer, 1973: 25)

These notions of language, thought, the individual and the
community are recurring themes which appeared a generation

later in the work of Heidegger. His suggestion that "language is neither an expression nor an activity of man. Language speaks" (1971: 197), and his reflections on language as thought, on the importance of (cultural) contexts for the creation of meaning, and the intersubjectivity of communication, are similar to the writings of Peirce. They retained a modern appeal, particularly with the contributions of Jürgen Habermas (1979) and Karl-Otto Apel (1973), whose theories of communicative competence and communicative ethics, respectively, reflect the influence of Peirce and his pragmaticism.

Peirce did not provide suggestions for the advancement of society toward the ideal of the community; he was primarily interested in the state of theory, in the progress of science, and the pursuit of scientific truth in an atmosphere of complete freedom for scientific endeavors. In this sense, he yielded to the authority of science, aware, however, of the conditions of everyday life and the consequences of scientific discoveries for the advancement of society.

The search for scientific truths, or the verification of theories, has social and political consequences; thus, the assertion of such truths through a process of popularization by the media or educational institutions becomes a considerable component in the development of social criticism. In fact, a separation of science and society during the time of Peirce's writings when the miracles of technology contributed to the industrialization and urbanization of the United States, seems difficult, if not impossible. He did not offer a comprehensive attack on social problems; however, Peirce combined scholarly insights with practical observations to warn against excessive reliance on reason for the conduct of life in this age of technological reason. He emphasized the importance of feelings and sentiments as part of human nature and therefore as part of the social response to the deviations of an industrialized society.

Peirce saw the individual not as autonomous, but as a social being with his own history, experiences and adaptability to change. The relationship between individual and society was determined by being in communication and participating with others in the experiences of the community. His condemnation of contemporary ideas of individualism and materialism emerged most clearly perhaps when he addressed the passing of the "Economical" or nineteenth century. Peirce said that the great attention paid to economical questions during our century has induced an exaggeration of the beneficial effects of greed and of the unfortunate results of sentiment, until there has resulted a philosophy which comes unwittingly to this, that greed is the great agent in the elevation of the human race and in the evolution of the universe.

(1935: 193)

And he continued elsewhere that

the conviction of the nineteenth century is that progress takes place by virtue of every individual's striving for himself with all his might and trampling his neighbor under foot whenever he gets a chance to do so. This may accurately be called the Gospel of Greed.

(1935: 196)

C. Wright Mills has concluded that Peirce's own position as an outsider in "the academies" resulted in "opposing the legitimating ideologies which they carried" and therefore "he came to oppose the practices they legitimated. These were the dominant practices of a rising capitalist society; individuality and calculating greed were seen at their center." Mills' social-psychological analysis of Peirce suggested that

Since this was both the practice and thought of his milieu, and since he was deeply against it he came to be against all mingling of "practice" and "theory" and to join action and thought on an ontological level with the underlying sentiment which he called love.

(1964: 211)

Peirce located the potential (and necessity) for social criticism in the process of cooperative inquiry, that is, in the role of communities (of investigators) to encourage and sustain self-critical conduct among participants. In this sense, at least, he provided a model for the articulation of criticism of social institutions, for instance, and its position in society with respect to the workings of public institutions, e.g., their alliances with political and economic power, and private enterprise. He also described the potential for a challenge of authority.

The intellectual power of Peirce's arguments was clearly understood by James, who was also affected by Darwinism and a vision of individuals as material organisms rooted in the natural order of things. He was different from Peirce, however, successful as a public individual, informed about the world, articulate, and comfortable among people. James became the recognized public champion of American Pragmatism among his contemporaries, because he addressed himself to the concerns and considerations of common people. In many ways, he

> was a typical product of the main stream of western thought since the Reformation; he was an individualist, interested in the experiences, perplexities, and satisfactions of individual souls, and anything claiming to be more-than-individual he distrusted from the depths of his own Protestant and American soul.
>
> (Gallie, 1966: 29)

It could be expected that he would turn "towards concreteness and adequacy, towards facts, towards action and towards power" (James, 1970a: 213), rejecting the traditional path of metaphysics. In fact, James suggested that theories *"become instruments, not answers to enigmas, in which we can rest"* (1970a: 213).

Pragmatism was a "mediator and reconciler," and, according to James, "has no prejudices whatever, no obstructive dogmas, no rigid canons of what shall count as proof. She is completely genial. She will entertain any hypothesis, she will consider any evidence" (1970a: 225).

James, too, invoked the power of inquiry within the bounds of the community in his discussion of Pragmatism as a method for clarifying the meaning and nature of truth. There is strength and confidence in the realization that all truths are man-made (1963: 159), and that truth is what works, and what is expedient and useful, on the whole and in the long run, for the individual in consultation with others. "Her only test of probable truth is what works best in the way of leading us, what fits every part of life best and combines with the collectivity of experience's demands, nothing being omitted" (James, 1970a: 225).

James reflected the essence of American culture in his thoughts on pluralism, which determines the contours of democracy, where the demands for satisfaction are met through cooperation and compromise among individuals. He believed in the power of direct knowledge and embraced the empiricist notion of testing ideas through "the use of the concrete way of seeing," which, in any event, incorporated the "whole originality of pragmatism"

(1909: 216); thus knowing is witnessing, and the structure of the concrete experience becomes the focus of his philosophical concerns. He believed that human beings are actors, not spectators in a changing world, who make reality emerge in a continuous and changing process of becoming. According to Whitehead, James was "essentially a modern man," whose "intellectual life was one protest against the dismissal of experience in the interest of system" (1968: 3).

The potential for social criticism rests in the ability to think and to act upon thoughts; it is also rooted in a sense of social responsibility. According to James, "the *use* of most of our thinking is to help us to *change* the world. We must for this know definitely *what* we have to change; and thus theoretic truth must at all times come before practical application" (1970b: 133). Pragmatism frees the individual to consider alternative visions of society, for instance, and encourages the emergence of a critical mind. James said that "we seem set free to use our theoretical as well as our practical faculties . . . to get the world into a better shape, and all with a good conscience" (1970b: 133). His understanding of discourse in the context of non-scientific, social (and religious) matters, in particular, allows for the introduction of standards of truth or validity that respond to social, and moral (or religious) commitments or preferences. In other words, he recognized the importance of moral issues in society and provided for a different process of reflection and determination of courses of action.

James acknowledged the urgency of moral questions in modern society, which

> immediately present themselves as questions whose solutions cannot wait for sensible proof. A moral question is a question not of what sensibly exists, but of what is good, or would be good if it did exist. Science can tell us what exists; but to compare the *worths*, both of what exists and of what does not exist, we must consult not science, but what Pascal calls our heart.
>
> (1970c: 201–2)

In this sense, the break with absolutism also meant a reconsideration of "good" or "bad" in the context of man-made theories of truth, or the creation of realities in which culture, discourse and language offer "genuine possibilities" for the advancement of society.

James shared his social and political sentiments generously and believed "in the reign of peace and in the gradual advent of some sort of socialistic equilibrium" (Perry, 1948: 237). It was clear to James that society has "undoubtedly got to pass toward some newer and better equilibrium, and the distribution of wealth has doubtless slowly got to change: such changes have always happened, and will happen to the end of time" (H. James, 1920: 286). Elsewhere he confided to a friend, "I am against bigness and greatness in all their forms," and he continued,

> The bigger the unit you deal with, the hollower, the more brutal, the more mendacious is the life displayed. So I am against all big organizations as such, national ones first and foremost; against all big successes and big results; and in favor of the eternal forces of truth which always work in the individual and immediately unsuccessful way, under-dogs always, till history comes, after they are long dead, and puts them on the top.
>
> (H. James, 1920: 90)

He believed in "real fights," taking risks as part of a significant life, and he fought for a number of social causes, while critical, but always firm in his patriotism. Although, as Mills has suggested, James "never fully articulated, much less systematized, his social and political opinions. They are more properly called 'sentiments'" (1964: 260).

The philosophy of William James places questions of participation and social communication in proximity to responsibility. Although he did not address the relationship between ethics and communication, his theoretical stance reflects the importance of faith and the power of personal freedom to engage in a critical examination of the social and economic environment.

James' concerns were reflected in Dewey's contribution to Pragmatism; his prolific writings on societal questions, based upon his interest in the social, his belief in the centrality of community, and his faith in the workings of democracy, supplied a theoretical context for the growing interest among social scientists in social problems. Their activities grew out of the realization that with an increasing concentration of political and economic power, the study of institutions and collective activities was an appropriate and necessary direction for social-scientific inquiry. The results were efforts to disclose the predatory nature of American industry (Veblen, 1899), to render an economic interpretation of history (Beard, 1914), and to offer a sociological critique of traditional thoughts about individuality and morality (Small, 1910; Ross, 1918; Park, 1938), in an effort to expose and share with others their understanding of the harsh reality of American life. The emphasis in these inquiries was on the social processes and the prospects for a perfect society, which would be identical with a perfect democracy.

Dewey viewed Pragmatism as a theory of logic and ethical conduct, although his interests ranged from the technical nature of philosophy to the variety of social problems facing democratic societies. In fact, he wrote that "Philosophy recovers itself when it ceases to be a device for dealing with the problems of philosophers and becomes a method, cultivated by philosophers, for dealing with the problems of men" (1917: 65). He felt that

> philosophy is inherently criticism, having its distinctive position among various modes of criticism in its generality; a criticism of criticisms, as it were. Criticism is discriminating judgment, careful appraisal, and judgment is appropriately termed criticism wherever the subject-matter of discrimination concerns goods or values.
>
> (1925: 322)

At the same time, Dewey considered the importance of inquiry in the search for norms of conduct in democracy as a way of life. He summarized his concern about questions of ethics and democracy as a major social problem by stating that

> The problem of restoring integration and coöperation between man's belief about the world in which he lives and his beliefs about the values and purposes that should direct his conduct is the deepest problem of modern life. It is the problem of any philosophy that is not isolated from that life.
>
> (1929: 255)

His sense of the practical combined with his belief in the potential of human expansion and development contributed to his popularity as a social philosopher.

For Dewey the world is evolutionary and people are creations and creators of their physical and social environments and communication

> is the familiar and constant feature of social life. We tend, accordingly, to regard it as just one phenomenon among others

of what we must in any case accept without question. We pass over the fact that it is the foundation and source of all activities and relations that are distinctive of internal union of human beings with one another.

(1934: 334–5)

Thus, communication established the individual in a system of mutual relationships and common purposes and offered opportunities of shared experiences, discourse and reflective thinking. Dewey maintained that "Of all affairs, communication is the most wonderful" (1925: 166); it is also

uniquely instrumental and uniquely final. It is instrumental as liberating us from the otherwise overwhelming pressure of events and enabling us to live in a world of things that have meaning. It is final as a sharing in the objects and arts precious to a community, a sharing whereby meanings are enhanced, deepened and solidified in the sense of communion.

(1925: 204–5)

Culture is the result of shared social and individual experiences which supply meaning and direction for the conduct of life; it is cumulative and complex and subject to domination and control through communication.

Communication as the foundation of society and a necessary condition for the working of democracy became the nexus of a critical perspective on American culture. The evolving critique of society was also a critique of an atomistic view of the individual which had become incompatible with the ideas of democracy when it disregarded the collective interests under the technological and economic consequences of a new era in American life. At the same time, industrialization and the rapid growth of society had also led to the creation of a "public" which was disoriented and unable to identify itself. Dewey lamented the fact that "the machine age in developing the Great Society has invaded and partially disintegrated the small communities of former times without generating a Great Community" (1927: 126–7). His goal, and that of others, was the perfection of the "machine age," which would eventually lead to a democratic way of life. According to Jean Quandt, they

saw the new machinery as a means to scale the obstacles to moral unity – ignorance, parochialism, and antagonism between classes. They believed that the new technology would encourage the growth of a mutual sympathy and a rational public opinion that transcended the boundaries of class and locality.

(1970: 34)

The rapid growth of information and the need for specialized knowledge encouraged and supported the rise of technocratic power. Dewey proposed that

it is not necessary that the many should have the knowledge and skill to carry on the needed investigations; what is required is that they have the ability to judge of the bearing of the knowledge supplied by others upon common concerns.

(1927: 209)

He favored a process of expert inquiry by social scientists, whose participation would not only confer upon them a special status, but also imply societal trust and confidence in the judgments of experts.

In a series of lectures published as *The Public and Its Problems* (1927), five years after the appearance of Walter Lippmann's *Public Opinion* (1922), Dewey presented his contribution to an ongoing debate about the conditions of society and the future of an American democracy. The work reflects an emerging sense of the importance of intellectual leadership in the critique of society at that time, and accentuates the political role of social scientists as expert representatives of a variety of societal interests.

A similar position had been expressed at the University of Chicago by Albion Small, who felt that consensus in society should be reached by "scientists representing the largest possible variety of human interests" (1910: 242). Such a sentiment would dramatically increase in later years, when mass communication research became entrenched in the academic environment which catered to specific political and economic interests. *The Public and Its Problems* also confirmed Dewey's belief in the power of human relationships and the strength of community. He said, "The local is the ultimate universal, and as near an absolute as exists" (1927: 215).

Dewey was a keen observer of the impact of social change on American society and recognized the potential of violence; he warned that "the control of the means of production by the few in legal possession operates as a standing agency of coercion of the many" (1935: 63), and suggested that "the use of symbols in place of arbitrary power was another great invention" (1935: 72) which created realities that shaped the sense of people about their place in society; and "Popular literacy, in connection with the telegraph, cheap postage and the printing press, has enormously multiplied the number of those influenced" (1935: 72). He concluded that

> established material security is a prerequisite of the ends which it cherishes, so that, the basis of life being secure, individuals may actively share in the wealth of cultural resources that now exist and may contribute . . . to their further enrichment.
>
> (1935: 57)

Consequently, he argued that a "renascent liberalism" adopt a "radical" position toward change which recognizes the importance of the social (besides the individual) as a category of action. This includes the realization that "intelligence is a social asset and is clothed with a function as public as is its origin, in the concrete, in social coöperation" (1935: 67).

Dewey was fully aware of the decline of individualism as a philosophy of life and the rise of forms of integration or socialization that had resulted in a "corporization" of society. Therefore, "the need of the present is to apprehend the fact that, for better or worse, we are living in a corporate age" (1930: 49).

He raised the notion of democracy to mean an active, cooperative life, in which individual differences merge in common interests, based on protected opportunities for communication, while the search for knowledge and the shared experience of social inquiry promotes individual and social development and secures the idea of democracy as an ideal environment in the face of permanent change, and as a continuing challenge to human creativity. A critique of social relations, that is, the installation of criticism as a method of social inquiry, was understood as the condition of social communication. It appears as an aspect of culture and is issued as a responsibility of the community of inquirers.

His views on a desirable society were most succinctly expressed in *Democracy and Education*, where he formulated two measures of the quality of social existence. They are "the extent in which the interests of a group are shared by all its members, and the fullness and freedom with which it interacts with other groups," while an "undesirable" society "is one which internally and externally sets up barriers to free intercourse and communication of experience" (1916: 99).

Similar ideas were expressed in the work of George Herbert Mead, which placed the study of human nature and the ability to communicate in a social context. His social behaviorism represents a continuation of Pragmatism as a philosophy of the social as opposed to the individualism of William James. He established the authority of the social as a category of analysis by suggesting that

> the behavior of an individual can be understood only in terms of the behavior of the whole social group of which he is a member, since his individual acts are involved in larger, social acts which go beyond himself and which implicate the other members of the group.
>
> (1967: 6)

Indebted to the thoughts of Darwin and Wilhelm Wundt, as well as to the contributions of his contemporaries, James and Dewey, Mead developed a theory of the self and mind which focuses on language and symbolization as a universal social activity. He stressed the importance of the social when he concluded that

> The human animal as an individual could never have attained control over the environment. It is a control which has arisen through social organization. The very speech he uses, the very mechanism of thought which is given, are social products. His own self is attained only through his taking the attitude of the social group to which he belongs. He must be socialized to become himself.
>
> (1936: 168)

For these reasons, communication, that is the use of language, becomes a social act through which the individual experiences himself, confronts himself as an object and recognizes his own reflexivity. Mead observed,

> I know of no other form of behavior than the linguistic in which the individual is an object to himself, and so far as I can see, the individual is not a self in the reflexive sense unless he is an object to himself. It is this fact that gives a critical importance to communication, since this is the type of behavior in which the individual does not respond to himself.
>
> (1967: 142)

The result is an individual as a self-conscious self who realizes the necessity of social dependence upon others.

Such a conclusion implied a model of society in which the development of the self through communication reflects the boundaries of community. In fact, Mead had already described an ideal society as one "which does bring people so closely together in their interrelationships, so fully develops the necessary system of communication, that the individuals who exercise their own peculiar functions can take the attitude of those whom they affect" (1967: 327).

It seemed plausible for Mead, who proceeded to demonstrate in his own work how the self emerges through communication, that democracy would emerge from such perfect and ideal conditions of a community of selves. He spoke of "the kind of democracy . . . in which each individual would carry just the response in himself that he knows he calls out in the community" (1967: 327). These visions of a universal discourse reflect the idealism of Josiah Royce, who had maintained personal contacts with Peirce, James and Mead, in particular. His understanding of communication (and the ideal society) always involved "participation in the other" (1967: 253); therefore, the rise of democracy remained a question of "organizing a community which makes this possible" (1967: 327).

Communication becomes the organizing process of community. That is to say, Mead pleaded for a definition of communication which stressed the significance of the social and the shared experience of individuals. For this reason, communication is never "simply a process of transferring abstract symbols; it is always a gesture in a social act which calls out in the individual himself the tendency to the same act that is called out in others" (1964: 281). This is important for an understanding of his critique of a society which lacks the type of communication that allows for "entering into the attitudes" (1964: 282) of others. Imperfect or incomplete communication affects the nature of "democracy" and leads to distorted realities. When Mead referred to the need for cooperation and sympathy among individuals, he emphasized the importance of the moral self as a participant in the process of democracy. The expression of an ethical consciousness, e.g., the feeling of belonging and interdependence, however, does not produce a leveling effect, but encourages diversity and excellence. In fact, individuals live and thrive in the reality of shared experiences, and according to Mead, "it is as social beings that we are moral beings" (1967: 385). Since sharing as a social aspect of society involves communication, Mead's work also indicates the dependence of ethical ideas on considerations of communication. Specifically, since his critique of society evolves from the position of the self *vis-à-vis* others and their definition of interests, communication as the locus of the social becomes a source of conflicts or agreements.

Mead's social theory and his understanding of the individual in society were informed by his social and political commitment to bring about changes in the everyday realities of life in the United States. Mead had also recognized the plight of the working class in the United States, the problems of technology as a dehumanizing experience and the failures of the community to control its destiny. In a review of Jane Addams's *The Newer Ideals of Peace* (1907) he concluded that

> the machine is a social product for which no individual can claim complete responsibility. Its economic efficiency is as dependent on the presence of the laborer and the market for its products as mechanical structure is dependent upon the inventor, and its exploitation upon the capitalist. But the group morality under which the community suffers, recognizes no responsibility of the exploiter to the laborer, but leaves him free to exhaust and even maim the operator, as if the community had placed a sword in his hand with which to subjugate.
>
> (1907: 127)

Mead's concerns about the nature of a democratic life as an expression of the values of the community were based upon what Shalin has called Mead's "radically democratic convictions" and his keen awareness of "social inequality." He described Mead's acute awareness of the social and political conditions of American society and his political engagements in the tradition of the progressive movement and concluded that "Mead's life can be seen as an attempt to prove in both theory and practice that revolutionary objectives can be achieved by essentially conservative means" (1988: 914).

Mead's notions of a democratic life were related to Dewey's appreciation of communication and his mythical and powerful explanation of communication, involving the idea of democracy.

Discussing the ideal of universal discourse and democracy, Mead suggested that

> If communication can be carried through and made perfect, then there would exist the kind of democracy to which we have referred, in which each individual would carry just the response in himself that he knows he calls out in the community.
>
> (1967: 327)

Mead's ideas were also related to the work of Charles Horton Cooley, another member of the Chicago School, for whom social communication was fundamental to an understanding of the self, and whose *Human Nature and Social Order* (1902) may be considered one of the earliest texts on the process of social communication. Cooley's conclusions that "without communication the mind does not develop a true human nature" (1909: 62), and that society is "simply the collective aspect of personal thought" (1902: 134) are reflected in the work of Mead and Dewey.

The proponents of community, then, emerged as critics of their social and economic environment, which typically celebrated the spirit of individualism and the rise of industrial capitalism. But this was also the time when political dissent became a formidable movement with demands for direct popular participation in government and discussions of "natural rights," including women's rights and political equality. There was more than a passing intellectual interest in socialism, spurred by social conflicts, labor unrest, and the attacks on nineteenth-century capitalism. Social scientists lived consciously in the proximity of history and had a keen sense of the contemporary conditions of American society. Such an awareness encouraged theoretical and practical activities and amounted to what Charles Beard has called a "counter-reformation" in American history. He described the atmosphere of change, which produced a different outlook on society and concluded that the "widespread and radical discontent of the working classes with the capitalist system hitherto obtaining produced a counter-reformation on the part of those who wish to preserve its essentials while curtailing some of its excesses." Beard continued that these developments impressed political thinking and affected legislation when it became obvious that "unrestricted competition and private property had produced a mass of poverty and wretchedness in the great cities which constituted a growing menace to society and furnished themes for socialist orators" (1914: 303–4).

There was also an active socialist movement which, according to Beard, had clearly recognized that

> the capitalist class, though few in numbers, absolutely controls the government – legislative, executive, and judicial. This class owns the machinery of gathering and disseminating news through its organized press. It subsidizes seats of learning – the colleges and the schools – even religious and moral agencies.
>
> (1914: 300)

The result was an engaged intellectual debate and the emergence of a critical literature about the failures of democratic promises, as well as the need for legislative action at all levels of political life to deal with the variety of social problems that had beset the nation. This was the setting for what Morton White later called the revolt against formalism in his review of liberal social philosophy during the early part of this century. For White, the attack on formalism led to "historicism" and "cultural organicism" referring to attempts by historians to "reach back in time" and by social scientists to "reach into the social space" (1949: 12) for explanations.

Social theorists faced the notion of change in their critique of the process of social communication and the role of societal institutions. But Pragmatism projected a definition of evolution (under the influence of Darwinism) which emphasized the processes of gradual change, adjustment and continuity. In contrast, a dialectical definition recognized discontinuity, abrupt changes of existing structures, or even the prospects of regression, as Trent Schroyer has suggested (1975: 108–9). Thus social theorists, who had acknowledged the problems of existing social structures, were ideologically committed to support continuity, and they responded to the needs and requirements of an urban, industrialized society by advocating various measures of adjustment. Among them were those members of the Chicago School who shared in the criticism of economic and social injustices in society and provided theoretical and moral support for the just and humane distribution of material resources. For instance, Simon Patten, speaking in the language of a new economics around the turn of the century about the "surfeited and exploited," stressed the importance of communication in an effort to help large numbers of Americans adapt to abundance.

> His social concerns and the expressed need to decrease social and economic differences through communication and coopera-tion resulted in the development of economic rights that extended traditional political rights and were designed to protect individuals who were adjusting to the new American environment.
>
> (Hardt, 1987: 151)

Such positions were developed with a growing appreciation of the cultural context of political and economic decisions and their effect upon the survival of the community as a cultural and spiritual resource. In the past, the American perspective on culture had been more closely related to a biological approach toward the individual and was less committed to emphasizing the differences between natural and cultural disciplines than the German tradition, which began to influence American social sciences after the turn of the century. This position was reflected in the struggle against the biological bias of Spencer's sociological methods which had occupied a generation of social scientists and continued to do so while the trend toward a cultural analysis of social phenomena gained ground with the coming of the Progressive era in American social history.

The context of culture had become a significant feature of the sociological enterprise, particularly with the rising spirit of collectivism in American thought before the First World War, when its theoretical position was a reflection of European and American influences. Similarly, a cultural-historical approach emerged from the writings of political economists, like Patten, who described the common ground of social research by insisting that "Pragmatism, sociology, economics, and history are not distinct sciences, but merely different ways of looking at the same facts." He added that all of them, however, "must accept consequences as the ultimate test of truth, and these consequences are measured in the same broad field of social endeavor" (1924: 264).

Similarly, Ogburn observed about ten years later that although the "trend toward specialization and that toward the solution of practical problems are at times in conflict," nevertheless, a "trend toward fluidity in boundary lines" had become quite noticeable because of the changing conditions of society and the nature of the search for knowledge (1964: 213–14). Thus, the study of communication as a social phenomenon and a potential source of social problems defied disciplinary boundaries and invited investigations from a number of perspectives, including sociology, economics, political science, psychology, as well as philosophy. The possible range for such an analysis of communication phenomena was also indicated by Charles Cooley's early definition of communication which embraced both language and methods of interaction. He had stated that by

> communication is meant the mechanism through which human relations exist and develop – all the symbols of the mind, together with the means of conveying them through space and preserving them in time. It includes the expression of the face, attitude and gesture, the tones of the voice, words, writing, printing, railways, telegraphs, telephones and whatever else may be the latest achievement in the conquest of space and time.
>
> (1909: 61)

His description stressed the importance of culture in the process of communication, and its comprehensive nature continues to reflect the original understanding of communication as a consequence of being in the world.

Under the leadership of Pragmatism social theorists focused upon the idea of the social, the role of community and the process of communication. These concepts suggested, particularly to Dewey, that communication as a life process would eventually and undoubtedly lead to democratic practice. At the same time, this conclusion constituted the beginning of a critical position in social science theory and research which understood itself as serving the cause of democracy. But there was no radical break with dominant traditional values, whose consequences were still found to be a desirable goal for society. Instead, it meant supporting political or economic conditions which would allow for the gradual adjustment of people to new and different environments. People were seen as consumer-participants in the great community, in which cultural or economic structures could be controlled by a call for the creation of alternative institutions, i.e., endowed newspapers, or activities, i.e., educational reforms, while science would serve the interests of all members of society. Such an equation of the political and economic interests of individuals with the interests of the scientific establishment revealed an attempt to join traditional values, i.e., the idea of democracy, with the interpretation of scientific knowledge, i.e., the consequences of technology, for society. It suggested an integration of democratic goals and scientific progress without accounting for the presence of political and economic power *vis-à-vis* the cultural diversity of groups or individuals and their needs for the acquisition of knowledge.

Accordingly, Dewey had defined the methods of such success in terms of freedom and access to knowledge, stating that "freedom of inquiry, toleration of diverse views, freedom of communication, the distribution of what is found out to every individual as the ultimate intellectual consumer, are involved in the democratic as in the scientific method" (1939: 102). The social sciences had become democratic sciences in the sense of involving and being involved in society in the name of progress and enlightenment.

On the other hand, social critics clearly recognized that the dangers for American society and its traditional vision of a democratic way of life did not emanate from government inter-ference or control alone, but that freedom could be restricted by economic factors. These limitations were the results of Darwinism and capitalism, which shaped American society and marginalized intellectuals who were opposed to these developments.

While Peirce may be celebrated as the father of American Pragmatism, his insistence upon the importance of a community of love against the advances of greed also made him a radical thinker, alienated from America and its gospel of individualism.

Those equally committed to the idea of community, like Dewey, produced a vision of community as an active, intelligent force that would be able to utilize the powers of political economy to (re)es-tablish the domain of the public and the life of the community. The critical position taken by Dewey and other members of the Chicago School consisted of an attempt to bring philosophy into the practi-cal arena of dealing with the problems of society. At the same time, Dewey realized the dangers for public communication, since

> all economic conditions tending toward centralization and con-centration of the means of production and distribution affect the public press, whether individuals so desire or not. The causes which require large corporate capital to carry on modern business, naturally influence the publishing business.
>
> (1939: 149)

In this particular context, there was a suspicion of the press as a potential (or real) instrument of suppression and deceit. Dewey warned that the factors which made the press an ideal mechanism for the transmission of ideas and information could also

> create a problem for a democracy instead of providing a final solution. Aside from the fact that the press may distract with trivialities or be an agent of a faction, or be an instrument of inculcating ideas in support of the hidden interest of a group or class (all in the name of public interest), the wide-world present scene is such that individuals are overwhelmed and emotionally confused by publicized reverberation of isolated events.
>
> (1939: 42)

Dewey's observations addressed most directly a system of communication which was created outside the community and hence would neither respond to its specific needs nor be responsible to it. Indeed, the media operated with information which constantly challenged people to assess and make judgments about events outside their control (and also outside their own interests). He concluded, for instance, that

> there is much information about which judgment is not called upon to respond, and where even if it wanted to, it cannot act effectively so dispersive is the material about which it is called upon to exert itself. The average person is surrounded today by readymade intellectual goods as he is by readymade foods, articles, and all kinds of gadgets. He has not the personal share in making either intellectual or material goods that his pioneer ancestors had. Consequently they knew better what they themselves were about, though they knew infinitely less concerning what the world at large was doing.
>
> (1939: 45–6)

Although there was a perceived lag between the production of information in society, particularly by the media, exerting control over the social environment, and the needs or desires of individuals as members of a community, there was no radical suggestion by Dewey for bringing the press into the community as a necessary condition for participation in the democratic process. On the other hand, Dewey's involvement in *Thought News* (together with Franklin Ford and Robert Park) was quite obviously based upon a vision of his social philosophy in action. As he reported to William James in 1891,

> the intellectual forces which have been gathering since the Renaissance and Reformation, shall demand complete free movement, and by getting their physical leverage in the tele-graph and printing press, shall, through free inquiry in a central-ized way, demand the authority of all other social authorities.
>
> (Perry, 1935: 518–19)

The critical perspective of social science scholarship emerged most clearly with an extended analysis of the instruments of change, e.g., the corporate power of American business and industry, including the press. Newspapers had become a frequent target of criticism for social activists and critics within the social science enterprise. Indeed, concerns about the proper role of the press, as defined by its idealized position within Dewey's expec-tations of community/democracy, and by its traditional function in American history, became widespread. They were reflected in the pages of the *American Journal of Sociology*, which served as an important academic forum of debates ranging from journalism education to press ethics and the effects of press coverage. The result was the first appearance of a diverse and critical literature of the media and a scholarly concern about issues of public communication combined with an articulated, reformist desire for a regular and systematic treatment of questions concerning the position of the media in American society (Yarros, 1899; 1916; Fenton, 1910–11; Vincent, 1905). Although published two generations ago, these contributions to a critique of the media are reminders of the universal problem of communication and media in society and the number of unresolved issues, despite enormous efforts throughout the last forty years, to understand the workings of the communication process.

The strength of the critique arose from an alliance between social reformers and social scientists. It was based upon a need to justify scientifically the variety of reform activities. More specifically, reformers had "faith in the capacity of social science to translate ethics into action. They hoped to find in social science not merely a description of society but the means of social change for democratic ends" (Oberschall, 1972: 206).

These were the years of encounters between the reigning ideology – liberalism – and the experience of socio-political changes in the United States. They resulted in the articulation of issues and potential solutions to "social problems" in the form of philosophical and social-scientific categories of thought. This was the era of the social fact which rose in the consciousness of intellectual and political leaders; it included the discovery of the significance of the communicative behavior of individuals and its socializing effects, which contributed to the consideration of society in a new light. The imagined (or real) freedom of scientific endeavors not only contained hope for solutions to social and economic inequality, it also secured the opposition to dominant interpretations of social facts and embraced the potential for criticism.

For instance, the writings of individuals like Lester Ward, Thorstein Veblen or John Dewey, driven by a faith in progress and an ethical concern for the welfare of individuals, reflected a critique of power and suggested an increased role of the state in the development of Western civilization. Accordingly, modern society, shaped by the forces of technology and industrialization, must turn to government and education for guidance in the production and distribution of knowledge and the protection of individuals against arbitrary rule and disregard of civil liberties.

Thus, Ward preached against the dangers of plutocracy, suggesting that "There is no greater danger to civilization than the threatened absorption by a few individuals of all the natural resources of the earth, so that they can literally extort tribute from the rest of mankind" (Commager, 1967: 186), while Veblen attacked capitalism and sought redress for common people in his *Theory of the Leisure Class* (1899), in which he offered a critique of conspicuous consumption and a view of individuals as victims of economic processes.

Speculating about Veblen's sympathies for social outcasts, including Wobblies, who "encouraged their members to commit sabotage with precision in order to preserve their sense of workmanship," David Riesman concluded that "To commit sabotage with precision is a highly skilled and individualistic thing. Perhaps it could be said that Veblen devoted much of his life to the art, as theorist and as practitioner" (1953: 140).

But this time was also devoted to a search for truth, and Dewey's social thought appears as a contribution to a larger, intellectual tradition that offered a critique of American society from the perspective of an engaged social science which viewed the world with detailed and specific practicality. It was joined by a belief in the strength of the individual and the potential of the social as a sphere of ethical conduct. Thus, when William James observed that "*Every* great institution is perforce a means of corruption – whatever good it may also do. Only in the free personal relation is full ideality to be found" (1920: 101), he implied the importance of independent intellectuals and their potential role in rethinking modern society.

The scientific struggle for change in the spirit of a liberal-pluralist tradition, and the critique of America as it turned from a rural idyll to an urban complex, resulted in appeals to specific norms, imbedded in ideas of community and democracy, and in the communication of these values; they were also instances of a desire to control. Thus, the beginnings of communication and media research fell into a period of intense engagement, if not preoccupation, with issues of improvement and progress, and, in this connection, also with the study of social control and its agencies. These studies ranged from the pioneering efforts of Edward A. Ross (*Social Control*, 1901) and William Graham Sumner (*Folkways: A Study of the Sociological Importance of Usage, Manners, Customs, and Morals*, 1906) to Charles H. Cooley (*Social Organization: A Study of the Larger Mind*, 1909 and *Social Process*, 1918).

The realization that underlying the workings of society is the transfer of meaning resulted not only in the recognition of communication as a significant social process, but it also led to a considerable interest in the opinion process among social and political theorists. The rise of modern publics, typically tied to the development of communication technologies, and the development of democracies, frequently identified with the existence of freedom of opinion, encouraged investigations of public opinion as a form of social communication. They included control of opinion, issues of political and economic propaganda, and the relationship between news and truthful information. Peters has written about the role of mass communication and its importance for progressive intellectuals who "conceived of the mass media as an integral part of a social order whose scale and mass requires systematic means of self-representation" (1989: 261).

It was the academy which led an assault on the increasing power of social institutions, including the press. Concomitantly it attacked the failures of American society to create favorable conditions for the exchange of information, including the failure to maintain a public sphere in which societal discourse would determine the cultural agenda and prepare individuals in the interest of the common good for participation in society.

Specifically, Albion Small, as an organizer of sociological research, his colleagues at the University of Chicago, and the reform-oriented Ross represent a generation of sociologists whose work offered an initial definition of a critical approach to communication and media studies.

Both Small and Ross had been influenced by the activist sociology of Ward, his distinction between physical and human evolution, and his development of a social theory that led to social reform. Ward had advocated collectivism during a time of *laissez-faire* individualism and a planned society, when government interference had become commonplace. Ross was intensively involved in radical reform and combined his interests in the politics of change with a critical assessment of societal institutions, including the media. His understanding of sociology as a guide to radical action was supported by Veblen with his economic critique of American society. They were joined by Robert Park who, under the influence of Georg Simmel and John Dewey, was particularly interested in problems of social process rather than structure and the potential of an enlightened public. Park sought to elaborate on the community of discourse and the rise of a democratic public, stressing the importance of people and the need to improve communication rather than to seek solutions from social institutions.

Small, who had been influenced by the writings of Spencer and Schäffle, which committed him to an organismic view of society, advanced an idea of society as

> a plexus of personal reactions mediated through institutions or groups. One among these reaction-exchanges was the state; but the state was no longer presumed to be in the last analysis of a radically different origin, office or essence from any other group in the system.
>
> (1912: 206)

This theoretical perspective was the basis for an extensive, contemporary critique of the social system, including communication and the media.

Therefore, in *An Introduction to the Study of Society* (with George Vincent), which appeared in 1894, Small developed an understanding of communication that reflected Schäffle's organismic vision of society in which the press, among other systems, was "incorporated in nearly every division of the psycho-physical communicating apparatus" (Hardt, 1979: 199). Both Small and Vincent recognized the pervasive influence of the press in modern society and described a *de facto* two-step flow of information when they concluded that

> the impulses communicated by this organ, regarded as a whole, give stimulus and direction to social activities of every kind. The fact that large numbers of individuals are not reached directly by the newspaper does not materially weaken this statement. The press influences all, at least, who are capable of exercising leadership, and through them makes itself felt to the very limits of the psychical organism.
>
> (1894: 326)

At the same time they described the economic dependence of the press, criticized its sensational and irresponsible conduct, and raised questions about the qualities of the press as a dependable source of knowledge. Their writings anticipated major areas of (mass) communication research devoted to gatekeeping and the two-step flow theory of the media (Hardt, 1979: 203).

Ross, not unlike Cooley, considered communication as embracing "all symbols of experience together with the means by which they are swung across gulfs of space and time" (1938: 140). Throughout his writings he remained highly sensitive to the power of the press as a potential instrument of public manipulation. In particular, he deplored the influence of economic interests on the press and, consequently, criticized the commercialization of the newspaper. Since Ross combined his scholarship with an intense engagement in social issues, he was bound to encounter the self-serving activities of the press and other media. He concluded that the

> clandestine prostitution of the great bulk of the newspapers to advertisers is the secret of the astounding domination the business class have gradually gained over us, a domination which arrests the attention of every philosophic foreigner on his first visit to the United States.
>
> (1938: 564)

Ross staked his hopes for society to strengthen corrective influences on a belief in the alertness and intelligence of the reading public to control the excesses of the media and to adjust deviations from their public role as disseminators of facts and opinions (Ross, 1910: 303–11; 1918: 620–32). However, he gained national fame with the publication of *Sin and Society: An Analysis of Latter-Day Iniquity* (1907), a book that attacked corporate imperialism in America and provided Progressive reformers with a moral justification for their advocacy of change. In it, Ross addressed the problems of material culture and the failure of society to adapt its norms to a rapidly changing technological environment. But the book also confirmed the limitation of reformist ideas; its radicalism was an expression of confidence in the dominant political and economic system.

Like others, the author appealed for social justice and sought control of the social and economic system through balance or moderation. Specifically, Ross counted on the power of public opinion to bring about change and offer salvation, and he chided the "revolutionary socialist," proclaiming that "Infatuated with his chimera, he lifts no finger to reach the near-by good, while his wild proposals excite apprehensions which hinder the progress of genuine constructive work" (1907: 148–9).

Park developed a theory of communication that was built upon Dewey's notion that "society exists in and through communication" and on his insight that communication also produces conflict and, potentially, collision with another mind or culture. This argument was a reflection of Georg Simmel's subjectivist perspective which had appealed to Park (as did the idea of "social distance" which influenced his extensive work on racial problems). Park's sensitivity to the role of the individual in society – which was also expressed through his work on the marginal man – shaped his definition of communication as a confrontational process. Communication served not only to attain community and define mutually agreeable goals; it could also be used to benefit different, even antagonistic causes. In his "Reflections on Communication and Culture," Park offered the view that communication also fosters competition and conflict, but that

it is always possible to come to terms with an enemy . . . with

whom one can communicate, and, in the long run, greater inti-
macy inevitably brings with it more profound understanding, the
result of which is to humanize social relations and to substitute
a moral order for one that is fundamentally symbiotic rather
than social.

(1938: 195–6)

Communication is also a process of interaction which is completed only when understanding occurs. Park differentiated between older, stimulus–response notions of communication and a
cultural vision. He stated that "communication is never merely a
case of stimulus and response in the sense in which the terms are
used in individual psychology. It is rather expression, interpretation, and response" (1938: 196). His discussion of communication
and culture concentrated on issues of competition, diffusion and
acculturation, reflecting the proximity of contemporary social
concerns in his work.

Park's analysis of the foreign language press furnished examples
of how minorities would gain knowledge and understanding of their
environment and, more importantly, of themselves. For instance,
talking about the foreign language press, he observed that the
desire to know created unrest, even conflict, and changed the
goals and perspectives of a younger generation. Thus, the Yiddish
socialist press

ceased to be a mere organ of the doctrinaries, and became
an instrument of general culture. All the intimate, human,
and practical problems of life found place in its columns. It
founded a new literature and a new culture, based on the life
of the common man.

(1967: 143)

In short, a return to community was essential for retaining the
stability of social relationships.

Park, too, warned against the potentially destructive power of
technological society. The media were means of creating fictitious
communities and a false sense of proximity. They were imperfect,
but then, so was society. Park placed the media as a surviving
species in the context of a struggle of existence that affected all
members of society. The press was part of the natural history
of society; in fact, it had its own natural history which included
competing interests and degrees of insight or understanding of the

social and political activities among members of the public (1923). His visions of society stressed the cultural context of individuals and promoted a brand of humanism that became popular in the cultural productions of these years. Indeed, Park felt that sociology could serve to provide a humanistic approach to the problems of the modern world and that it would be a "healing study, a 'science' in the older sense, a body of knowledge and insight that made man more at home in the world . . ." (Matthews, 1977: 193).

These early sociological considerations reflect the concerns of a generation of American social scientists who witnessed decisive social and economic changes. Although different enough in their particular interests, they ultimately shared the vision of a pluralistic model of society; and they welcomed an alternative to the potential excesses of individualism *and* socialism as reflected in *laissez-faire* theories and Marxist doctrines of the times. Indeed, the prominence of issues like socialization or cooperation, and the stress on balance, represented notions of change; the goal was always to establish democracy in the United States. Such ideas reduced the potential richness and variety of American culture to considerations of the United States as an undifferentiated, homogeneous culture, burdened with the expectation of being or becoming a "good" or "great" society. For instance, the debates over immigration as a process of assimilating individuals and the role of ethnic media in social communication are the most obvious contemporary examples of an applied social science inquiry that ignored social structures and concentrated on case studies. C. Wright Mills captured the mood of American social sciences by reminding his readers in an essay on textbooks and their ideological nature that the "ideal of practicality . . . operated, in conjunction with other factors, as a polemic against the 'philosophy of history' brought into American sociology by men trained in Germany" (1943: 168) with the result of shifting the focus of inquiry to "real" problems. In this connection he talked about the prevailing tendencies among social scientists to define problems in terms of deviations from norms, or standards of society, suggesting that "this mode of problematization shifts responsibility of 'taking a stand' away from the thinker and gives a 'democratic' rationale to his work" (1943: 169).

American Pragmatism also provided the foundations for a belief in an order made by individuals; when it opened the possibilities for conceiving of thoughts as instruments of action and constituted an environment, experiential knowledge rose to become creative, social practice. The likelihood of a social order determined by practice, based upon human experience and the pursuit of truth in the discoveries of inquiry, promoted not only experimentation and reform, but also supported the notion that questions of right or wrong rested in human experience. Truth had become a human affair, and language and communication became fundamental aspects of a quest for change. In this sense, the Pragmatism of Peirce, James and Dewey was a philosophy of modernity whose major component was a theory of moral criticism. It was a philosophy of experience that turned from religion and a traditional belief in ideal ends or intrinsic goods to human inquiry and an affirmation of a new belief in action. Under these circumstances, the community of inquirers was to search for appropriate methods to explore the shifting boundaries of human conduct or social standards.

The acquisition of knowledge in the pursuit of change, as a driving force behind a new understanding of moral judgments, involves communication; it also emphasizes the importance of language in defining social responsibility. The fact that habits lead to actions and that conscious reasoning leads to an understanding of right and wrong suggests a relationship between responsibility and communication. Thus, considerations of truth and understanding, of community and communication, are also articulations of ethical concerns. They were raised in an era of anxieties about the development of modern society only to disappear later on, particularly during the rapid development of social-scientific approaches to the study of communication and media. When they resurfaced during recent years, the field had undergone significant changes.

Throughout the period of Dewey's theoretical contributions to social-scientific inquiries into the conditions of American society by Chicago sociologists, communication remained an abstract idea, although a critical stance suggested concrete analyses of the media in the context of exploring the notion of democracy as a modern problematic. The resulting ideas of communication described a process which differentiated between those in control of the technology (the operators of the press) and those receiving the messages (the public); but they failed to recognize the effects of cultural or economic differences of the communication process on the workings of society. In the minds of the social critics, the Great Community, or the ideal democracy, was populated by individuals whose interests, capabilities and understandings coincided with the essence of the community, while communication became the vital, integrating and socializing force in the process of democratization and, as such, remained a major concept in social theory and research.

At the time, there was little disagreement over the suggestion that there can be no human nature independent of culture. The question was rather how to deal conceptually with the historical components in an examination of social and cultural processes. Indeed, at the beginning of the twentieth century, there was a strong movement among the first generation of American social scientists, which reflected a sophisticated understanding and appreciation of the German historical school, including socialist writings. As exponents of a cultural-historical tradition in social science scholarship, its most prominent representatives provided academic leadership in the critique of social and political conditions of society with works which were a direct response to the reality of their own age. However, in their writings they sought to reach an accommodation with existing economic structures and political power, and their solutions to the problems of modern capitalism were based upon the conviction that, despite its failures, capitalism offered an appropriate context for the growth and success of a great society.

The underlying assumption of theoretical discourse during these years was the prevalence of a harmonious state of mind and matter; hence opposition and conflict were treated as deviations and not as radical departures from traditional ways of thinking about communication, media, or democracy. There was something irresistible about the idea that the spirit of equal opportunity, shared experience and fair treatment permeated American culture and directed the course of participation.

A major argument for the failure of the prevailing democratic theory and, implicitly at least, for the failure of communication to work the magic of establishing and perpetuating the democratic experience, was advanced by Walter Lippmann in a series of books. Beginning with *Liberty and the News* (1920), he contradicted the pronouncements of progressive reformers and others, like Dewey, who still believed in the potential of a democratic society. In the wake of the experiences of the First World War, Lippmann began to raise questions about the role of the press in modern society and the relationship of individuals to the state and to the process of political decision-making. Based upon his readings of Freud and influenced by the writings of George Wallas, he introduced the notion of the irrational to the political process and argued for the importance of considering biases, prejudices and feelings in people's attempts to grapple with the notion of facts and reality. Lippmann's writings are central to understanding the dilemma of communication in modern society; they return to the question of power in a democratic state, e.g., the position of institutions and the role of individuals in the creation of knowledge, which includes the responsibility of the press to serve the truth, to inform and educate rather than to amuse or excite.

Lippmann's critique of communication and media in modern society also reflected the presence of a rising generation of social critics whose attacks on American institutions typically included the press for failing to occupy its envisioned role as the organ of representative democracy. They included Upton Sinclair (*The Brass Check*, 1919), Oswald Garrison Villard (*Some Newspapers and Newspaper-Men*, 1923), and George Seldes (*Lords of the Press*, 1938), who recalled the problems of commercialism with its enthusiastic response to mass appeals, and dwelt on the lack of freedom in the workplace for journalists and editors. They issued fiery indictments and warned about the dangers of an ailing press for the democratic system, recognizing that the quality of political life depended on the nature of the media system.

But the contributions of this generation of critics remained "inadequate or impotent," according to Lee Brown, who concluded his study of press criticism with the observation that historically it had been "of uneven quality and inwardly directed" (1974: 98). Indeed, early press criticism operated on the assumption that the requirement of responsible journalism was professional service rather than participation by the public, with decisions about the flow of information generated by advertising revenues and modified by editorial reasoning. The emphasis, again, rested on advice for adjustment and correction of excessive commercialism.

A last attempt to offer such an extensive and qualitative critique of the media and their failure in American society to participate in the search for the Great Community was the report by the Commission on Freedom of the Press, issued as *A Free and Responsible Press* (1947). Although published after the war, its reformist spirit and recommendations reflect the critical position of earlier writings and signal the end of an era of critical discourse in American social sciences. In fact, the Commission report summarized the critique of previous decades; it reaffirmed a belief in the free flow of information and the diversity of ideas, and it reiterated the dangers of a press dominated by the ideas of owners and those who control the press through economic or political means. As an indictment of the contemporary media, the report was a remarkable document. Based upon broad principles and general truths, it called for an "accountable freedom" of the press. Jerilyn McIntyre has suggested that the "most enduring legacy of the commission is that it draws attention to the connection between the continuing problems of mass communication in a modern democratic society and some of the most fundamental and enduring questions of modern political thought" (1987: 153).

The report also reflected an appreciation of human values and a sensitivity to the interdependence of human affairs, which Thomas Haskell has identified with Dewey and his generation as a product of social experience. He found that

> they experienced society not only in the vicarious, deliberate, rational manner of the social researcher – presumably always master of his data, holding society at arm's length as a mere object of examination – but also in the immediate, haphazard, unaware manner of the voter, lover, consumer, and job-seeker who is himself an object and onrushing element of the social process. Both kinds of experience prompted their recognition of interdependence.
>
> (1977: 16)

Nevertheless, the report failed to persuade the public or the media. Instead, it remained a thoughtful and eloquent appeal by a group of scholars, who were unable to overcome the political reality of their own positions *vis-à-vis* the commercial interests of the culture industry. If anything, the report continues to serve as a reminder that social institutions, like the media, and the economic interests which hold their future, will not be moved by the intelligence or conviction of theoretical propositions. Instead, the fate of the Commission report demonstrates the existing gap between intellectual positions and political practice, that is, the isolation of informed judgment from the public sphere and the inability of the media to consider the ethical dimensions of their professional practice.

Over time the analysis of society became increasingly empirical, behavioristic and scientistic in the consideration of the individual, the role of communication and the effects of the media. Mass communication research followed the route of atomistic positivism in its analysis of democratic practices. Implicit in this direction of social-scientific inquiry was an assumption of shared cultural and social values across American society. Thus, the specter of mass society as an aggregate of individuals united in a shared consciousness of individualism would also be conceived of as holding the promise of an emancipatory movement, involving all people and reflecting a triumph of individualism under bureaucratic guidance and in an age of technology.

The confrontation of an emerging social science with a nineteenth-century philosophical tradition represented a major turning-point when the locus of interpretation of reality moved into the realm of empirical observations. As William Albig has observed,

> While it was necessary for the social science to free itself from 19th century philosophical and ethical preoccupations . . . there was no need to reverse the values and encourage an often spurious objectivity and cultivated illiteracy. While it was necessary to retreat from over-facile generalization unsupported by any significant accumulation of data, there was no need to abjure generalization to the extent found at present in the frequently desiccated and relatively meaningless fragments of data accumulated by empirical statistical research.
>
> (1957: 17)

Indeed, the development of social theories in the United States under the guidance of a liberal-pluralist perspective was based upon an assumption of consensual unity. Under its influence complex social and political issues of power and authority were reduced to an examination and legitimation of the dominant social system; that is to say, the practice of normative functionalism, including the assumptions of behavioral research, surveys and the contributions of social psychology, led to the reproduction of the dominant view of society in mass communication research.

The critical writings of social theorists and sociologists from Dewey to Park are also reminiscent of prevalent "socialist" ideas and raise questions about the premises of progressive reformers in the United States and the ways in which communication suggests itself as a social process. There has always been some socialism since society came into being (Freeden, 1978: 27). However, Cooley specifically confirmed that he could "not see that life presents two distinct and opposing tendencies that can properly be called individualism and socialism, any more than that there are two distinct and opposing entities, society and the individual, to embody these tendencies"; accordingly, "the phenomena usually called individualistic are always socialistic in the sense that they are expressive of tendencies growing out of the general life, and, contrariwise, the so-called socialistic phenomena have always an obvious individual aspect" (1902: 40).

The discussion of human existence in an age of despair, the realization of change, and the potential of the community of inquiry and the challenge of participation were central to Pragmatism (and, particularly, to the work of Dewey); they were also familiar aspects of Marxist thought. Underlying both is the notion of social praxis. According to Richard Bernstein,

> Like Marx, Dewey believed that the only way to bring about a freer, more humane society in which creative individuality can flourish is by the transformation of objective social institutions. Like Marx, Dewey calls for a criticism of criticisms that is directed towards controlled change.
>
> (1971: 228)

Indeed, there were discussions about individualism and assumptions about human nature, including an ethical conception of the individual, which were widely shared among progressive thinkers, pragmatists and socialists. After all, the actions of individuals were of social significance and the potential of technology offered hope for the improvement of society and the emergence of ethical principles from the experiences of community and communal existence. These considerations were based on everyday practices, including encounters with an active, if not vigorous, immigrant culture that flourished in the United States.

Enriched by theories of socialism and the experiences of European labor movements, a leftist intellectual culture critique appeared with considerable vigor. Among its most prominent representatives was Victor Francis Calverton, who offered a comprehensive critique of American culture. He attempted to organize a collective effort among Marxist intellectuals to comprehend the psychological conditions of society and to overcome the disillusionment with capitalism. As Daniel Aaron remarked, "Calverton's career is almost a one-man history of the American radical movement between 1920 and 1940" (1965: 337).

But regular discussions by Marxist and non-Marxist intellectuals in journals like *The Modern Quarterly*, *The Masses*, *The Liberator*, or *The New Masses* also reflected the level of concern about the importance of culture and helped establish a Marxist tradition in the United States of searching for a theory of culture in the shadow of economic and social determinants. Its presence, however, was marked by a failure to attract widespread attention and to recover political influence in the face of criticism which may have held, as Reinhold Niebuhr suggested, that "Marxism is not so much the natural political philosophy of proletarians, as it is a disease with which they have become infected" (1932: 144).

Radical ideas also fell victim to government suppression of socialists and their press during the First World War, and to an effective anti-communist (and anti-foreign) propaganda throughout later years. The results were disappointing for the cause of socialism which failed in the age of Americanism and its broad definition of an American way of life which may well have included socialist notions of public service in the name of the community. Thus Paul Buhle, who has chronicled the presence of Marxist thought in the American environment, albeit misconstrued or misunderstood by its proponents during these years, concluded that "what passed for Marxist thinking could be more accurately placed somewhere between the margins of Progressive thought . . . and a rough understanding of Marxian economics." He also observed that authors had difficulties "reconciling Marxist theories with contemporary reality as well as academic orthodoxy" and observed that under changing political conditions "they returned chastened, almost without exception, to the familiarity and warmth of mainstream American thought: on one side to the Pragmatism and empiricism of the social sciences; on the other, to the aestheticism of high culture" (1987: 164).

Earlier, Leon Samson had provided a plausible, contemporary explanation for the failure of socialism in the United States. He talked about Americanism as "substitutive socialism" and declared that Americanism is looked upon as a highly attenuated, conceptualized, platonic, impersonal, attraction toward a system of ideas, a solemn assent to a handful of final notions – democracy, liberty, opportunity, to all of which the American adheres rationalistically much as a socialist adheres to his socialism – because it does him good, because it gives him work, because, so he thinks, it guarantees him happiness. Americanism has thus served as a substitute for socialism. Every concept in socialism has its substitutive counter-concept in Americanism, and that is why the socialist argument falls so fruitlessly on the American ear.

(1933: 16)

On the other hand, Marxists recognized the power of progressive thought, including Dewey's accomplishments as a theorist and "leader of the advanced intellectuals" whose philosophy served specific historical functions in its class specificity. According to Novack,

Dewey performed for the philosophy of Progressivism a service similar to that performed by Henry George and Veblen for its economics, Beard for its history, Parrington for its literary criticism, Holmes and Brandeis for its jurisprudence, Sandburg for its poetry, Charles Edward Russell and Lincoln Steffens for its journalism.

(1975: 40)

It is even possible that the contributions of these individuals were influenced by contemporary socialist ideas, yet the same author dismissed Dewey's philosophy as a "theoretical expression of the outlook of the educated petty bourgeois in the epoch of the climb of American capitalism to world domination and the transformation of bourgeois democracy into imperialist reaction" (1975: 41).

Thus, the first encounter with a critical perspective of society, and specifically with the study of "mass" communication as a direct concern of modern American sociology, reflected more accurately a level of tolerance for dissent within the academic establishment, and therefore within the dominant theoretical paradigm, than the emergence of an alternative, let alone Marxist theory of society. Although socialism probably enriched the emergence of Americanism, the result was a critique of communication in the process of emancipation, e.g., the achievement of individualism in an industrialized society and in the production of mass – not class – society.

Nevertheless, the influence of Pragmatism, rising through the social reform movement of the 1920s and supported by social research of the 1940s and 1950s, would remain a strong and persistent element in the changing climate of the 1960s and guided the expressions of the social sciences in the 1970s and 1980s. Its prevailing disposition was the result of an optimistic belief in the individual as a free and creative participant in the social and political life of the community. The promise of a place and a share in the benefits of the Great Community for everyone continued to be reflected in theoretical issues and practical concerns and produced a vision of mass society as a community of cultures, while it reproduced the weaknesses of American sociological contributions of that period, which Gouldner has identified as "a lack of historicity" and "an insensitivity to class stratification, domination, and to the property ramifications of their problem" (1976: 118).

Pragmatism as a method of clarification of ideas promoted the study of communication as a social process. It sought a common ground for thought and meaning in the notion of shared experiences and introduced socially founded ideas of truth and reality. The prevalence of doubt and the need for (self-)control – that is, certainty – over the social environment encouraged and sustained criticism. The result was a process of reasoning about the conditions of life. The real emerged with the aid of the social sciences in their quest for truth, which had turned into a search for the spirit that created American society and for answers to the desire to build on such inspirations. When the religious foundations of the American Dream were replaced by the fervor of scientific inquiry, the importance of non-scientific knowledge remained a significant influence. Thus, the age of Pragmatism accommodated ideas about society as one nation under God and an almost righteous belief in the success of democracy and the power of empiricism. Religion as a way of life and the struggle for scientific truth were deemed compatible as humanism and empiricism were consciously joined by a generation of social philosophers cognizant of the religious traditions of their disciplines. The considerations, however, had shifted to worldly concerns and the state of society, in particular, under the pressures of change and the experiences of modernization. The cult(ure) of Pragmatism had led to a preoccupation with the question of social cohesion; American sociology during these years had found its legitimation through scientific practice and would continue to be absorbed in methodological issues affecting the analysis of communication and media. Its critique remained identified with attempts to secure a coherent liberal *Weltanschauung* and ultimately strengthened an ideology of social control.

The writings of American pragmatists and their followers were also a defense of the ideal political community. They reflected the tendency to embrace the virtues of classical liberalism at a time when the economic (and political) structure of society changed with a loss of community and the rise of urban power from emphasizing individual identity and equality to social anonymity and conformity. The values of immediacy or direct participation in the political and social life were translated into ideas of representation in government and mediation in communication. The United States had become a pluralist society and communication and the role of the media were no longer issues of individual expression. Instead, they were relevant social practices with assigned roles in the organization and control of a complex federation of communities of interests. The dehumanization of modern society began with the use of media technologies as political instrumentalities when individual expressions were replaced by media presentations of public consciousness, transforming individual acts of social or political participation into forms of representation. It was the result of an emerging technological society whose modes of production and communication offered not only social cohesion but also an increasing centralization of power and control over people.

American social theorists had realized the potential consequences of change and offered their own solutions toward stabilization and the improvement of society in the spirit of a social and economic reform movement. But they also shared the conditions of a technological civilization, that is, a universe of thought and practice which had elevated scientific knowledge to a powerful position *vis-à-vis* political practice. The idea of social engineering permeated democratic decision-making processes, which were dominated by professional elites who produced the definitions and explanations of public opinion. The social sciences had become part of an administrative structure that relied on the power of technological rationality. As a result, the prevalent discourse about culture and communication during the first decades of this century was directed toward the confirmation of the relationship between science and political practice which ultimately served the interests of elites and their desires for the rational organization and satisfaction of material needs. The Pragmatism of Dewey and others included visions of democracy which were based on the enabling power of communication and on the workings of interactive processes between communities of experts and a public that lacked the communicative and democratic competencies of informed political decision-making. The result was a theory of communication and the media that was doomed to collapse under the impact of cultural and economic conditions of inequality.

The development of the social sciences – and communication and media studies, in particular – continued to rely on faith in progress, namely, a widely shared belief in the superiority of American society (and Western civilization) and its technological-industrial nature, and the trust in scientific knowledge, despite a growing atmosphere of doubts and serious challenges. The secret of its strength may be found in an adherence to a type of Pragmatism which Samson described as a

> lever whereby the American by an act of criticism reads himself out of the institutions and ideas that annoy him, but does not really do away with them. . . . He does away with them, in other words, in his mind. Here is where the pragmatist turns up a utopian face. The pragmatist substitutes for the political process a purely psychologic As-If.
>
> (1933: 41–2)

The failure of Pragmatism rested in its inability to produce a radical critique of society which would overcome the built-in constraints of an idealistic or utopian way of thinking in the face of severe political and economic crises which would not respond to visions of an educated and informed community of inquirers engaged in deliberating reforms and contemplating social change. Bernstein argued that Dewey's

> faith in creative intelligence is naive because he underestimates the powerful social, political, and economic forces that distort and corrupt this "ideal." Despite Dewey's intention, the consequence of his own philosophy is to perpetuate the social evils that it seeks to overcome.
>
> (1971: 228)

During the latter part of the 1930s, however, the interest in questions of communication and media changed from theoretical considerations and social criticism, based upon the expectation of progressive thought, to practical concerns and specific problems within the scope of emerging research methodologies. The deficiencies of the reigning social philosophy were masked by a turn to considerations of inquiry, the testing of specific ideas, and the development of methodologies in pursuit of an objective analysis of the social and political environment. By now sociology was rapidly expanding to provide knowledge through the procurement of facts and their relationships. In fact, Charles Beard observed that "the spirit of American scholarship in the social sciences is intensely empirical" (1935: 63). But he also predicted the ultimate failure of empirical research to provide a theoretical synthesis based on the accumulated knowledge of society when he wrote that

> American scholarship runs its course. Its statistical and factual studies produced materials and work of immense value to future thought and use. . . . But efforts of American scholars to bring to pass a social synthesis by the application of the empirical method have come to a dead end. This fact is not generally admitted. Indeed it is stubbornly contested.
>
> (1935: 64)

His remarks foreshadowed the response of Critical Theory to the American social sciences a few years later.

Still, Pragmatism remained the dominant influence on American social theory. The radical critique of American sociology beyond the 1940s by C. Wright Mills, for instance, also includes a debate with the Pragmatism of Peirce, James and Dewey and a realization of the need to confront the everyday problems of society. His sociological study of Pragmatism (1964) was not only a major contribution to the literature of American social theory, but also an example of his philosophical grounding in preparation for his later work. However, his reflection on social theory in light of Pragmatism and the criticism of modern pragmatists declined with his increasing ideological conformity; Mills decidedly turned to the "radical aspects of the 'classic tradition' in sociology from Marx to Mannheim" and to "more universal concerns with contributions of radical European thought," according to Horowitz (1964: 26). This included Western European Marxism and the Frankfurt School.

Emerging from the work of Harold Lasswell, another student of American Pragmatism, was the idea of "mass communication" and the growing political need to define and study communication phenomena. The ensuing specter of empirical social science research coincided with commercial and public demands for information about the processes of mass society; the belief in progress provided confidence for the establishment of communication research which would soon move into a visible (or public) phase of its development as a modern approach to help explain and solve the problems of society. Thus, when a new generation of social scientists opened the era of "mass" communication research, its representatives appeared with hypotheses, a considerable interest in acquiring methodological expertise, and the desire to move issues of communication in society on to center stage.

This was a time when the conscience of history was buried in the pursuit of the present, and American communication research turned in its quest for knowledge from the possibilities of understanding to the certainties of empiricism.

Chapter 3

On ignoring history
Mass communication research and the critique of society

> Most of the critics in this country want to see their criticisms within the present framework of the industry.
>
> Paul Lazarsfeld

By the 1940s the United States had made the transition into an age of mass societies, when dreams of the Great Community were reconstituted as opportunities for participation in a collective life, with promises of protection from mass manipulation and loss of liberty. Social theorists had become preoccupied with notions of depersonalization and the atomization of society, reflecting upon a hostile world that was increasingly dominated by totalitarian regimes. Their claims of authority championed the need for individuals to share a sense of community under the guise of their respective ideologies. Some of the circulating theories of American social scientists rested on analyses of modernization and its effects upon social organizations, taking into account the shift from notions of "community" to considerations of "society." Other theories addressed the study of collective behavior, that is, the effects of mass manipulation, including propaganda and advertising, on the nature of the social environment.

Under these circumstances, issues of communication and society figured prominently in the work of Chicago sociologists, who questioned the direction of urban growth and social commitment. In their writings public opinion was recognized as a powerful and essential source of strength for the maintenance of a democratic society and remained a major focus of theorizing about the nature of pluralism. Indeed, the character and conduct of large numbers of people coping with technological change and searching for meaningful conditions of existence, in an environment that had become more difficult to understand and almost impossible to conquer, had presented new opportunities for the study of social behavior and control.

For instance, Herbert Blumer, whose work in the tradition

of Mead and symbolic interactionism represented a Pragmatist approach to the pathology of mass society, provided a now classic discussion of collective behavior as a study of "ways by which the social order comes into existence, in the sense of the emergence and solidification of new forms of collective behavior" (1939: 223). For Blumer, communication played a significant role in his discussion of the processes of social movements. He differentiated among collectivities, such as publics, crowds and masses, and suggested that social movements centering on the mechanisms of the public or crowd give rise to the political and moral phases of the social order, while those which "stress the mechanisms of the mass, yield subjective orientations in the form of common tastes and inclinations" (1939: 280). Accordingly, his presentation of public opinion and propaganda appears related to public activities, while issues of advertising ("mass advertising") are addressed as appeals to members of the mass.

In contrast to European discussions of mass society and the dangers of totalitarianism, Blumer and others provided an explanation of mass phenomena which rested on American middle-class experiences of massification, describing the conditions of social change under the pressures of technology and industrialization. Other groups or classes also involved in this process, like the "proletarian mass," consisted of people "with little organization or effective communication," they were "wrested loose from a stable group life" and

> usually disturbed, even though it be only in the form of vague hopes or new tastes or interests. Consequently, there is a lot of groping in their behavior – an uncertain process of selection among objects and ideas that come to their attention.
>
> (1939: 45)

The frequent observations of media involvement in the process of organizing and manipulating people served as an obvious agenda for the study of communication. At about this time, in the early 1940s, Harold D. Lasswell had introduced the term "mass communication" in his work about political power and propaganda. The term was meant to signify the modern conditions under which society is organized and to emphasize the role of bureaucracies and their communication technologies in political decision-making processes. It was also an acknowledgment of the importance of communication for the analysis of social phenomena.

The decline of community and its authority in an industrialized and urbanized society resulted in new patterns of social organization with potential consequences for the social and political understanding of democracy. In fact, the idea of mass society emerged in the United States as a theory of pluralism that offered a new sense of freedom and the possibility of participation to various social groups. Kornhauser concluded in the late 1950s that the conditions of mass society "carry with them both the heightened possibility of social alienation *and* enhanced opportunities for the creation of new forms of association." He also observed that

> Modern industry destroys the conditions for a society of small enterprises, but it also provides the condition of abundance which frees people to seek new ways of life. Modern urban life atomizes traditional social groups, but it also provides a variety of contacts and experiences that broaden social horizons and the range of social participation.
>
> (1959: 237–8)

Consequently, the media, in seeking to shape public opinion around the potential of participation, assumed an important social and political position of influence which invited public scrutiny and attracted close scientific analysis.

Hence, following the tradition of American sociology as a study of human relations, social theorists were especially concerned with the conditions of mass society. Their emphasis remained either on the study of relationships between people and the elite, encompassing the shifting social or political power, or on analyses of collective behavior under changing social realities. Another tradition of social-scientific scholarship concentrated on issues of culture and cultural change under the pressures of mass society. Such topics ranged from the impact of political and economic issues on everyday life, for instance, the nature of ethnicity or race and the growth of a consumer society, to the powerful position of media enterprises in the relationship between individuals, institutions and the state. There was always at least an implicit expression of hope for a better way of life in mass society. Accordingly, Edward Shils concluded that

> as the mass of the population comes awake when its curiosity and sensibility and its moral responsiveness are aroused, it begins to become capable of a more subtle perception, more appreciative

of the more general elements in a concrete representation, and more complex in its aesthetic reception and expression.

(1961: 4)

Consequently, some investigations focused on aspects of participation in the cultural life of society, like the production of material culture and the capacity for expression and understanding. The resulting debates about the nature of culture under the influence of mass movements, including the rise of popular culture and the position of high culture in American society, provided yet another intellectual source of communication and media studies in the United States.

Such optimistic views of mass society and mass culture, embracing critical observations about the progress toward freedom or individuality, supported the rationale of a functioning liberal-pluralist democracy in the United States. They also conferred relevance and special importance on issues of communication, and – appropriately so – on the function of media and media technologies in mass society.

When the demands of the marketplace, combined with the rise of social-scientific methodologies which served the expanding interest in questions of communication and people, prevailed, the decline of a critical approach to the study of society and communication under the theoretical influence of Pragmatism and its application by Chicago School sociologists seemed complete. By the 1940s, however, a new generation of social theorists continued the search for ways in which "social science [could] be used in order to realise liberal values and goals in modern society" (Smith, 1988: 5). Undoubtedly there had been changes as a result of

an increasing concern with the scientific status of the field, reflected in the preoccupation with methodology; the rise of other sociology departments as centers of research and graduate instruction; the absorption of major European sociological theories; and changing concepts of the proper role of the sociologist in relation to the society he studied.

(Matthews, 1977: 179)

Throughout the ensuing debates about mass society theories and their impact on the American experience, warnings about the dangers of powerful media and their effects on the welfare of society and the expression of democratic practices resurfaced in the literature. For instance, Louis Wirth wrote that in "mass communications we have unlocked a new social force of as yet uncalculable magnitude" which "has the power to build loyalties, to undermine them, and thus by furthering or hindering consensus to affect all other sources of power." And he urged that it is important "that we understand its nature, its possibilities, its limits, and the means of harnessing it to human purposes" (1948: 12). His words reflect the spirit of American Pragmatism and the traditional concerns of its sociological dimension, namely, the utilization of a new social force for the benefit of society and the creation of a better world.

Thus, when American communication and media studies emerged in the 1940s, their initial concerns reflected the needs of an expanding society, including the positioning of political and economic interests, while their intellectual foundations rested on the influence of the critical tradition of Pragmatism and the sociology of the Chicago School. That is, the basic commitment to enlightenment and the improvement of society *qua* society was replaced by a definition of allegiance to special interests that equated the rising demands of the political and economic systems with serving the welfare of society. Along the way, the process of (mass) communication became identified with the creation and maintenance of the necessary conditions of the social environment and the quality of the democratic experience, while issues of communication and media rose to become commercially and politically relevant topics of social-scientific inquiry.

Although significant contributions to the field of communication and media research were made initially by individuals working in the traditions of sociology, social psychology or political science, there were also expectations for the creation of a separate discipline. With these promising beginnings of modern (mass) communication research grew an implicit assumption that its praxis could not only produce a theoretical understanding of the role of media and communication in a liberal-pluralist society, but also help legitimate social-scientific concerns about the nature of communication and establish mass communication as a scientific discipline. These hopes seemed particularly strong among those whose scholarship was organized exclusively around problems of media and communication, often under the auspices of journalism or mass communication departments within American colleges and universities, where contemporary references to mass communication research as a discipline continue to reside.

Shearon A. Lowery has provided a typical description suggesting that the "move towards becoming a discipline" began with the institutionalization of mass communication research in university programs, and is reflected in the presence of "scholarly journals, scientific associations, textbooks, and the other trappings of a discipline" (1988: ix). Others, with strong academic groundings in sociology or social psychology, for instance, seemed less inclined to contemplate the status of the field. Although considerations of communication in the context of social theories, in particular, remained a considerable but never exclusive concern of most major contributors to the field, including Lasswell, Lazarsfeld, Deutsch, Lewin and Hovland, they never precluded other, related investigations of human relations or social structures. In fact, the ability to contextualize questions of communication in the specific problematic of established disciplines contributed significantly to insights into human nature and conduct.

On the other hand, individuals like Wilbur Schramm, who emerged (from journalism education) during this period as a leader in the field, yearned for a systematic and unified theory of communication. He repeatedly expressed his disappointment in the failure of contemporary mass communication research to produce a theoretical framework for the study of communication during the latter part of his career. At other times his proposal for uniting sociological and psychological insights into a powerful model of communication (1971: 7) became a curious reminder of earlier movements toward building a unified science, when scholarly debates among logical positivists concerned a successful combination of inner and outer worlds constructed through experience.

The discoveries of mass society and mass culture phenomena, however, were also accompanied by a decided turn away from the contributions of American Pragmatism and the sociology of the Chicago School. In fact, traditional sociology had rediscovered nature, and, under the influence of Talcott Parsons, embraced structural functionalism with its claim to move steadily in the direction of a theoretical system, not unlike classical mechanics (Parsons and Shils, 1951: 51). Beginning with the 1940s there was a decisive shift toward functional analysis, which focused on the study of social phenomena and their

consequences for social structures. The idea that society consisted of a system of interrelated parts striving toward a state
of dynamic equilibrium determined, in turn, the site and range
of social and political activities. In fact, the notion of functional
analysis, as related to serving specific needs or ends, meant
that the study of communication, including "mass" communication, became identified with the search for dependencies or
consequences of activities by communicators and their audiences that would challenge or maintain the stability of the
social system. The need to watch for these functions, that
is, for intended or unintended media effects had significant
consequences for the ensuing analysis of communication and
media within a cultural frame. Specifically, under the influence
of Parsons (and Clyde Kluckhohn), A. L. Kroeber's concept
of culture was significantly modified to restrict its definition
to behavior shaped by "patterns of values, ideas, and other
symbolic-meaningful systems" (Harris, 1979: 281), reflecting
an idealist notion of culture and an attempt to accommodate
a structural functionalist explanation of society. Harris argued
that such emerging idealistic cultural anthropology fulfilled not
only "the conservative bias inherent in institutionalized social
science," but it was also prone to follow Parsonians who "accept
the system as a given and seek to account for its stability" (1979:
284–5).

The interest in culture also surfaced in the discussions about
the relationship between personality and culture by Ralph Linton
(*The Cultural Background of Personality*, 1945), Musafer Sherif
(*The Psychology of Social Norms*, 1936), and Hadley Cantril
(*The Psychology of Social Movements*, 1941), among others. A
few years later Gerbner included a cultural perspective in his
definition of communication when he suggested that individuals
must understand their social environment in order to "come
to grips (and not unconsciously to terms) with the sweeping
undercurrents of their culture" (1958: 107).

Most recently, DeFleur and Ball-Rokeach have offered a broad
and "tentative" definition of culture as "solutions to problems
of living that are passed on to following generations" (1989: 6),
marking the continuation of an equally confining, functionalist
perspective in mass communication literature.

Earlier, the continuing problems caused by the depression, the
increasing importance of the media as political and economic

institutions, and the rise of fascism and communism in Europe had helped shift the focus of social-scientific research. There had been a loss of confidence in American society and the promise of a rediscovery of the self, with the help of psychoanalysis and the work of John B. Watson and Sigmund Freud, in particular.

This had also been the time when modern science became a social and political force and a source of social knowledge, constituting a significant departure from the historical scholarship of the early twentieth century. These changes were accompanied by the decline of common sense and the rise of expert opinion represented by social scientists and their obsession with society as an object of study. Robert Park observed at the time that "scholars were being replaced by intellectuals, men of wisdom, knowledge, and balance by men with a drive for maximum conceptual abstraction and an outcaste sensibility" (Matthews, 1977: 186). Similarly, Michael Sproule has observed that critical social analysis in the field of propaganda, which had gathered momentum between 1919 and 1937, based on a "reemergence of rhetorical consciousness" (1987: 60) in society, began to fade and eventually lose to the ability of communication research to produce reliable knowledge about social influences and to cater expediently to commerce and government without raising many "troubling questions about the interests and motives of persuaders" (1987: 68).

When the field of (mass) communication theory and research turned from a cultural/historical interpretation of communication, reminiscent of Pragmatism and the work of the Chicago School, to a social-scientific explanation, ideas of communication and media were processed in the context of quantitative analyses and investigations. These changes were most graphically reflected in the vastly different treatment of communication between the 1930 and 1968 editions of the (International) Encyclopedia of the Social Sciences. For instance, the two-page essay by Edward Sapir in the 1930 edition suggested the pervasiveness of communication throughout society. Sapir wrote that "every cultural pattern and every single act of social behavior involve communication in either an explicit or an implicit sense," and he offered a definition of society that was based on a cultural network, consisting of partial or complete understandings between the members of organizational units of every degree of size and complexity, ranging from a pair of lovers or a family to a league of nations or that ever increasing portion of humanity which can be reached by the press through all its transnational ramifications.

(1930: 78)

Almost forty years later, the original entry was revised by Ray L. Birdwhistell, and the concept of communication was enlarged to include nearly fifty pages about the phenomenon of "mass" communication. In his introductory essay, Morris Janowitz ascertained that

the social-scientific view must reject the notion that the growth of the mass media necessarily produces an undifferentiated society with a general lack of articulation and an inability to make collective decisions. Researchers must see the mass media as instruments of social control and social change that may have either positive or negative consequences, depending upon their organization and content.

(1968: 41)

Additional entries about "Control and Public Policy" (Wilbur Schramm), "TV and Its Place in Mass Culture" (Richard Hoggart), "Audience" (Leo Bogart) and "Effects" (Joseph T. Klapper) completed the discussion, with Hoggart introducing ideas about alternative, non-commercial television, based on British experiences. A separate entry dealt with political communication. The overall tone of these entries, however, confirmed the social-scientific bias toward the study of production, processes and effects. They reflected what George Gerbner called a central concern of the study of communications, namely, "the production, organization, composition, structure, distribution, and functions of message systems in society" (1967: 52), and promoted an understanding of a mass media theory that would concentrate on questions related to the "composition and structure of mass-produced message systems" (1967: 55).

These developments in the definition and scope of communication research, as reflected in the encyclopedia entries and their range of coverage, and supported by the extensive publication of books and journals in the field, occurred within a generation. They enabled individuals, like Lasswell, to reflect on the experiences of those years as an encounter with a *tabula rasa* of theories and practices. He recalled that when he "became acquainted with the field of public opinion and communications research there was no Roper, no Gallup, no Cantril, no Stouffer, no Hovland. Lazarsfeld was neither a person, nor a measuring unit; or even a category" (1972: 301).

The fast rise of communication and media research paralleled social and political needs for knowledge about the power of information and its role in the control of society. It also reflected the presence of a social-scientific *instrumentarium*, like survey research or content analysis, to capture and describe the process of communication. Accordingly, in their recent retrospective look at "milestones in mass communication research," Lowery and DeFleur selected "studies of media effects [which were] empirical, quantitative, social science investigations, carried out in the main-line academic tradition of North American functionalist theory" (1988: ix).

Earlier, Wilbur Schramm had identified Lazarsfeld, Lewin, Lasswell and Hovland as the "'founding fathers' of communication research in the United States" (1963: 2), following Berelson's designation of these individuals as leading social scientists (1959: 1), but completely ignoring the history of concerns about communication and culture that had characterized the Chicago School and continued to surface in literary and anthropological writings at the time. Instead, Schramm insisted on characterizing communication research as an exclusive exercise of a behavioral science orientation by suggesting that it "is quantitative, rather than speculative. Its practitioners are deeply interested in theory, but in the theory they can test." He insisted that "they are behavioral researchers: they are trying to find out something about why humans behave as they do, and how communication can make it possible for them to live together more happily and productively" (1963: 5–6).

According to Schramm, the "science of human communication" had arrived only with the development of "audience measurement, public opinion sampling, content study, and the measurement of social effect" (1948: 5). Such definitions would coincide with rising interests in methodological issues rather than with specific social or political problems of a postwar society that attempted a gradual adjustment to normalcy. In his own retrospective assessment of these developments, Lasswell identified the growth of communication research as a

> response to a remarkable convergence of favoring conditions. The social sciences were in a spasm of inferiority when they compared themselves with their brothers, sisters, and cousins in the physical and biological sciences. Many of the leading figures were convinced that unless the specialists on society were able to "quantify" their propositions, they were doomed to the permanent status of second-class citizens in the universe of secular knowledge.
>
> (1972: 302)

Conversely, Lasswell insisted on being quantitative about communication, because

> of the scientific and policy gains that can come of it. The social process is one of *collaboration* and *communication*; and quantitative methods have already demonstrated their usefulness in dealing with the former. Further understanding and control depend upon equalizing our skills in relation to both.
>
> (Lasswell *et al.* 1949: 52)

His own views on the necessity for quantitative analysis had been solidified in his integrative work of classical and empirical political science, and emerged with his extensive involvement in the analyses of communication flows ranging from psychiatric reports to propaganda campaigns. By denying the dualism of individual and society, and utilizing Freudian analysis as an instrument of thought, which let him move between and within logical thought and free-floating fantasy, Lasswell also stressed the pluralism of possibilities and an all-encompassing totality. He argued that

> sound political analysis is nothing less than correct orientation in the continuum which embraces the past, present, and future. Unless the salient features of the all-inclusive whole are discerned, details will be incorrectly located. Without the symbol of the total context the symbols of details cannot be data.
>
> (1935: 4)

Lasswell foresaw the necessary developments of social analysis long before political science, and for that matter communication research, recognized them; Heinz Eulau has observed that

> in utilizing the ideas of emergence and wholeness he was anticipating the course of social-scientific inquiry in the next few decades, with its emphasis on *gestalt* thinking, interdisciplinary frames of references, development, functional categories and procedures, and, last but not least, the distinction between levels of analysis.
>
> (1969: 26)

Lasswell's imaginative contribution to an analysis of the symbolic aspects of politics and his wide-ranging and prolific writings on theoretical and methodological questions of politics, personality and culture, however, remained rather peripheral to communication research. In fact, his work on communication in the context of politics seemed to have shared the fate of other views on communication and human relations often associated with anthropology or literature and languages: they retained their significance or usefulness only by their ability to contribute to the dominant, sociological view of communication and media and never realized their potential as alternative explanations.

The primacy of sociological concerns about communication was reflected in a 1933 presidential report by Willey and Rice about the "agencies of communication," in which the authors concentrated on the transmission of messages under rapid technological changes. Their lengthy narrative suggested that "agencies of mass impression" would make millions of individuals think and act alike and that "the concentration of these agencies" would also mean an increased control over behavior. The result would be a "pervasive system of communication from which it is difficult to escape. Each new device provides one more channel that has its ultimate focus in the individual," and people become "dependent upon the new instruments and their use becomes a part of routine." They concluded in a strangely prophetic way that communication in its commodified form was a powerful element, capable of transforming the behavior of individuals and social organizations alike. They also noted that communication in society developed "without plan or aim" and as a "consequence of competitive forces, not social desirability," which also threatened the destruction of traditional agencies (1933: 216–17). The report furnished not only data about the state of communication in the

United States; the authors also offered hypotheses which lent support to a critical analysis of American culture by Critical Theory only a few years later.

The decisive shift to a scientific/empirical definition of the field emerged with a series of scientific models of communication and mass communication, particularly from the late 1940s and throughout the 1950s, which were preoccupied with functional aspects of various (mass) communication models and reinforced by specific positivistic methods. These activities served a number of immediate goals, specifically, the definition of the field, or, as some would argue, the discipline, the demonstration of its scientific nature, and finally its legitimation as a social-scientific enterprise.

Thus, when Lasswell offered a "convenient way to describe an act of communication" (1948: 37), he proposed what became an influential and considerably powerful formula for understanding human communication. He proceeded to identify not only the elements of the communication process – communicator, message, medium, receiver, and effects – but he also labeled the corresponding fields of communication research: media analysis, audience analysis and effect analysis (1948: 37). The description revealed Lasswell's primary interest in the power of persuasive (political) communication, but also referred to organismic equivalencies within an approach dominated by the intent of the communicator and the effect of messages (1948: 41). As such, his definition of communication harks back to the stimulus–response model, rooted in learning theory, which became a significant force in mass communication theory. Focused upon effects, this approach implied a concept of society as an aggregate of anonymous, isolated individuals exposed to powerful media institutions engaged in reinforcing or changing social behavior.

Equally important and quite persuasive in its scientific, mathematical intent was the work of Claude Shannon and Warren Weaver (1949), whose model described communication as a linear, one-way process. Their successful efforts can be traced to a series of subsequent constructions of behavioral and linguistic models of communication. In their assessment of such model-building activities, Johnson and Klare concluded that among "all single contributions to the widespread interest in models today, Shannon's is the most important. For the technical side of communication research, Shannon's mathematical formulations were the stimulus to much of the later effort in this area" (1961: 15).

In the following years, mass communication research was informed by a variety of communication and mass communication models. Stimulated by earlier efforts and by the rise of psychological models, which included aspects of balance theory and co-orientation (Heider, 1946; Newcomb, 1953; Festinger, 1957), they provided an attempt to order and systematize the study of mass communication phenomena (Schramm, 1954; Gerbner, 1956; Westley and MacLean, 1957). Their authors shared an understanding of the complexity of mass communication and its integration in society. At the same time, the impact of these models directed mass communication research toward an investigation of specific components and encouraged or reinforced a preoccupation with questions of communication effects. Furthermore, it accommodated the development and critique of research methodologies based upon a functional theory of society that had been firmly established with the creation of mass communication models.

McQuail and Windahl (1981) documented the unfolding of these models and confirmed the pervasive influence of mathematico-quantitative ideas on communication research. Consequently, the field offered social-scientific explanations for the stability of the social, political and commercial system without critically evaluating its own communication-and-society paradigm. Indeed, it was not until a widespread paradigm crisis reached the social science establishment, particularly in the 1970s and 1980s, that communication and media research turned to acknowledge the importance of culture.

Nevertheless, even throughout these years, the field of (mass) communication research continued to be identified overwhelmingly with the mainstream perspective of social science research. Both shared the implications of a pragmatic model of society. Their investigations related to the values of individualism and operated on the strength of efficiency and instrumental values in their pursuit of democracy as the goal of individual members of a large-scale, consensual society.

The commercialization of everyday life, particularly prior to the Second World War, provoked an atmosphere of experimentation and innovation that raised questions about the expanding role of communication and media in society. The requirements of propaganda analysis, including the production, dissemination and reception of persuasive messages during the war, and the demands of a postwar economy, helped accelerate the study of communication in society without the need to reflect on the nature and intent of communication research.

The resulting research agenda at US universities revealed not only a substantial social-scientific bias, but it also perpetuated an acquired taste in communication and media research with the production and distribution of edited volumes of mostly dominant research positions. These books, or readers, created useful and expedient sources for understanding various contributions to communication research; they also helped develop an almost instantaneous working definition of the field. These emerging collections soon identified the social-scientific leadership in communication research; they provided a feeling for the breadth of academic interests (including some minority positions) in issues concerning the spectacle of mass society and the impact of media technologies on culture; and their contents proved to be instructive examples of how editors defined the nature of communication inquiry, including its methodology.

The first series of texts were generated after the Second World War. They included *Communications in Modern Society* (1948), *Mass Communications* (1949) and *The Process and Effects of Mass Communication* (1954), edited by Wilbur Schramm, as well as *Communication of Ideas* (1948), edited by Lyman Bryson, and *Reader in Public Opinion and Communication* (1950), edited by Bernard Berelson and Morris Janowitz.

There were other, more specialized works, notably Paul F. Lazarsfeld and Frank Stanton, *Communication Research, 1948–49* (1949), or Carl I. Hovland, Arthur A. Lumsdaine and Fred D. Sheffield, *Experiments in Mass Communication* (1949), which represented major sociological and psychological research perspectives on communication in the United States. Finally and considerably later, Bernard Rosenberg and David Manning White edited *Mass Culture: The Popular Arts in America* (1957) to provide the first comprehensive look at theoretical and practical aspects of mass culture, followed a few years later by *Culture for the Millions? Mass Media in Modern Society* (1961), edited by Norman Jacobs.

In his introduction to *Communications in Modern Society*, which was based on conference reports presented at the University of Illinois, Schramm suggested that this was "a good time for communications men to look around them and take stock, and ask where do we go from here" (1948: 4). His resulting catalogue of questions concerning the role of the media and audiences within the democratic system was similar to earlier attempts to assess the place of communication in society. However, times had changed and Schramm noted that the "techniques of scientific research" would now be able to "supply verifiable information in areas where the hunch, the tradition, the theory, and the thumb have ruled" (1948: 5).

The book was intended to define the status of the field and its future, and its contributors represented the social sciences, journalism education and the media.[1] Their presentations, with few exceptions, identified major problems in communication and marked the beginning of a search for definitive answers to the lack of concrete information about people as audiences, media content and the location of responsibility within the political framework of American democracy. They affirmed private ownership of the media, commercialism, and the social responsibility of audiences which "can be best inculcated in a scientific age, by reliable knowledge about social consequences" (1948: 55). Discussions of the nature of communication in terms of cultural or social determinants based on literary or philosophical sources were rare (among the exceptions were contributions by Leo Lowenthal) and accentuated the general lack of a historical perspective. Instead, a historical outlook on the development of applied communication research featured the improvement of technical and economic conditions (for media operations), the increase in potential audience shares, and clarified the role of government, particularly with the introduction of television, and, last but not least, explained media effects.

During the same year, Lyman Bryson published *The Communication of Ideas*.[2] The book was based upon lectures presented at the Institute for Religious and Social Studies of the Jewish Theological Seminary in New York. Although the scholarly perspectives on communication revealed "no systematic outline of a theory of communication" (1948: 1), they offered a theoretical antidote to the one-dimensionality of the Schramm collection. They also contributed to a basic concern about the nature of community, and Bryson acknowledged the pivotal role of communication which "makes community possible and community is both the location of our interest and the basic concept of our present thinking" (1948: 2).

Bryson also argued that considerations of communication reflected a reaction against "the dominant intellectual tendency of our time, which is to think more of processes and less of things" (1948: 2). He attempted to address the complexity of things *and* processes in modern communities; he observed the inevitable fact of technological change and that the achievements of modern communication, like all modern inventions, "can be either good or evil and are both good and evil most of the time" (1948: 6). The volume reflected more accurately than Schramm's earlier publication the range of interests in communication studies, in particular, the diversity of potential contributions to the debate about culture and communication. From this compilation emerged a strong sense of the historical and cultural positioning of questions related to the meaning of communication, either as a philosophical issue or as an everyday event in the context of interpersonal relations or media activities. Social-scientific treatments of communication were tempered by the presence of literary and artistic perspectives, and the critique of communication concentrated on the potential for the media with their political power to maintain an irresponsible and dysfunctional role in a democratic society. One of the persistent conclusions of the book is that "mass communication has this inescapable character: it is a relation between a single point of diffusion and a great mass of audience," raising serious questions about the "mass production of ideas" (1948: 7).

The increasing demands for suitable texts resulted in the publication of *Mass Communications* (1949), intended by Schramm to help produce an "integrated introduction to mass communications for persons who would like to study them through the windows of the social sciences" (1949: vii). This volume contained material, including extensive bibliographies and statistical information, that spanned the development of the field, including excerpts from classic works, like Lippmann's *Public Opinion*, or Park's "The Natural History of the Newspaper." By and large Schramm relied on contributors to earlier readers (his own and that of Bryson) and drew on individuals at major research institutions.[3] His selections continued to reflect the shift to a social-scientific perspective on mass communication issues; they also recognized private or corporate media research as a significant component of the mass communication research environment. The content of the book itself is evidence of the status of "mass communications" as an object of scientific analysis, supported by descriptive/analytical materials about the history and social control of the media, raising by now familiar questions about the position of mass communication in the United States.

Schramm's compilation remained well within the expected boundaries of describing specific "target" areas of social-scientific analyses: communication processes, contents, audiences and effects, without reflecting the need for a critical understanding of the role of research, for instance, *vis-à-vis* private (commercial) and public interests.

The *Reader in Public Opinion and Communication*, edited by Bernard Berelson and Morris Janowitz at the University of Chicago and published in 1950, grew out of their realization that theoretical and practical interests in public opinion and communication needed a comprehensive and cohesive treatment which "adequately synthesizes and collates the available concepts and propositions in the field" (1950: ix). The resulting book was a first attempt to move in this direction with the preparation of a single volume of representative readings. The "major criterion" for the selection was "the quality of the contribution," representing the "major streams of interests and modes of thought now active in the field" (1950: x). Thus, the book combined a number of disciplines, including sociology, psychology, political science, history, economics, anthropology, and fields like law, journalism and librarianship.[4] It also provided a historical dimension of theoretical thought, since, contrary "to popular notions and even to the ideas of some practitioners in the field, the study of public opinion did not spring full-panoplied from the brow of George Gallup in the 1930s" (1950: 1). Consequently, the selections reflect the continuity of scholarly investigations of the relationship between notions of public opinion and communication in society. The volume offers a sense of theoretical concerns that reach from the works of Cooley, Mead and Park, and the later contributions by Riesmann, Lowenthal and Adorno, to those social-scientific attempts which "delimit and define the theoretical aspects of communication into formulations which can be subjected to empirical research" (1950: 143).

The *Reader in Public Opinion and Communication* constituted a work in the tradition of Chicago School sociology; it represents an attempt to create intellectual conditions for dealing with public opinion and communication with its bias toward the need to understand theoretical developments, its inclusion of a

variety of cultural or historical considerations, and its appreciation of communication not just as a process, but as a necessary condition for the existence and survival of a democratic
society.

In 1954 *The Process and Effects of Mass Communication*
appeared as a result of demands for a training manual in
communication "research and evaluation" by the United States
Information Agency (1954: i). Schramm had based his selections
on classroom materials used by the Institute for Communication
Research at the University of Illinois. Although aimed at the
international communication expert, the book became a major
text in the field of American mass communication studies; its
first edition reached six printings, and a second revised edition
in 1971, with significant changes and a co-editor, is in its fourth
printing in 1990.

Despite its title, the book dealt almost exclusively with
the notion of effects, reflecting an increasing social-scientific
preoccupation with questions of message construction, audience behavior and the impact of communication. Schramm
relied on what were by now standard sources, adding those
communication experts who worked for USIA, including Ralph
White and Joseph Klapper.[5] His extensive introductory notes
to various sections of the book reflected an attempt to summarize the discussions of communication research and provide a
focus on the requirements of international communication. He
advocated

> the clearest possible understanding of the target culture, . . .
> adequate tools and skills of communication and a clear under-
> standing of the use and capabilities of these tools, . . . a working
> relationship between the communicators and the sources of
> policy, and . . . constantly updated intelligence not only on
> the opinions and situation of the target audience but also on
> the effects of communication on them.

> (1954: 432)

In his selection and substantive presentation Schramm sought to
emphasize the specific, task-oriented approach of communication
research, thereby reinforcing the direction of the field as a social-
scientific enterprise, while reducing the utility of the volume as a
source of understanding communication in the context of culture
and society.

By the middle of the 1950s, then, a visible college of communication research emerged, formed by the literature of these collections, and suggesting a decisive development of the field during these years. Collectively, these books identified a small number of individuals and research institutes as the knowledge brokers of a new field of social-scientific endeavor. They became a major source of information about the nature of (mass) communication and its effects on all segments of society. They also identified acceptable research methodologies and provided evidence of the advancement of research techniques, however, without offering sufficient theoretical support.

The predominant position of Wilbur Schramm as a major producer of collections of mass communication research during these crucial years is undeniable; his sense of the "field" shaped questions about the role and function of communication and created an agenda for instituting research programs, particularly in the Midwest. He had come out of the University of Iowa, where he had known Kurt Lewin and was part of a Second World War group in Washington, DC, working on propaganda analysis that included individuals like Carl Hovland, Samuel Stouffer, Nathan Maccoby, Rensis Likert, Ralph Nafziger, John Gardner and Bernard Berelson; others, like Leo Rosten, Margaret Mead, Paul Lazarsfeld and Frank Stanton, also influenced him during these years (Cartier, 1988: 170).

When Schramm returned to Iowa, he had a strong sense of the interdisciplinary nature of communication research, the potential of social science methodology, and its capability to answer practical questions, but no apparent theoretical framework for a critical assessment of the role of the media in American society. This was the beginning of a period when the search for improved research tools obfuscated the rationale for communication research, except to respond to a rather vague idea of the relationship between communication, media and democracy. Although Schramm may have been ideally prepared to serve in the role of a shaper of theory, given his wide-ranging, interdisciplinary interests, he missed this opportunity and continued a successful career as a promoter of the field and a popularizer of new research areas, ranging from television and children to new communication technologies.

Schramm avoided controversy with his sense of accommodation and, undoubtedly, his knowledge of the politics of academic research. For instance, Cartier has noted that Schramm's work at Iowa "was oriented toward cooperation with the press, and was not constituted from a critical stance." She noted that

> Schramm thought of press lapses as failures to live up to a high calling, not as endemic problems. He planned to offer a revolutionary cure, partly in a subversive manner: he would *educate* these trade-oriented folks to prepare them for their calling; and he would continue to do so after they got into the field.
>
> (1988: 274)

Consequently, Schramm's initial contribution was journalistic rather than scientific; he reported about the state of communication research, but he did not engage in an informed critique of theories and methodologies of the field and their appropriateness for the study of society. However, he adopted a strong interest in the growth and development of the academic field, coupled with questions of freedom and responsibility, in which the support of communication research becomes a public responsibility in an effort to create and sustain a level of media performance that contributes to the development of a democratic society (1957).

When Rosenberg and White created the first viable textbook on mass culture, they deliberately ignored "artificial academic boundaries" to offer "the insights of fifty-one observers commonly concerned with the social effects of the media on American life" (1957: v). Consequently, *Mass Culture* includes historical perspectives from Alexis de Tocqueville and Walt Whitman to Leo Lowenthal, sections on specific media activities, as well as theoretical discussions of culture and the impact of modern communication on people.[6] The collection featured opposing positions in an assessment of American culture and provided "the viewpoints of both those who look with optimism at the media and those who scrutinize them with great anxiety" (1957: v). Accordingly, White suggested that "it is just these mass media that hold out the greatest promise to the 'average' man that a cultural richness no previous age could give him is at hand" (1957: 17), while for Rosenberg "Contemporary man commonly finds that his life has been emptied of meaning, that it has been trivialized. He is alienated from the past, from his work, from his community, and possibly from himself – although this 'self' is hard to locate" (1957:

7). The volume was a unique addition to the field, since it not only introduced age-old concerns about the preservation of culture, but also offered insights into emerging discussions about the conditions of modernization, the destructive forces of commercialism, and the impact of the mass media on interpretations of democracy and culture.

This dialogical approach to the cultural debate was supplemented two years later by the publication of *Culture for the Millions? Mass Media in Modern Society*. The book was based upon a seminar sponsored by the Tamiment Institute and *Daedalus*, the journal of the American Academy of Arts and Sciences; it was edited by Norman Jacobs. The collection demonstrated that the concerns over the production and consumption of culture, the power of the media, and the failures of criticism had remained an important agenda in the academy. The participants included social historians, philosophers and social scientists, critics and artists.[7] Their presentations and discussions reflected a sophisticated and engaged debate about the status of mass culture – and the future of mass culture theory in the United States. The contributors focused on the dilemma of a society drifting into the future without a cause or a vision of utopia; but their work was frequently informed by a strong sense of history and was conscious of the presence of other individuals who would raise questions about the quality of mass culture or about its existence and utility as a consumer item. The volume offered opportunities for sharing intellectual concerns about the state of society and provided a rationale for a critique of mass society by giving arguments for or against notions of mass culture as expressions of democratic experiences which would stress usefulness (and effectiveness) rather than excellence, consumption rather than production, and entertainment rather than education. In his preface to a 1961 edition of the book, Paul Lazarsfeld suggested that contemporary social criticism, which he identified with the reaction of "liberals" to the state of society, was a response to their own disappointment over the way in which people used their freedom of choice rather than a substantive comment about the cultural conditions of society. His observation that people "instead of listening to Beethoven" or "going to Columbia University" would "listen to Johnny Mercer" or "go to the Columbia Broadcasting System," underscored the success of popular culture (1961: xiv). But his comments also reflected a strong belief in the survival of society and the possibility of reform not because, but *in spite* of the presence of cultural elites. Lazarsfeld must have realized that social criticism plays a major role in the creation of an atmosphere of change, and that change itself had become an integral aspect of modern society, and, in due time, a focus of communication research. He was convinced that a "continuous stream of criticism" prepares society to "take advantage" of change and that it "is the tragic story of the cultural crusader in a mass society that he cannot win, but that we would be lost without him" (1961: xxiv).

Lazarsfeld was among those European (and particularly German-speaking) philosophers and social scientists who had arrived with the beginning of the Second World War. He called himself a "European positivist" who had been influenced by Ernst Mach, Henri Poincaré and Albert Einstein, and who felt intellectually close to members of the Vienna Circle (1969: 273). When he encountered members of the Frankfurt School, particularly Theodor Adorno and Max Horkheimer, who were in their first years of exile, Lazarsfeld was not particularly familiar with Critical Theory. But he discovered a mutual interest in the problems of mass culture, which he had begun to analyze in his studies of audiences and media contents. On the other hand, in his association with Columbia University, Lazarsfeld was introduced to the theoretical work of Robert Merton, and the evolving collaborative efforts in the area of mass communication and community studies "became an integral part of the 'Columbia' version of structural functionalism," testifying to Merton's involvement in the rise of communication research (Robinson, 1988).

Undoubtedly, Lazarsfeld also recognized the importance of critique within the social sciences. His own complex intellectual interests and his life-long commitment to applied research in general, and sociological research in particular, kept him involved in the process of assessing methodological and substantive contributions to the creation and transfer of knowledge. Thus, his understanding of "mass" society included the challenge to social scientists to help improve the standards of people living under the conditions of industrialization.

Elsewhere, Gerbner would offer a definition of "masses" that emphasized the movement of messages rather than the organization of people. He argued that the "key to the historic significance of mass media is . . . the association of 'mass' with a process of production and distribution"; consequently, "Mass communication is the technologically and institutionally based mass production and distribution of the most broadly shared continuous flow of public messages in industrial societies" (1967: 53–4).

While Schramm defined the parameters of the field through the continuous publication of textbooks throughout the 1950s, Lazarsfeld delivered the social-scientific expertise and new insights into the role of communication in American society. With its display of professional ingenuity and political astuteness, his work emerged as a definitive contribution to American leadership in (mass) communication research. His initial interest in methodological problems, applied to the study of media effects, resulted in a number of studies which helped mold the communication and mass communication establishment. Although communication research in the guise of propaganda and advertising analyses had existed for some time, Lazarsfeld helped establish the credibility of the field as a social-scientific endeavor in the university environment. He must be considered a major force in the definition of modern communication research, and his pronouncements about the nature of media research have remained relevant contributions to the current rationale of the field and are important for understanding its development.

For instance, it is significant that Lazarsfeld was more than an academic researcher; he had also recognized the potential of (mass) communication research in the field of marketing and attempted to define and secure his position between academic pursuits and commercial interests. In this context, he became particularly sensitive to reactions from the media industry and realized the precarious nature of communication research as an expression of academic endeavors, concluding that

> we academic people always have a certain sense of tightrope walking: at what point will the commercial partners find some necessary conclusion too hard to take and at what point will they shut us off from the indispensable sources of funds and data?

(1969: 314)

Lazarsfeld consistently felt that contemporary criticism of the media belonged to and was "part of the liberal creed" and that intellectuals were too strict in their indictment of the media, but he also thought that the media were overly sensitive to such criticism (1969: 315). Facing a dilemma, he sought to avert a possible disenchantment of commercial partners in media research projects by raising media criticism to a legitimate intellectual activity, proposing the use of journalism schools as training grounds for media personnel. He suggested ways to make "criticism more bearable, both for those who offer it and for those who receive it," by advocating that a division be set up (at the University of Illinois) "to deal with nothing but these problems of criticism. Students and researchers should come to think of criticism as something being systematically studied." Lazarsfeld hoped that, once institutionalized, "there would be less emotionalism connected with it" (1948: 188). However, journalism education never succeeded in elevating criticism of or by the media to the level of general practice.

Lazarsfeld's understanding of social research, through his involvement in American radio research, serves as one of the earliest examples of a systematic social-scientific study of a new medium and its social and political impact on society; in fact, his early career was built upon the need for information about people as audiences and audiences as potential markets.

His notion about the establishment of research bureaus, coupled with his entrepreneurial talents and thus his (conscious or unconscious) break with American traditions of academic research, created the most favorable conditions for the development of radio research, while enhancing his own position of leadership. Morrison, in particular, has documented Lazarsfeld's rise in the academy, his enthusiasm for non-academic research and his "emerging role of managerial scholar [which] demanded many of the skills associated with commerce: most notably, the business acumen necessary to secure a steady flow of work contracts" (1988: 195). Although there may have been detractors among his colleagues at Columbia University, Lazarsfeld's approach to a systematic, efficient and practical analysis of the media was also much admired. Schramm, who had met Lazarsfeld during the war in Washington, DC, was among those who began to lay the groundwork for a similar research bureau at the University of Iowa, before he moved to the University of Illinois and founded the Institute of Communications Research. Schramm emulated Lazarsfeld's broad notion of communication research during his career at the University of Illinois and Stanford University (Cartier, 1988), and he dedicated his book, *Mass Communications*, to "Paul F. Lazarsfeld who has done perhaps more than any other man toward bringing the social sciences to bear on the problems of communications" (1949: v).

When the Office of Radio Research at Columbia University was started with a grant from the Rockefeller Foundation, Lazarsfeld reported that it was "to study what radio means in the lives of the listeners" (Lazarsfeld and Stanton, 1944: vii). This was not Lazarsfeld's first encounter with radio research, however. He had conducted audience research in connection with the Princeton Radio Research Project and in Austria as early as 1932.

Lazarsfeld considered the study of radio a major undertaking which could provide insights into American culture and society, assuming that "the operation of radio certainly bears the imprint of the present social system and is, in turn, bound to have certain effects upon social institutions" (1939: 5). He asserted that the investigation of radio could also lead to understanding social and cultural values in society, since "what is or is not going on the air is greatly influenced by the respect for existing moral codes, the acceptance of today's distribution of property, and other features of American culture" (1939: 5). However, there is no indication here that Lazarsfeld entertained ideas about the social or political problematic of the power of ownership, or the control of content and its impact on other groups or classes in society, except to speculate about the social and economic consequences for established institutions, like the press and education. He identified the problems of joint ownership which arose a few years later with the profitability of radio and raised ethical questions about its effects upon news coverage. Concerned about the relationship between radio and newspapers, Lazarsfeld asked, "What is the advertising policy resulting from joint ownership? How is news of social importance such as that of labor disputes and racial problems, handled under varying ownership structures of newspapers and radio stations?" (1941b: 13). Lazarsfeld's questions revealed a major problematic of commercialism and a specific weakness of contemporary media coverage. Discriminatory news gathering and dissemination practices involving the organization of labor and the participation of the black community were rarely addressed, and Lazarsfeld contributed a concrete and insightful comment on the need for socially relevant investigations of media behavior.

Subsequently, radio research took on a specific, relevant and important role in social research, providing a guide to practical concerns. Indeed, Lazarsfeld was keenly aware of the location of radio research in a considerably larger field of studies; the interdisciplinary nature of radio research was reflected as early as the beginning of the Princeton Project, when he and his colleagues (Hadley Cantril and Frank Stanton, both associate directors) outlined some basic principles of their research procedures. They emphasized the lack of adequate funding, the need for a theoretical concept, and the effects of radio on contemporary life, with special reference to "social, regional and other differences" among audiences (1939: 203). Specifically, Lazarsfeld and his colleagues argued for the development of "listener research," the utilization of commercial research results, and the cooperation with other non-profit organizations. But they also felt that a theoretical framework was needed to "guide us in empirical research and in our interpretation of the findings" (1939: 203). The Princeton Project group also speculated that radio has greater effects in specific areas, such as music, news and politics.

By 1940 Lazarsfeld visualized the outlines of an academic discipline when *The Journal of Applied Psychology* devoted another special issue to the problems of radio research, and within a few years analyses of radio had become a major source of information about communication behavior, while Lazarsfeld had succeeded in promoting a common interest in communication research among colleagues and professional broadcasters. By the early 1940s radio research had become a cooperative venture between commercial interests and academic pursuits under Lazarsfeld's guidance and methodological expertise.

During the war Lazarsfeld continued his research in the Office of Radio Research at Columbia University. The results became evident by 1944, when he reported that the development of radio research had led to the integration of different, methodological approaches; to innovative uses of the Audience Analyzer, aimed at learning more about the effects of radio; and to the further exploration of research techniques (Lazarsfeld and Stanton, 1944). But by this time Lazarsfeld seemed to have lost his interest in radio research, cast about for other, perhaps more challenging projects, particularly television research, and supported the use of "communications research" to define these activities (Lazarsfeld and Stanton, 1949: xi). According to Morrison, "Insofar as Lazarsfeld was concerned, the field for him had been exhausted by 1943 – some sixteen years before Berelson wrote his bitterly controversial paper on the withering away of mass communication research" (1988: 206). However, Lazarsfeld did not succeed in executing a television research agenda while the medium swept the country; he continued with other interests, while the analysis of television proceeded elsewhere.

In the meantime, the publication of other radio studies continued. For instance, the first nation-wide study of the public's attitudes toward radio was commissioned by the National Association of Broadcasters, planned in 1943, and executed in 1945 by the National Opinion Research Center at the University of Denver. Columbia University's Bureau of Applied Social Research cooperated with the analysis and interpretation of the findings. In his introduction to the final report on the growing professionalism of the industry, entitled *The People Look at Radio*, Lazarsfeld and Field suggested that the fact that

> the National Association of Broadcasters sought out independent research experts to prepare and report such a survey is a sign that the industry is doing its best to mold a constructive program of action from the great variety of forces which impinge upon it.
>
> (1946: ix)

There is a recognition here of the mounting pressures on the industry to be responsive to their respective communities and to curb their enormous appetite for economic success.

But there was no attempt at this time to project the consequences of a public service model on the prevailing conditions or to find *basic* ideological differences in the critique of contemporary radio. In fact, Lazarsfeld found that broadcasters and their critics shared a fundamental belief in the social and political system, and he observed that "most of the critics in this country have one outstanding characteristic. Most of them want to see their criticisms met within the present framework of the industry" (1948: 86–7).

Such a pronouncement also implied that mainstream academic or social-scientific criticism of radio as a social, economic and political instrument, including Lazarsfeld's own position, was located within the boundaries of industrial practice and federal regulations. The emphasis was placed on improvement rather than on revolutionary change, and the book concluded on a rather conciliatory note. He observed that the

> survey has shown in a variety of ways that people are, by and large, satisfied with what American radio does for them. Still the progressive elements in the radio industry are only too right to be sensitive to the critics, especially to ask for criticisms as they have done in this survey. Radio, which reaches the ears of all the people, seems to have listened well to their voices. People say radio is fine; they want it to develop ever more so.
>
> (Lazarsfeld and Field, 1946: 90)

A few years later, when Lazarsfeld and Stanton recognized and acted upon the emergence of a field of communication research, they returned to the need for "a general philosophical orientation and a systematic body of research techniques" to launch such an effort (1949: xiii). They identified a need for theoretical and methodological support in reaction to major social developments brought on by the rise of literacy and the offerings of a "large-scale, fairly centralized communications industry," and they wondered about "the effects of this general development on the spiritual and social life of our times," specifically about the relationship between the "wants of the audience and the cultural function of the industry." These comments reflected the ongoing mass society debate among American intellectuals and helped locate Lazarsfeld and Stanton as caught between competing interests. They realized the commercial nature of the communication industry, but they also insisted that "in order to best serve the whole community, the industry should be the voice of its intellectually and morally most advanced sector" (1949: xiv). In fact, communication research would become an important source of media policy and social philosophy.

Throughout these years, the broadcasting industry had maintained a rhetoric of compliance with democratic ideals. While the American Broadcasting Company saw itself as reflecting a "tradition of independence and of free enterprise, liberality in social philosophy, belief in free education for all and in public service" (Bittner, 1985: 84), the National Association of Broadcasters had declared "American broadcasting as a living symbol of democracy [whose] only proper measure of its responsibility is the common good of the whole people" (Siepmann, 1950: 60).

From his own political assessment of American society, and

perhaps after his professional analysis of the economic power of the broadcasting industry, Lazarsfeld had come to the conclusion that "freedom of speech is now a three-cornered proposition between the government, the communications industry and the individual citizen" (Lazarsfeld and Field, 1946: 74). His model assumed a separation of power and conveyed the impression that individuals were actually in control of their political or economic destiny, and, thus, viable partners in any alliance of power, while any notions of collective representation of various social, cultural or political interests remained unexplored.

Specifically, Lazarsfeld's research strategy was built upon the idea that such alliances shift depending upon the issues and their varying implications. Indeed, the demands of individuals for freedom of speech and the role of the broadcasting industry to "maintain a vigilance to see that the government does not interfere with the freedom of radio as an institution" and to defend "its commercial interests under the formula of free speech" (Lazarsfeld and Field, 1946: 74) constituted a major political problematic. It also contained practical consequences for Lazarsfeld's work. His strategy was to "keep the Bureau [of Applied Social Research] maneuvering between the intellectual and political purist and an industry from which I wanted cooperation without having to 'sell out'" (1969: 321).

This period of communication research was also shaped by the political atmosphere leading up and through the experiences of the Second World War. Most obvious were the demands for information about propaganda effects; less visible, but equally important, were the encounters with *émigré* scholars whose presence in the traditions of logical positivism and Marxism began to enrich the intellectual climate of American universities. Both the search for specific answers to the power of communication and the availability of European expertise helped determine the development of the field into the 1980s.

For instance, Lazarsfeld continued to seek theoretical breakthroughs, and the subsequent presence of Theodor Adorno in the Princeton Office of Radio Research was based upon his hope to "develop a convergence of European theory and American empiricism" (Lazarsfeld, 1969: 323). However, opportunities for an exploration of theoretical foundations for the advanced study of communication passed when the proposed vehicle for such undertaking, the so-called music project, ultimately failed and the professional relationship between Lazarsfeld and Adorno ended. According to Lazarsfeld, Adorno's instructions "could hardly be translated into empirical terms" and Rockefeller Foundation funding was eventually terminated (1969: 324).

Lazarsfeld's preconceived notions of what constituted valid research surfaced in an unpublished critical response to Adorno's 161-page memorandum, *Music in Radio* (June 26, 1938) that left no room for compromise with Adorno's own understanding of the problematic. He wrote to Adorno,

> You know that I have an unchanging respect for your ideas and that I am sure our project will . . . profit greatly by your cooperation. But you also know that I have great objections against the way you present your ideas and against your disregard of evidence and systematic empirical research.

Lazarsfeld's response was that of a fund raiser, sensitive to the prospective sources and critical of the style and content of the funding proposal; he concluded by saying that

> you think because you are basicly [*sic*] right somewhere you are right everywhere. Whereas I think that because you are right somewhere you overlook the fact that you are terrible in other respects, and the final reader will think that because you are outrageous in some part of your work where he can easily catch you, you are impossible altogether.
>
> (Lazarsfeld, 1938)

Adorno, on the other hand, remembered his encounter with American mass communication research years later when he concluded that "theoretical reflections upon society as a whole cannot be completely realized by empirical findings" (1976: 69). He recognized the primacy of empirical sociology, because of its "immediate practical utilizability, and its affinity to every type of administration" (1976: 70), and he implicated academic communication research for the failure to acknowledge and to clarify the complexity of "societal objectivity" by suggesting that those who fund media research projects are only partly to blame for making sure "that only reactions within the dominant 'commercial system' are recorded and that the structure and implications of the system itself are not analyzed" (1976: 71).

Lazarsfeld's encounter with Adorno and Horkheimer was fruit-ful only in that it led to a joint publishing effort and to his own definition of critical research. About thirty years later, Lazarsfeld recalled Adorno as a "major figure in German sociology," identifying him as a representative of "one side in a continuing debate between two positions, often distinguished as critical and positivistic sociology" (1969: 322). On the other hand, while Lazarsfeld had attempted to engage in a discourse with members of the Frankfurt School, subsequent representatives of empirical communication research remained uninvolved. McLuskie has observed that the dialogue between "'the Lazarsfeldian paradigm' and the variety of so-called 'critical paradigms' mentioned in leading Anglo-American journals of communication research occurs without engagement, without working relationships, from a distance quite safer than that which existed between Adorno and Lazarsfeld" (1988: 33–4).

The Institute of Social Research and the Office of Radio Research at Columbia University collaborated in 1941 on a special issue of *Studies in Philosophy and Social Science*, which was devoted to problems of mass communication. The edition included Lazarsfeld's frequently cited "Remarks on Administrative and Critical Communications Research" among other contributions from Adorno ("On Popular Music"), Harold Lasswell ("Radio as an Instrument of Reducing Personal Insecurity"), Herta Herzog ("On Borrowed Experience: An Analysis of Listening to Daytime Sketches"), William Dieterle ("Hollywood and the European Crisis") and Charles Siepmann ("Radio and Education"). In his brief introductory statement, Horkheimer emphasized that "some of our ideas have been applied to specifically American subject matters and introduced into the American methodological debate" (1941: 1).

Lazarsfeld, however, used this occasion to offer his own understanding of the mass communication research establishment in the United States by drawing on his encounter with Critical Theory in the American context of social research. According to Lazarsfeld, "*administrative research* . . . is carried through in the service of some kind of administrative agency of public or private character," while "*critical research* is posed against the practice of administrative research, requiring that, prior and in addition to whatever special purpose is to be served, the general role of our media of communication in the present social system should be studied" (1941a: 8–9).

Lazarsfeld credited Horkheimer with the idea of critical research,

but he did not pursue the philosophical or theoretical implications
of Critical Theory for media research, particularly in the American
context. Nevertheless, Lazarsfeld reportedly was serious about
coming

> to terms with something which seemed to me to have a core of
> intellectual integrity, and at the same time seemed to be foolish
> and irresponsible. It was always a mixture of curiosity, interest,
> respect and irritation. So anything, any contact with the Institute
> was always quite a sincere quality.
>
> (Morrison, 1988: 207)

Lazarsfeld's definition of critical research ignored the historical
nature of critical research in the tradition of the Frankfurt School
and failed to consider the role of culture in the positioning of the
media, opting instead for his own ideological position. He has
commented on his attitude toward Critical Theory, acknowledging
his "tendency towards cannibalism. In order to understand another
system of thought I have to translate it into my own terms. It never
occurred to me that I might thereby try to exercise dominance over
the other fellow" (1975, cited in McLuskie, 1988: 34). Although
sympathetic toward Critical Theory, Lazarsfeld insisted upon a
deductive form of critical research, misunderstanding Adorno's
theory of society, in which data are not phenomena which express a
general theory, but "mere epiphenomena upon the theory" (Rose,
1978: 98).

Indeed, Lazarsfeld, and many of his contemporaries, saw the
problems of media and society in technological terms, dealing with
the inevitability of industrialization, the massification of audiences,
and the effects of these "mass" media on people. They adopted
a technological rationale, which Horkheimer and Adorno once
defined as "the rationale of domination itself" (1972: 121), and
which could only provide solutions consistent with the prevailing
theory of society.

Furthermore, over time American (mass) communication research
has remained insensitive to changing historical conditions which
effectively define problems of communication. Instead, communication research typically aligned itself with the social and economic
power structure and maintained an ideological position that would
be exposed and attacked by Horkheimer and Adorno.

Reviews of Lazarsfeld's work by Gitlin (1981), Morrison (1978),
McLuskie (1975), and Mills (1970), as well as his own discussion

of the definition and organization of empirical social research, support the conclusion that mass communication research under the intellectual leadership of Lazarsfeld concentrated on the existing conditions of the media and society. According to Gitlin, Lazarsfeld was engaged in a search "for models of mass media effects that are *predictive*, which in the context can mean only that results can be predicted from, or for, the commanding heights of the media" (1981: 93). His sense of criticism was fueled by his own intellectual curiosity and strengthened by his belief in the function of criticism within a liberal-pluralist society.

The role of the critical in this context of Lazarsfeld's writings was still one of providing a scientific rationale for an adjustment to the dominant forces in American society. It was not a critique of the political-economic system or a challenge of positivism as a foundation of media research at that time, nor was it an attempt to impose a new vision of a (social) democratic society upon the political system, his Austrian experience with socialist ideas notwithstanding. In fact, there is no evidence in his writings on radio research, for instance, which suggests that Lazarsfeld considered, or was sympathetic to, a radical critique of the commercial model of broadcasting, or that he was committed to a Marxist challenge of American positivism as it began to reach the social sciences during the 1930s. Alternative ideological positions were certainly not impossible.

For instance, the early history of American broadcasting between 1922 and 1927, in particular, is replete with alternatives to the commercial structure of the industry and advertising revenues. Also, the stimulating insights of the Frankfurt School, if not of American Marxist scholars, invited a response to theoretical debates about the future of society and the role of the social sciences. Thus, Borchers' recent suggestion that "Lazarsfeld withdrew to the purer realms of the social sciences on the other side of the Atlantic" after a confrontation with the socialist ideas of Hendrik de Man in Austria, is a recognition of Lazarsfeld's political ambivalence (1988: 219). Similarly, Bernard Berelson observed that Lazarsfeld's "socialist background was there, but his foreground was with American business and Paul was always delighted that he could phone up the President of Columbia Broadcasting System to get him on the phone" (Morrison, 1988: 195). It was an additional indication of Lazarsfeld's inclination to act upon his immediate environment. In addition, "the prohibition on political self-consciousness'" as

John Peters has called it, included the terrain of American (mass) communication research and involved the rules of separating facts and values under which expressed commitments and claims of objectivity would clash (1989: 217). These restrictions were spread throughout the social science establishment; they encouraged self-denial or deception and may have had a particular influence on *émigrés*, like Lazarsfeld, whose cultural adjustments remained under scrutiny.

It makes sense, then, that critical research in Lazarsfeld's view was identical with maintaining the traditional pattern of domination and control, reinforcing "three-cornered" relationships, which could be analyzed in terms of influences or effects, and producing a sense of real and potential imbalances. Lazarsfeld's arguments represented an administrative research perspective, as Gitlin concluded in his critique of the dominant paradigm in mass communication research (1981: 93). Elsewhere, McLuskie has maintained that "Lazarsfeld's idea was to institutionalize critical research, make it a tradition – in part to sensitize clients to criticism. But behind this heuristic role was Lazarsfeld's agenda to force the critical theorist 'to separate clearly fact from judgment'" (McLuskie, 1977: 25). By doing so, Lazarsfeld strengthened the hegemony of administrative research and secured his own place in the hierarchy of American (mass) communication research.

Mass communication research of this period, with its intensive effort to produce a variety of mass communication models since the 1950s, had also sought the theoretical unity and, therefore, political strength of the field. It had moved from a sociological perspective to a multi-disciplinary area of communication and mass communication studies, which offered new opportunities for critical research. Lazarsfeld had recognized this trend, but he was unable to forge his critical research perspective into a major, theoretical statement. Indeed, when he began to formulate his position *vis-à-vis* the reality of economic and political authority in mass communication research, he offered a reading of Critical Theory (and the Frankfurt School) which ignored the theoretical premises and their practical consequences, particularly as suggested in the works of Horkheimer and Adorno. His approach to Adorno and Critical Theory was an indication, however, of Lazarsfeld's search for convergence, which David Sills has identified as a consequence of his "sense of marginality for his intellectual activity" (1979: 422). It explains his attempted crossings into other theoretical and methodological traditions or fields of inquiry. But his own claims for critical research remained theoretically and practically (politically) within the traditional bourgeois context of the social science enterprise. The notion of a critical position ultimately meant a recognition of authority and a reconciliation with power; it also meant working with the necessity for change within the dominant paradigm and arguing for the convergence of existing theoretical or practical perspectives.

The critical research of Lazarsfeld was neither based upon a Marxist critique of society nor founded on traditional social criticism in the United States, with its questioning of authority in the populist, reformist sense. Nevertheless, Lazarsfeld's work helped define the American domain of communication research for decades to come. His remarks about critical research represented the repositioning of traditional social science research *within* the practice of what C. Wright Mills has called abstracted empiricism (1970: 60). The notion of critical research, as opposed to administrative research, became a point of legitimation in the development of (mass) communication research. Its presence asserted the neutral and independent position of communication research as an established and recognized field of study and helped justify its claims as an administrative unit within the organization of American universities.

The field also represented a relevant and important *methodological* specialization as a branch of sociology. As a result, scholarly interests in methodological issues frequently became priorities and, ultimately, determinants of social research and research agendas. A reason for the failure to advance a unified theoretical proposition has been the legitimation of communication research through its methodological expertise combined with its service function for government and commerce, including media enterprises. Gitlin talked about the "bargaining mentality . . . within a common, hegemonic ideological frame" (Gitlin, 1981: 101). And almost thirty years after Lazarsfeld's initial writings, Dallas Smythe has commented upon the "oversupply" of administrative research at the expense of critical inquiry (1969: vii).

Also, the accommodation of a critical position within (mass) communication research in this form, and as suggested by Lazarsfeld, may have served as a convenient strategy for defusing potentially controversial (since ideologically unacceptable) and challenging threats to the authority of the sociological enterprise in (mass) communication studies, including public opinion research. These threats arose from two directions: traditional social criticism, latent in American social-scientific scholarship since the turn of the century, and post-Second World War Western European Marxism, engaged as a theoretical force in the explanation of historical conditions and social changes in Western Europe since the end of the war.

Lazarsfeld's contributions to media studies also created a sense of urgency in the analysis of communication and its effects upon society. There was much more to know, and society needed explanations and solutions to a variety of social, political and economic problems in the aftermath of the Second World War and in preparation for the anticipated return to normalcy. Lazarsfeld and others moved the field into a prominent and politically relevant position among legitimate academic disciplines. The persistent growth of their communication research agendas, involving conspicuous topics like children, advertising, pornography, violence or crime, produced spontaneous definitions of social problems related inescapably to media performance.

For instance, responding to Lazarsfeld's notion of critical research, George Gerbner summarized social-scientific contributions to the identification of social problems (through content analysis) and came to the conclusion that the liberal-pluralist system, founded upon a "community of publics," was endangered by the creation of mass markets and mass market research. Echoing C. Wright Mills, Gerbner observed that the

> dissolution of publics into markets for mass media conceived and conducted in the increasingly demanding framework of commodity merchandizing is the cultural (and political) specter of our age. This fear is now joined by a growing concern over the trend of social science research, especially in the field of communications. More and more of this research is seen to succumb to the fate of mass media content itself in being implicitly tailored to the specifications of industrial and market operations.
>
> (1964: 498)

In his review of the "consequential meaning of media content," however, he failed to clarify the fundamental ideological differences between the cultural criticism based upon a Marxist critique of capitalist society, which he cited, and the critical position of some social-scientific inquiries into media content.

Mass communication research in this era of economic recovery and existential dilemmas typically isolated specific conditions of the environment. It delved into relationships among people, investigated questions of social identity, and, generally speaking, raised some doubts about the stability of individuals in their social relations. At the same time, there was a marked absence, however, of questions about the role of the media in the process of culture and ideological struggle, including the location of authority and the distribution of power. Thus, Gerbner's "challenge for mass communications research" reflected his own commitment to a liberal-pluralist vision of society, based upon the participation of individuals in a "genuine" public. He asked communication scholars

> to combine the empirical methods with the critical aims of social science, to join rigorous practice with value-conscious theory, and thus to gather the insight the knowledgeable individual in a genuine public must have if he is to come to grips (and not unconsciously to terms) with the sweeping undercurrents of his culture.
>
> (1958: 106–7)

His challenge was a confirmation of Lazarsfeld's call for critical research, but it was also a reflection of a democratic ideal which characterized earlier reformist notions in American social science research. Although reform-minded in the sense of understanding itself as contributing to the betterment of society, (mass) communication research remained committed to a traditionally conservative approach to the study of social and cultural phenomena, in which instrumental values merged and identified with moral values.

Under Lazarsfeld's leadership communication research in the United States had become a formidable enterprise which was deeply committed to the commercial interests of the culture industry and the political concerns of government. For instance, in 1957 Robert Merton suggested that the major intellectual and theoretical conditions of the field, including the potential consequences of applied social research, were shaped by "market and military demands" (1957: 451). He specifically acknowledged that "in the field of mass communications research, industry and government have largely supplied the venture-capital in support of social research needed for their own ends" and wondered whether such administrative research had "been too closely harnessed to the immediate pressing problems, providing too little occasion for dealing with more nearly fundamental questions of social science" (1957: 452).

In fact, both Lazarsfeld and Merton agreed that "increasingly the chief power groups, among which organized business occupies the most spectacular place, have come to adopt techniques for manipulating mass publics through propaganda in place of more direct means of control," and they asserted that "Economic power seems to have turned to a subtler type of psychological exploitation, achieved largely by disseminating propaganda through the mass media of communication." The authors concluded that these "media have taken on the job of rendering mass publics conformative to the social and economic status quo" (1957: 457). Consequently, the "third" corner of Lazarsfeld's model as an object of media and government intervention provided a profitable area of scientific study and analysis.

Lazarsfeld's suggestion of critical research as a socially desirable goal within the limits of the dominant perspective of democratic practice was an anachronism. It appealed to a common-sense notion of criticism at a time when common sense was being replaced by expert opinion. In addition, by arguing the primacy of empiricism as the basis of social theory, Lazarsfeld successfully excluded Critical Theory from social theory (McLuskie, 1977: 26–33). On the other hand, his introduction of critical research alternatives represented a successful attempt to create a pseudo-confrontation with research practices which, in fact, occupied the same theoretical (and political) premises. It reflected an unwillingness to explore alternative explanations, which was not a particularly unique characteristic of communication research at that time. For instance, Robert Sklar has found that American Studies was similarly disadvantaged with its "reluctance to utilize one of the most extensive literatures of cultural theory in modern scholarship, coming out of the Marxist intellectual tradition." He concluded his assessment of that field with the suggestion that "to have left untouched such a potential resource exposes one of the essential causes of the problem of theory in American Studies" (1975: 260).

Ultimately, however, such "reluctance" to utilize a Marxist approach for an analysis of culture and communication has its roots in the conservative tradition of the social sciences, including the field of communication research, whose practitioners were occupied with a search for causes underlying the decline of political authority in American society. In a variety of ways, they defined media as indicators of social integration to explain and reaffirm the workings of the democratic system, particularly with the emergence of new social movements and the pressures of increasing material needs. In fact, communication research claimed a significant share of the attempt to preserve and support the ideological status quo with its explorations of the decline of credibility and legitimacy of the system, or the threats to populism. Consequently, in the prevailing atmosphere of anti-communism any Marxist critique of culture and society would continue to be defined as alien, that is, as constituting an adversarial, if not hostile position on questions of media and communication in the United States, which could only aggravate the crisis of democracy.

In general, there was a lack of articulation of larger, more fundamental questions in the literature of (mass) communication theory and research, not only about the failure of the liberal-pluralist vision of American society, but also about its own theoretical foundation. As Albig noted, the "study of mass communication content and effects has been conducted with enormous gusto." But he was discouraged by the fact that, although many

> research studies have avoided broad generalizations; skillful synthese [*sic*] have been rare. The intellectual climate has been unfavorable to the emergence of logical theory, while objectively accumulated data have been far too fragmentary to provide the basis for much generalization or grand theory.

And he concluded that "Ingenious and imaginative forays into minutiae have not been paralleled by imaginative and skillful generalizations, and by elaborations of theories concerning the broader processes of opinion formation and change" (1957: 15).

Gerbner also voiced his concern over the fact that even an interdisciplinary search for a "theory that might help us to study, understand, judge, and control the conduct of events in which mass media and mass communications play an increasingly significant role" had been unsuccessful. He added that "There is no such theory now. Most attempts to construct theories have taken parochial or tangential approaches of established disciplines or the partial view of journalistic scholarship" (1967: 43).

Finally, Wilbur Schramm voiced his disappointment over having failed in the creation of a central theory and concluded toward the end of his career that "communication has developed like a scholarly discipline. But has it produced a central, interrelated body of theory on which the practitioners of a discipline can build and unify their thinking? I am afraid that it has not" (1983: 14).

With the end of the Second World War American scientific know-how had become an important commodity, and the export of social-scientific theory and methodology involving communication and media studies through various educational programs and extensive travel by American experts was significant. Among the most widely distributed works were collections of communication research literature, compiled by Wilbur Schramm. His *The Process and Effects of Mass Communication* (1954) originated in work for the United States Information Agency, while a series of radio talks for the Voice of America in 1962 was later published under *The Science of Human Communication* (1963). These books, and others like *Mass Communications* (1949), became major sources for understanding American approaches to the study of mass communication, determined definitions of communication, and for years served as models of scientific analysis in many foreign countries.

During this period communication research had also come under the scrutiny of its own practitioners, but with rather limited and disappointing results, since social scientists practiced a form of self-critique that was, for the most part, aimed at the methodological issues of the field. For instance, when Joseph Klapper published his research survey in *The Effects of Mass Media* (in mimeographed form in 1949 and as a book, *The Effects of Mass Communication*, in 1960), Lazarsfeld speculated in his introduction to the 1949 edition about the lack of knowledge concerning media effects, suggesting that the

> main difficulty probably lies in formulating the problem correctly. For the trouble started exactly when empirical research stepped in where once the social philosopher had reigned supreme. To the latter there was never any doubt that first the orator and then the newspaper and now television are social forces of great power.

And he concluded that a lack of sophisticated measurement techniques combined with the complexity of media effects were responsible for the current state of information about what media do to people (1949: 1–2).

Lazarsfeld implied that empirical communication research must break with the line of argument and the logic of historical and theoretical analyses, and replace rather than supplement the previously held views on the power of communication in the hands of those who control it with the newly established truths of empirical research. However, a few years later Smythe began to raise a number of substantial issues pertaining to the conduct of communication research. He, not unlike Lasswell, exposed the dangers of scientism, observing that the "bulk of the research in the interdisciplinary field coming to be known as 'communication research' has been in the hands of persons who more or less consciously adopt the stance of 'scientism'." Consequently, the "evidence from the fields of history, sociology, political science and economics are ignored as being unfit for acceptance as 'science'" (1954: 24–7).

Smythe argued for a combination of empirical methodologies and rigorous logic to create "non-scientistic" conditions for the pursuit of communication research and the development of a general theory of communication with premises and preconceptions that are rooted in historical consciousness. His sense of history demanded a recognition of the importance of culture and cultural institutions for an assessment of contemporary media effects, and he produced a "substantive" thesis which held that over time and "as our culture has developed it has built into itself increasing concentrations of authority" which are nowhere "more evident than in our communications activities" (1954: 24–7). He developed a historical scenario and reached the "hypothetical conclusion" that "as our social organization has become more tightly integrated on the basis of modern technology, authority has increasingly been built into it"; and he advocated that a further hypothesis be tested

> that our mass media, through cutting off feedback, through dealing in stereotypes, through specializing in a manipulative view of humanity (both directly through advertising and indirectly through the plot structures and motivations portrayed in entertainment and other program material), are capable of molding us more and more into authoritarianism.
>
> (1954: 21–4)

These observations, combined with his suggestions, did not provoke a major theoretical discourse, however, although calls for more theory could be heard throughout these years and into the 1980s. However, they were reminiscent of Lasswell's much earlier work about the use and effectiveness of symbols in specific political and cultural environments. But while Smythe had raised critical issues from a theoretical perspective, Berelson now pronounced the end of communication research from within the establishment a few years later. His review of the field in terms of its "distinguished past" (1959: 5) included a series of minor or less influential positions (besides those represented by Lasswell, Lazarsfeld, Lewin and Hovland) that consisted of a reformist approach (Hutchins Commission), a historical approach (Riesman, Innis), both of questionable scientific value, according to critics, as well as a series of perspectives represented by journalism (Schramm, Casey, Nixon), mathematics (Shannon, Weaver), psycholinguistics (Osgood, Miller) and psychiatry (Ruesch, Bateson). Interestingly enough, Berelson omitted significant contributions in other disciplines, revealing a blind-spot for considerations of communication and language in such areas as anthropology, linguistics and literature. On the other hand, he characterized Lazarsfeld as the only one "who centered on communication *per se*" (1959: 5). But his solutions were rather disappointing; they followed established lines of communication research, observing new developments in popular culture and mass communication, and urging the adoption of an economic perspective on communication. Berelson failed to address specifically the poverty of the theoretical discourse, but seemed content with defining the "vitality" and "breakthroughs" of the field in terms of research activities and methodological advancements (1959: 6). In addition, there was no attempt on his part to connect (old and new) pursuits of communication research with questions of society, let alone issues of enlightenment and culture. Unlike other fields, mass communication studies had not specifically attracted the work of social theorists, but provided opportunities for specific research interests which were widely accepted, imitated and published. The theoretical debates in other disciplines, however, were not as readily reflected in the (mass) communication literature. Berelson's failure to respond to the interdisciplinary nature of the theoretical discourse serves as an additional indication that (mass) communication research had been project-oriented and dedicated to the practical application of research methodologies.

The expert respondents to Berelson's myopic vision of the field were Wilbur Schramm, David Riesman and Raymond Bauer. Schramm denied the existence of a discipline to justify the various contributions and recommended "not to look for the unique theory in communication which we are accustomed to see in disciplines." He reaffirmed the viability of the field by alluding to the dedication of "young scholars" and defended their work toward the "day when we may have a science of man" (1959: 9). His argument seemed to tie the rise of communication research to the progress of the social sciences and the idea that practice will inevitably lead to theory.

Riesman placed Berelson's remarks in the broader context of academic endeavors and came to the conclusion that the dilemma of the field may be based on the intimidation of "adventurous research" in a methodological monoculture coupled with the possibility of theoretical work "which offered at once quick pay-off for the capable student and elegant models for the meek and timid" (1959: 11). Riesman encouraged the enterprising spirit of independent research and its potential of enlightenment; in fact, he warned that "conceptual schemes, while essential and inevitable, can serve to alienate the worker from his material as well as bring him closer to it" (1959: 13). His view of communication research was informed by the experiences of a dominant research ideology and its consequences for the American social science establishment.

Bauer argued that "with the possible exception of some of Lasswell's work, the early period was not marked by great ideas but by diverse methodological approaches" with the gravity shifting "from the exploitation of a method to the substance of problems which demand diverse methods for their exploitation" (1959: 14–15). He recognized the traditional tendency of the field toward procedural issues, but was cautiously optimistic about the future of mass communication research, particularly in the area of media effects.

Despite their different perspectives, the respondents agreed on the need for more detailed information about the place of communication and the role of the media in modern society. They trusted either their level of methodological sophistication or their creative insights to help push the field of communication research beyond its contemporary position. Riesman's comments also reflected an appreciation of the cultural and historical context for the study of communication; and they raised larger issues about the state of communication research as a closed professional enterprise or as an open field of intellectual endeavor.

Although questions of communication have traditionally been the concern of many disciplines, the investigation of specific communication phenomena had become a separate activity during these years, defined by social-scientific methodologies and the bias of research issues. It even seems that a political theorist like Lasswell, whose philosophical groundings in the Pragmatism of the Chicago School (Mead and Dewey), and the Positivism of the Cambridge School (Whitehead), combined with his recognition of the centrality of communication in the social process, had remained inaccessible as a potential source of theoretical insights.

At the conclusion of his own appraisal of mass communication, which had been "a vital and productive field in academic socio-logical research" in the 1930s and 1940s, Herbert Gans echoed Riesman's earlier observations. He felt that "mass-media research should also be part of the study of American society and culture as a whole, but this large subject has, perhaps because of its vast-ness, not been popular with sociologists, or with anthropologists" (1972: 700).

On the other hand, Lazarsfeld exemplified the success of a sociological enterprise that was located at Columbia University and that had, primarily through his own efforts, succeeded in inventing and defining mass communication research under conditions of increasing media attention, based on the need of an industry to know more about its potential in the marketplace. The idea of communication as a promising field of research about human relations and the relationship between society and a rapidly developing media industry, particularly advertising and television, had attracted an active community of researchers from several disciplines. Questions about communication or the role of the media were reduced to practical issues, while theoretical interests in the development of a communication-based theory of society, for instance, surfaced as a critical position outside the (sociological) mainstream. They were identified with a particular concern about language and culture, reminiscent of the earlier work by Mead and others, suggesting (mostly in vain) alternative perspectives for a media sociology.

This period of communication studies, however, was defined in terms of specific research objectives. It was characterized by a decided emphasis on the idea of society, which had become the focus of social-scientific analysis. The notion of critical research remained within the administrative considerations of communication research, while criticism often involved methodological issues and was bound to threaten creative or innovative modes of inquiry.

At the same time, the need for theoretical advancement was scarcely considered in the relevant literature of communication and media studies. Such activity occurred – outside of communication research – in an interdisciplinary context, typically combining philosophical, literary and anthropological insights into the nature of language and culture. The results were alternative explanations of communication and media, based on the use of symbols in private and public discourse, the power of myths, and the symbolic functions of democratic institutions, which replaced the idea of society with the notion of culture.

At the end of the period, mainstream communication and media research had failed to address critical developments from within and without its boundaries. It had remained within specified categories of interests, reflected in an academic specialization in the study of communication that was interdisciplinary by its commitment to a behavioral science orientation, but without any significant or successful attempt to break out of its monadic circle. With the acknowledgment of a cultural approach to the study of society during the following decades, the field would demonstrate a willingness to coopt specific theoretical or methodological aspects of a critical Marxist tradition, including Critical Theory, rather than to rethink its position in terms of the weaknesses or failures to produce a theory of communication that is also a theory of society.

Chapter 4

On introducing ideology
Critical Theory and the critique of culture

Pragmatism reflects a society that has no time to remember and meditate.

Max Horkheimer

The prevalence of a social-scientific vision of the world with its own positivistic claims on truth and reality remained a major issue following the introduction of communication research by Lazarsfeld and others. However, there were alternative visions of communication and society, although marginal at the time, which had always existed outside the social science establishment. They were expressed in the context of literature and sociology through a holistic approach to the study of society by those working with an understanding of culture as a dramaturgy of symbolic expression, and by others through a critique of mass culture which emerged from Marxism and, more specifically, from the contribution of Critical Theory to American social theory. Both traditions shared an abiding belief in the importance of exposing the destructive power of progress and the deprivation of the individual caught in an increasingly barbaric world, and working toward a more humane society. Thus, a critique of culture evolved from the writings of Kenneth Burke and sociologists like Hugh Dalziel Duncan, or the sociological work of David Riesman or C. Wright Mills next to intensely theoretical contributions by Horkheimer, Adorno, Marcuse and Lowenthal, in particular. Their ideas emerged during a period of political and social upheaval in the United States which provided the context for a significant critique of modern society.

The dilemma of a cultural approach to the study of society, which had been contested successfully by mainstream sociology, was reflected in Duncan's call for "a return to humanism, but a humanism conceived in a passion for understanding contemporary America." He added, "We must return to the belief that, while man has a nature and a history, he also has a community" (1953: ix). Duncan proposed to overcome the fixed belief in specific positivistic methods by offering a symbolic analysis of literature for the benefit of understanding contemporary society, fully "aware that many American social scientists consider inquiry into the structure and function of symbolic expression hardly a reputable preoccupation for a 'scientific' social scientist" (1953: ix). He saw himself surrounded by opponents and spoke in an indirect reference to Harvard sociology, and Talcott Parsons in particular, of the "mechanists, and particularly those whose signatures appear at the end of the 'General statement' of *Toward a General Theory of Action.*" Duncan did not believe that "roles should be studied as 'mechanisms,' nor that symbolic systems 'gear' or 'mesh'," and he thought that "Many sociologists (certainly many American sociologists) are mechanists" (1968: vii).

Although American sociology since Cooley, Dewey, Mead and Park, for example, had acknowledged the symbolic dimension of social relations with its extensive writings about the role of communication in society, it had failed to produce a social theory. Duncan insisted that communication theory as social theory had to be based on an analysis of symbolic forms and their effect on the social order. His reason was that traditional studies of communication had been "modeled after the study of material objects, as symbols were reduced to things in space" (1967b: 241), resulting in the emergence of techniques, like Bernard Berelson's influential *Content Analysis in Communication Research* (1952), which concentrated on the collection and processing of data "for the objective, systematic, and quantitative description of the manifest content of communication" (1952: 18). Duncan suggested that those who practice content analysis "are apt to confuse what they are doing as technicians with what should be done in theory and methodology. What can be quantified is studied, what cannot is neglected, and, among parochial behaviorists, is even described as 'beyond' science" (1967b: 260).

At the same time, he dismissed negative criticism of sociology, and, implicitly, empiricism in communication studies, as long as technicians dominate theoreticians, or, as long as theorists fail to produce theories "that can be reduced to hypotheses useful to technicians" (1967b: 260).

Duncan declared an end to the era of "American sociologists who have mortgaged the future of sociology to the methods of the physical sciences." It had become obvious to him that "such methods are not useful in discovering what we need to know, namely, the how and why of consensus as it arises in the most basic of all human experience – communication" (1962: ix). A few years later he proposed that a "break-through in communication theory that will advance social theory cannot come so long as we reduce communication to an event which must be studied by existing methods of research," and he warned against the appropriation of a physical science methodology that reveals answers about "motion in time and space, not about man in society. Questions about communication must be about communication as a social, not a physical event" (1968: 15).

Ultimately, his critique of sociology was a critique of mechanistic models which reduce communication to processes or states without providing knowledge about how words, or forms of communication, determine an individual's action in social relationships. Indeed, he felt that modern American sociology had produced theoretical monsters which "almost rival the chimeras of antiquity; firebreathing monsters, with a lion's head, a goat's body, and a serpent's tail, have been matched by grotesques with mechanical heads and symbolic bodies" (1968: 17).

Duncan attributed the change of perspective among those interested in communication theory, from sociology to anthropology and literature, to the lack of theory and the failure of sociology to come to terms with the need for symbolic analysis. In his words, "If communication was social, and the social was the communicative, something must be said about how communication determined social relationships, and, at the same time, something equally pertinent must be said about how social relations affected communication" (1967b: 241).

Duncan thought that the search for a theory of communication grounded in a theory of society could somehow reunite mainstream sociology with the tradition of Dewey, Mead, Cooley or Burke and form a coherent view of the symbolic nature of the world. He maintained that, despite their differing emphases, communication scholars could agree that social reality is constituted by symbolic forms. In fact, they shared the belief that "*how we communicate determines how we relate*, just as how we relate determines how we communicate" (1967b: 261).

Kenneth Burke represented this tradition which inquired about communication in terms of symbolic action, grammar, rhetoric and dialectic with sophistication and foresight. His discussion of "dramatism" in *A Grammar of Motives* (1945) "is full-blown structuralism well in advance, of course, of the French structuralist movement," according to Frank Lentricchia (1982: 130).

The publication of *Attitudes toward History* (1937), in particular, helped establish Burke's reputation as a social critic and theorist. It was received critically by a number of academic fields, including sociology and history, as a language-centered study of reality. Burke addressed the destruction of traditional values and the emergence of technical-political forces that resulted in the existential dilemma of modern individuals: the replacement of a faith in individuality by a submission to the rule of state or economic authority.

Burke, whose analyses frequently contained a sociological dimension, based his own contributions as a critic on an integration of technical criticism and social criticism "by taking the allegiance to the symbol of authority as our subject." He found that "Since the symbols of authority are radically linked with property relationships, this point of departure automatically involves us in socioeconomic criticism" (1937: 234). Burke offered views of the individual as a symbol-using animal and insisted throughout his work on the values of knowing the symbol systems that surround and affect the lives of people. His discussions of the historical process of maintaining authority and the desire for change, as well as his own role as an intellectual and participant in society, were based on understanding and expanding on the centrality of language. In fact, he demonstrated long before others had grasped the importance of language for the study of human relations, that the study of words and symbolic action was the most revealing, and therefore effective, exercise of helping expose and explain the problems of contemporary society, among them alienation and hegemonic struggle. People are connected by language, and the individual, "by reason of his 'property in' the public grammar, the 'collective' property of speech, becomes concerned with processes of socialization" (1937: 252). Burke argued that these needs "are implicit in the nature of language that gets its shape by reference to such economic foundations" as the "productive and distributive patterns" of human relations (1937: 252).

Burke identified the processes of history and the strategies of those in authority (and in possession of the authoritative symbols), by addressing the forces of alienation and suppression. He observed that although "the dispossessed struggle hard and long to remain loyal . . . the bureaucratic order tends simply 'to move in on' such patience and obedience." Moreover, authority will "drive the opposition into a corner by owning the priests (publicists, educators) who will rebuke the opposition for its disobedience to the reigning symbols" (1937: 68). When Burke elaborated on social relationships, he characterized the struggle between dominating forces in society and their efforts to survive in terms of a "stealing back and forth of symbols" (1937: 229), and he described the hopes of the "dispossessed" to regain possession as resting in an "allegiance to the structure that has dispossessed him" (1937: 232).

Burke developed a rationale of history as an organizing principle for recapturing or repossessing a sense of place, and the need to "own a 'myth' to take up the slack between what is desired and what is got" (1937: 212). In his *Attitudes toward History* (1937) – as well as in *Permanence and Change* (1935), *A Grammar of Motives* (1945), or *A Rhetoric of Motives* (1950) – Burke continued to offer not only an original, American perspective on authoritative strategies of domination in a manner that has now become known as a Gramscian approach to the struggle for hegemony, but, equally important, he advanced a theory and methodology for integrating questions of communication and media into an analysis of culture.

As early as 1951 Duncan had suggested the importance of Burke's intellectual contribution to the study of communication in his review of *A Rhetoric of Motives*. He said that it would be "unwise to talk about communication without some understanding of Burke, for he has assumed the burden of constructing hypotheses on the social effects of communication in terms of the process of identification as this takes place through the use of symbols" (1951: 594). Although he urged that "particularistic studies in the field of communication research" should be continued, Duncan emphasized the need for theoretical contributions and concluded that "Burke is asking the important question which is not only who reads what but how those who read are affected by what they read" (1951: 594).

But even Duncan's own project to involve contemporary sociology in a meaningful dialogue with existing theoretical premises and his propositions toward a sociological theory of communication remained a partial success at best, despite a conciliatory attempt with assurances that the occasional sharpness or teasing in his disagreement with behaviorists was merely argumentative and not intended to insult or ridicule (1968: viii).

Nevertheless, Burke and Duncan raised the level of skepticism about the state of communication research not only by questioning the theoretical consequences of working with reified concepts and of being preoccupied with the processing of data, but also, and more importantly, by introducing a dialogic model of social-scientific inquiry. In addition, their work directed other disciplines or fields, such as literature, literary criticism, or social theory, to the exploration of language and the potential of communication as a theoretical framework for an analysis of social relations and processes, for instance, between artists and audiences, writers and readers, or leaders and followers of social and intellectual movements within a cultural context.

Duncan developed a dramatic model of social relations to explain the social use of symbols and to raise questions about how communication determines social order. He insisted that "*how* we communicate determines *what* we communicate" and reminded his readers that communication occurs in public and private forms and "if there are no common symbols there can be no common meanings, and hence no community" (1968: 32). His scholarly work also reflected the political conditions of a country in turmoil, and he observed decisive changes of the community in the presence of the Viet Nam War, which darkened his sense of the future. Duncan did not share the earlier faith of Dewey or Mead in the survival of democracy, or the blind confidence of his contemporaries in the success of modern society. Progress for Duncan meant becoming humane first, and he articulated a need for making future generations understand that "we cannot become humane until we understand our need to visit suffering and death on others – and ourselves" (1968: 39).

Consequently, Duncan urged the undertaking of "vast and profound changes . . . in the way we study society," beginning in "anguished awareness that victimage is the means by which people purge themselves of fear and guilt in their relations with each other" (1968: 39). This awesome perspective held a hope, however, for understanding what communication is by insisting on the dislocation of traditional communication research in favor of a cultural approach which would be invested by knowledge about the forms of social interaction and a profound interest in being.

Earlier, Burke suggested the importance of recognizing the

essence of being in the study of culture. He reminded his readers that science is involved with processes and not concerned with substance or being, and that "any attempt to deal with human relationships after the analogy of naturalistic correlations becomes necessarily the reduction of some higher or more complex realm of being to the terms of a less complex realm of being" (1945: 506). Consequently, social scientists must realize that to engage in the study of human communication, that is, to preserve and build on complexity which characterizes the substance of being, means taking into account the whole from all perspectives. The result is the creation of an environment in which a "dialectic of participation" produces certainty based on the requirement "that all the sub-certainties be considered as neither true nor false, but *contributory*" (1945: 513).

Thus, the conventional certainty of scientific knowledge gives way to the possibility of many insights or interpretations. In this spirit, for example, history appears as a "dialectic of characters," changing expectations, not "to see 'feudalism' overthrown by 'capitalism' and 'capitalism' succeeded by some manner of national or international or non-national or neo-national or post-national socialism," and emphasizing the permanent existence of elements of these positions "attaining greater clarity of expression or imperiousness of proportion of one period than another" (1945: 513).

This is not only a critique of the social sciences, but also encouragement to promote different ways of thinking about culture and communication. It breaks with scientific models of development and change, or with the flow or process of communication, by introducing the notion that final answers are unobtainable and that solutions are the interplay of positions or voices. In Joseph Gusfield's interpretation of Burke, the sociologist is "the critic whose task is to point to the multiple understandings, the alternative possibilities inhering in situations, to bring new meanings and metaphors to bear on taken-for-granted assumptions" (1989: 27). A sociology of communication, in this view, becomes a form of criticism and a creative activity that builds on knowledge without the constraints of a positivistic vision of communication and human behavior.

Burke contributed significantly to making rhetorical analysis available to communication and media research by suggesting its usefulness to the study of human interaction. According to Gusfield there are

> three ways in which Burke's rhetorical perspective has been productive for sociologists. The first is found in the enormously insightful approach to human interaction as persuasional. The second is in the understanding of social science research as affected by rhetorical elements.

And the last one is the "common framework, which literature and literary analysis, as rhetoric, share with sociology," providing "basic categories for seeing and interpreting social action" (1989: 19). It is especially this latter area of legitimate common concerns and scholarly interests that constituted the most fruitful environment for the development of a critique of culture and communication.

Burke may have anticipated modern ideas concerning the uses of language or symbolic analysis, but he received only marginal attention by (mass) communication scholarship between the 1940s and 1960s. In fact, Lentricchia's remark that "the ambitious studies of contemporary critical theory, with few exceptions, continue to ignore Burke almost totally" (1982: 119) can also be extended to include past and present activities of (mass) communication research. Similarly, Frederic Jameson has observed that Burke's "immense critical corpus" of work had "been utterly without influence in its fundamental lessons," namely, "as an interpretative model to be studied and a method to be emulated" (1982: 70). He proceeded to determine whether Burke's work "can be reread or rewritten as model for contemporary ideological analysis" (1982: 71) and concluded that since "Burke's system has no place for an unconscious," his "symbolic act is thus always serenely transparent to itself, in lucid blindness to the dark underside of language, to the ruses of history or desire" (1982: 88).

There is no evidence of Kenneth Burke in the major writings on communication and media in American culture and no significant impact of his scholarly contributions, which reflect the social and political engagements of an intellectual life in the 1930s and 1940s. At the same time, there is also no rediscovery of the potential of Burke's dramatistic paradigm in the contemporary pursuit of understanding the world of symbols. His work has simply failed to engage the imagination of social theorists and those who have been eager to analyze the symbolic environment in the guise of communication research or media studies.

Similarly, the work of Erving Goffman, who had continued the Burkean tradition with his specific interest in social reality and the development of a dramaturgy of human interaction, promised to advance the understanding of social communication and, therefore, the definition of social action. His contribution to a microanalysis of communication within the cultural contexts of individuals, consisting of image management and the staging of appearances before others, concentrated on the structure of individual experience and took role theory to its logical conclusions. Goffman described the individual actor operating in a social space that seemed out of institutional control, thus elevating the creation of social roles to a central concern in social thought and replacing the idea of society.

More recently, Richard Lanigan has argued that Goffman's claim that method alone is a sufficient theory was an example of "a-historical sophism by which much of positive science also justifies its claims to objectivity," and he called on phenomenological theorists "to improve on the legacy of Erving Goffman" (1988: 343). On the other hand, Goffman's ideas had a marginal impact on the field as a theory or method of critical communication research.

In discussing the contributions of Burke, Duncan and Goffman to the study of life as drama, Taline Voskeritchian has noted a "gradual tightening of the parameters of social life with a parallel diminution of the *philosophical* idea of man." Thus, "for Burke the problems of man are timeless, inborn, incurable," while "for Duncan and Goffman, man is a social problematic, a problematic formulated against the background of an increasingly ominous world which generates in its inhabitants a sense of marginality and exile" (1981: 279).

Together, their scholarship offered an opportunity to rethink the study of society; their works stand as a persuasive critique of modern life, and as a challenge to old ways of studying society. Dramaturgical analysis posed individuals in the context of a secularized, urban environment. It identified communication as a central problematic and proceeded to develop strategies of inquiry that focused on form instead of content. In so doing it turned from a mechanistic view of human conduct to offer an alternative, humanistic context for the study of communication in which the dialectic becomes the method of analysis. Voskeritchian talked about "skepticism and pluralism as the foundations of their methodology" (1981: 296).

Throughout their writings there is a recurring faith in the workings of democratic principles, that is, in the individual's power of self-regulation or correction, reflecting a continuation of the "optimistic mood" of Pragmatism. It permeates Burke's discussion of the dialectic as a source of reason that will prevail over dogmatism and Duncan's discussion of the power of the dramatic dialogue to sustain egalitarian conditions for participation in communication; it even surfaces in Goffman's view of individuals, who seem trapped in the modern world, but able to maintain continuity in their encounters.

Hugh Dalziel Duncan emerged during the 1960s as a major critic of traditional sociological approaches to the study of communication and society. Like Goffman, Duncan had been educated at Chicago and informed by the theoretical contributions of Pragmatism in the tradition of James, Dewey, Mead and Cooley. He had been encouraged by the work of Burke to refine his ideas about the importance of the symbolic environment. His theoretical position may also have grown out of his own biographical circumstances. For instance, Voskeritchian has noted that both Duncan and Goffman were non-Americans who displayed "an intellectual and methodological attitude which combines a European (in this case Anglo-Saxon) cosmopolitan sensibility with the empathetic, essentially optimistic mood of American Pragmatism and symbolic interactionism" (1981: 277).

However, when Duncan, in particular, insisted on the possibility of a theory of society that was grounded in the symbolic nature of the individual, his criticism of the dominant perspective was largely ignored. Indeed, the original efforts to establish a dramaturgical analysis of communication were replaced by a critique of mass culture which also questioned, albeit implicitly, the state of communication and media research in the United States.

Such a critique emerged from a tradition of Marxist scholarship in the United States, which was joined by the contributions of the Frankfurt School in the 1940s. Both formed a nucleus of alternative theories of society based on an intensive treatment of questions related to mass culture and mass society. In fact, they added a new perspective to an ongoing debate and examples of their work began to appear in the standard

communication literature, perhaps as an implicit acknowledgment of theoretical strengths in an era that lacked a sense of
theory.

In particular, the paucity of theoretical contributions to the study
of communication and society was a well-recognized dilemma of
the American social sciences. Duncan recalled its history and the
position of *émigré* scholarship by saying that

> Up to the thirties, we were producing an indigenous school of
> social theory in America that we had every reason to have
> hope for. We certainly were proud of it, and then we got
> fat and lazy. We began to rely far too much on the brains
> of refugee scholars, as we once did on European theorists.
> In our generation (with the notable exception of Talcott Par-
> sons), few American social scientists have made many con-
> tributions to social theory. We have been pilfering foreign
> brains so long now that it's getting to be downright embar-
> rassing.

He ended by urging the development of the American tradition of
theory (1967a: 226).

At the same time, the prevailing pressures of positivism and
an intellectually confining and dogmatic approach to communication research hardly left room for the type of critical research
proposed by Max Horkheimer and Theodor Adorno with their
introduction of Critical Theory to an American environment that
was not particularly receptive to Marxist theorists, especially
foreign ones. Sproule has reported that the "idea that critical social analysis was somehow unpatriotic" was even taken
up by Congress and its House Un-American Activities Committee (1987: 72). Carey's impression that "the term 'critical'
did not so much describe a position as a cover under which
Marxism might hide during a hostile period in exile" (1982:
22) alludes to the problems of Marxist scholarship as an alien
phenomenon in the United States. But he totally disregards
the history of Critical Theory, including the significance of its
earlier phase in Germany, the specificity of the concept itself,
and the relationship of Critical Theory to Marxism. The result
was the emergence of distinct philosophical perspectives by a
number of German *émigrés* who were also critics of contemporary bourgeois societies, including the practice of the social
sciences.

For instance, Adorno had always felt rather pessimistic about his work with Lazarsfeld. When stipulations concerning the Princeton radio project insisted that the limits of analyses be defined by the American commercial radio system, he concluded that "it was thereby implied that the system itself, its cultural and sociological consequences and its social and economic presuppositions were not to be analyzed" (1969: 343). More important perhaps was Lazarsfeld's insistence on the quantification of culture, which struck Adorno as a "demand to 'measure culture'," and as quite inappropriate for someone who had come to the conclusion that "culture might be precisely that condition that excludes a mentality capable of measuring it" (1969: 347).

Lazarsfeld, on the other hand, reported that he had drawn upon Adorno's studies for his version of critical research, but his own discussion of Critical Theory was limited to acknowledging its stimulating effects upon administrative research. There was no attempt to deal with the theoretical (and ideological) consequences of integrating Critical Theory into mainstream communication research. Lazarsfeld's conclusion – that "if it were included in the general stream of communications research, [Critical Theory] could contribute much in terms of challenging problems and new concepts useful in the interpretation of known, and in the search for new data" (1941: 16) – remained a vague and noncommittal statement. It also implied that Critical Theory would not determine the type of (mass) communication research, but would function as a source of ideas for the execution of administrative research. And finally, these remarks also help demonstrate Lazarsfeld's shotgun approach to rendering ideas capable of supporting his own research interests.

There were other, basic differences between German *Sozialforschung* and American social science research methodology, most importantly, perhaps, the question of empirical verification, which preoccupied American social scientists. Horkheimer had explained the methodological viewpoint of critical social research in the issue of *Studies in Philosophy and Social Science* that carried Lazarsfeld's article on administrative and critical communication research. His comments were concise and to the point; he explained that the formation of categories for critical research must consider "the historical character of the subject matter to which they pertain, and in such a way that the categories

are made to include the actual genesis of that subject matter."
Subsequently,

> the general concept is thus not dissolved into a multitude of
> empirical facts but is concretized in a theoretical analysis of
> a given social configuration and related to the whole of the
> historical process of which it is an indissoluble part.
>
> (1941b: 122)

Horkheimer developed a critical rationale for the formation of
social theory by describing one of the major issues in the relationship between individuals and media, and therefore in the realm of
communication research. He observed that public media

> constantly profess their adherence to the individual's ultimate
> value and his inalienable freedom, but they operate in such a
> way that they tend to forswear such values by fettering the
> individual to prescribed attitudes, thoughts, and buying habits.
> The ambivalent relation between prevailing values and the social
> context forces the categories of social theory to become critical
> and thus to reflect the actual rift between the social reality and
> the values it posits.
>
> (1941b: 122)

This was a clear challenge to traditional theories of communication
and a source of inspiration for new contributions to the field,
but it is difficult to imagine that Lazarsfeld or Schramm, for
that matter, would have joined forces with Horkheimer's critical
position.

In fact, Horkheimer argued that the "real social function
of philosophy lies in its criticism of what is prevalent" (1989:
264). What was prevalent was the replacement of philosophy by
sociology and the domination of the study of society by a social-
scientific perspective, which continued to excel in the production
of information about communication, media and people and their
social, political or economic relations. Horkheimer recognized the
American preoccupation with the

> assiduous collecting of facts in all the disciplines dealing with
> social life, the gathering of great masses of detail in connection
> with problems, the empirical enquiries, through careful ques-
> tionnaires and other means, which are a major part of scholarly
> activity,

and he suggested that all are adding up "to a pattern which is much like the rest of life in a society dominated by industrial production techniques" (1972: 190–1). A Critical Theory of society, however,

> has for its objects men as producers of their own historical way of life in its totality. The real situations which are the starting point of science are not regarded simply as data to be verified and to be predicted according to the laws of probability. Every datum depends not on nature alone but also on the power man has over it. Objects, the kind of perception, the questions asked, and the meaning of the answers all bear witness to human activity and the degree of man's power.
>
> (1972: 244)

Horkheimer insisted that the "chief aim of such criticism is to prevent mankind from losing itself in those ideas and activities which the existing organization of society instills in its members" (1972: 265). Therefore, it must be one of the goals of Critical Theory to make individuals realize their relationship to society and the differences between their everyday activities and the guiding ideas of society which they acknowledge.

Horkheimer's positioning of Critical Theory coincided with a period in the history of Western thought when fascism and communism threatened the existence of democracy, and when a critical attitude toward the social and economic consequences of late-industrial capitalism was needed to help redefine the nature of a democratic society. Indeed, it became a moral obligation to expose and learn from the failures and weaknesses of a capitalist system that provided the only alternative for creating desirable changes. In their 1972 preface to *Dialectic of Enlightenment*, Horkheimer and Adorno reflected on the continuing threat of totalitarianism and restated that "critical thought (which does not abandon its commitment even in the face of progress) demands support for the residues of freedom, and for tendencies toward true humanism, even if these seem powerless in regard to the main course of history" (1972: ix–x).

A critical analysis of society meant to engage in criticism which was an intellectual, and eventually practical, effort which is not satisfied to accept the prevailing ideas, actions, and social conditions unthinkingly and from mere habit; effort which aims to coordinate the individual sides of social life with each other and with the general ideas and aims of the epoch, to deduce them genetically, to distinguish the appearance from the essence, to examine the foundations of things, in short, really to know them.

(1972: 270)

But the recognition of a critical position, based on a notion that the substance of truth is historical, was rare in sociological analyses of communication and particularly absent from Lazarsfeld's discussion of critical research. It reflected fundamental differences between two intellectual traditions and their approach to culture, society and media phenomena. Pragmatism – with its suggestion that ideas or theories are plans of action and that truth is nothing but the success of an idea – had promoted the view that, in an atmosphere of competing statements or ideas, significance is defined in terms of consequences. According to Horkheimer, "Pragmatism has from its beginnings implicitly justified the current substitution of the logic of probability for that of truth, which has since become widely prevalent" (1947: 43). In such an atmosphere prediction becomes the mechanism of social thought, while practice replaces thought, like Dewey's idea that knowing is doing. Horkheimer charged that

pragmatism tries to retranslate any understanding into mere conduct. Its ambition is to be itself nothing else but practical activity, as distinct from theoretical insight, which, according to pragmatistic teachings, is either only a name for physical events or just meaningless.

(1947: 48)

He saw that the rise of Pragmatism coincided with the development of industrial power and technological superiority in the United States. It was the philosophy of an age of science in which experimentation succeeded over meditation and challenged a philosophical tradition which accepted the primacy of thought and theoretical insight. Horkheimer exposed the dangers of Pragmatism, which attempted "to model all spheres of intellectual life after the techniques of the laboratory," becoming the "counterpart of modern industrialism, for which the factory is the prototype of human existence, and which models all branches of culture after production on the conveyor belt, or after the rationalized front office." Accordingly,

> Thought must be gauged by something that is not thought, by its effect on production or its impact on social conduct, as art today is being ultimately gauged in every detail by something that is not art, be it box-office or propaganda value.
>
> (1947: 50–1)

The location of communication research in the scientific culture of society, its self-defined role of providing insights into the position and function of communication and media in American life, and its narrow understanding of the nature of communication in compliance with the needs of industry and politics, are evidence of its allegiance to a Pragmatic world view, and perhaps an explanation for the different nature of theoretical work in the field. Indeed, ideas about communication and media can be conceived as providing mechanisms to promote series of events toward specific practical goals; for instance, a conceptualization of models to serve experimentation and the verification of facts also helps determine the discourse about communication and media effects. The result is the production of "the knowledge of domination, not the knowledge of cultivation" (Frankfurt, 1972: 125). Under such conditions, there was no place for a historical process which provided knowledge about the relationship between individuals and technology and the processes of communication that locate and identify the individual in the age-old struggle for survival against domination or oppression. In fact, there was no time for history, or reflection in general.

The differences between the theoretical requirements of a critical analysis of contemporary society offered by Critical Theorists and the premises for observations of social phenomena occupied by American social scientists were significant and obviously unacceptable to those controlling communication research. Robert Merton once referred to these differences in the study of society in terms of knowledge and information. He suggested that knowledge

> implies a body of facts or ideas, whereas information carries no such implication of *systematically connected* facts or ideas. The American variant accordingly studies the isolated fragments of

information available to masses of people; the European variant typically *thinks about a total structure of knowledge* available to a few.

(1957: 441)

American communication research in the 1960s provided an example of information-gathering practices with a decidedly future-oriented frame of reference, which determined the nature of data collection concerning socially or economically relevant communication behavior. Specifically, public opinion research occurs as an information-gathering activity that has little potential for contributing to the knowledge about people and society. It reveals the commodification of information as the product of a mass culture industry which sells people a way of life that they may recognize as their own, while it remains ahistorical and divorced from the culture which it purports to understand and insists on interpreting.

Consequently, the approach to the study of culture by members of the Frankfurt School (and their development of an aesthetic theory that had originated during the early days of the Institute of Social Research) would be significantly different from American concerns with communication, mass society and mass culture. Horkheimer and Adorno presented their theory of mass culture as early as 1944 in *Die Dialektik der Aufklärung*, which was issued as *Dialectic of Enlightenment* in 1972 when it began to have an impact on the American mass society debate.

An understanding of a theory of culture by Horkheimer and Adorno, equally shared by Marcuse, Lowenthal and Benjamin, is based in the rise of civil society and, more specifically, the development of capitalism. The early work of Georg Lukács, particularly his *Theory of the Novel* (1916) and *History and Class Consciousness* (1923), addressed the contemporary crisis of culture, that is, the disintegration of community and the decline of the subject, and provided a Marxist perspective on the fate of the individual in modern society. Extrapolating from Marx, Lukács used the notion of commodity fetishism to introduce reification as a "deadening" of social and intellectual processes which extended beyond the economic to characterize bourgeois life and to confirm atomization and fragmentation under advanced capitalism.

Dialectic of Enlightenment introduced the specter of reification and its consequences for contemporary society, that is, the destruction of the Enlightenment and the dilemma of criticism. But while

Horkheimer and Adorno revealed a profound pessimism in face of the aftermath of the Second World War, the obscenity of fascism, the failure of socialism under Stalinist rule, and the increasingly authoritarian nature of American society, their work is also an expression of a need for the Enlightenment to "*consider itself*" and to redeem the "hopes of the past" (1972: xv). They acknowledged the paradox of human suffering and social progress and confronted conditions under which the "flood of detailed information and candy-floss entertainment simultaneously instructs and stultifies mankind" (1972: xv). *Dialectic of Enlightenment* contained a critique of mass culture, albeit truncated, that was revealing and instructive for those searching for a theory and method of dealing with communication and media.

The problematic of communication in the modern world emerges through an examination of the history of language and thought, the growth of civil society and the rise of capitalism, when the commodification of ideas resulted in the development of the culture industry. It is located in the social, political and economic conditions of contemporary mass culture and its understanding rests on the ability to trace the relationship between individuals and the alienating environment of modern institutions. Thus, the study of communication is also the study of alienation and desertion, while the history of the media is also the story of separation and isolation of individuals.

According to Horkheimer and Adorno, the formalized production of goods, including culture, aiming at uniformity and efficiency, is based on the "predominance of the effect" (1972: 125), which replaces the work or idea. Consequently, consumers choose technique over content, and perfection of the production over distraction of the arts. The culture industry embraces the ideology of business in its creation of needs; it obtains power from "its identification with a manufactured need" (1972: 137) and the promise of escape from the work process through its production of amusement. Escape, however, is nothing but an approximation or "prolongation" of work (1972: 137), since it makes no new demands and requires no independent thought from the audience.

Horkheimer and Adorno described the reduction of individuals to customers and therefore to elements or objects in the processing of information that serves to maintain the status quo, based on the vague and noncommittal nature of communication, which becomes the *modus vivendi* of the culture industry. They concluded that "Anyone who doubts the power of monotony is a fool" and reminded the reader that "the bread which the culture industry offers man is the stone of stereotype" (1972: 148).

Attacking the perpetuation of political values by the media, the authors suggested that the culture industry treats individuals as illusions and will tolerate them as long as they maintain an unquestioned identification with the public. In effect, "The peculiarity of the self is a monopoly commodity determined by society; it is falsely represented as natural" (1972: 154). In such a society, individuals, culture and advertising merge to produce a seamless stream of communication and images, strengthening the bonds between industry and consumers, between the media and audiences, and ultimately, serve to maintain the economic and political power structure. Consequently, "freedom to choose an ideology – since ideology always reflects economic coercion – everywhere proves to be freedom to choose what is always the same" (1972: 166–7).

Horkheimer and Adorno questioned not only the contemporary manifestations of the media industry; they also raised doubts about the values perpetuated in defense of the prevailing ideology and scrutinized the mechanisms of social criticism. In fact, Adorno proposed elsewhere that the

> task of criticism must be not so much to search for the particular interest-groups to which cultural phenomena are to be assigned, but rather to decipher the general social tendencies which are expressed in these phenomena and through which the most powerful interests realize themselves. Cultural criticism must become social physiognomy.
>
> (1981: 30)

Under such a redefinition of cultural criticism, Adorno suggested that Critical Theory could not accept alternatives or choices between transcendent or immanent criticism of culture, that is, "either calling culture as a whole into question from outside under the general notion of ideology, or confronting it with its norms which it itself has crystallized" (1981: 31).

As a contributor to US communication research literature, Adorno outlined the manner and methodology with which Critical Theory would attack the problems of media in contemporary society (1954). He suggested that historical insights into the

development of media in American culture were absolutely necessary to "do justice to all such complexities" that existed in the
rise of mass culture (1954: 214). But the quest for knowledge about
the nature of modern media also needed a "depth-psychological
approach," since the "media are not simply the sum total of
the actions they portray or of the messages that radiate from
these actions," but have a "heritage of polymorphic meaning"
which has been "taken over by the culture industry inasmuch as
what it conveys becomes itself organized in order to enthrall the
spectators on various psychological levels simultaneously" (1954:
221). Adorno provided a wide-ranging discussion of ways in which
to address the cultural problems of television and suggested that
the "effort here required is of a moral nature itself: knowingly to
face psychological mechanisms operating on various levels in order
not to become blind and passive victims" (1954: 235).

Critical research in the tradition of Critical Theory, with its
speculative approach to contemporary culture and society, sought
to challenge the theoretical basis of traditional social research.
Critical-administrative research, on the other hand, in the tradition
of a progressive American sociology, was driven by methodological
considerations and the immediacy and potential threat of mass
culture phenomena to the social or political status quo.

At this time American communication research had begun
to expand upon the pioneering work of Lazarsfeld, Hovland,
Lasswell and others, and was drifting into what Lazarsfeld had
labeled "administrative" research with an increasing sophistication
of its empirical methodology. Members of the Frankfurt School
identified this trend as market research, and Leo Lowenthal
suggested that it could only reflect "reified unmediated reactions
rather than the underlying social and psychological function of the
cultural phenomena under scrutiny" (Jay, 1985: 50).

The problems of mass society, with its feared cultural and
political consequences, particularly in the face of fascist and
communist threats from Europe, had encouraged an American response, when earlier research into questions of collective
behavior (Blumer), media and diffusion (Lazarsfeld), persuasion
(Hovland), and propaganda (Lasswell), sought empirical evidence
to demonstrate the workings of a pluralist society in the United
States. Among these contributors, Lasswell represented the most
knowledgeable theorist, whose appreciation of Marx and Freud as
major intellectual sources for the interpretation of cultures, and

whose familiarity with the structure of Marxist ideology offered a comparative perspective for the study of political behavior long before many of his American colleagues acknowledged its relevance.

Lasswell had to overcome the fact that political science theory and academic research in the 1920s had not considered the importance of Marxist thought, because "America was protected by geographic distance and its own affluence and provincialism from a realization of the significance of the class struggles in Europe, and in part by the 'red scares' of the early 1920s" (Smith, 1969: 64–5). He appreciated the importance of a cultural approach to the study of communication; and his writings, since the publication of *Propaganda Technique in the World War* in 1927, reflected the need to sensitize communication researchers to the uses of language. He had pondered these issues in the wake of a number of important publications, particularly Lippmann's *Public Opinion* (1922) and *The Phantom Public* (1925), on the question of the public and its role in the political system.

Lasswell also represented a long-standing interest in the study of culture and symbols in the context of political communication. He had raised significant possibilities for the analysis of politics in cultural settings, that is, for "the study of changes in the shape and composition of the value patterns of society" (1935: 3). He had recognized the proximity between political and social practices and the significance of the symbolic environment and began to formulate communication research strategies that would systematically embrace "patterns of personality and culture" (1935: 208). Lasswell was convinced of a relationship between subjective and objective aspects of existence, and concluded that "in the culture that we know best the rearrangement of inner experience has become intimately connected with overt materializations" (1935: 268). His approach consisted of historical analyses and the use of empirical data to compose pictures of political reality, as in "News Channels and Attention Areas: The Role of Secondary Contact," which also described a variety of creative procedures to assess public communication (1935: 185–206). Cartier has called Lasswell "a humanistic behaviorist" in the tradition of the scientific naturalism of the Chicago School (1988: 187), while Lerner has observed that "Lasswell always stressed the importance of normative functions in human enterprises. Although a behaviorist, he never became an addict of behaviorism (or any other ideological 'ism')" (1979: 406).

In fact, Lasswell provided communication research with ideas about effects, content analysis and an approach to communication which overcame the simplicity of (his own) earlier stimulus–response models, and by doing so, probably contributed more to the field than most of his contemporaries in communication and media research. But he could not prevail theoretically in the sociological circles that dominated the developing stages of the field. Leo Rosten has called him "the most fertile catalyst and theorist of his generation," adding that Lasswell's "pioneering contributions to propaganda analysis, the pyramid of power, content analysis, political symbols, and political psychology are indisputable and historic" (1969: 9).

Nevertheless, while Lasswell's scholarship was impressive in its scope, its criticism was confined to the study of political behavior and the uses of symbolic analysis, and therefore removed from the most active realm of communication research. His position also highlights the consequences of segmentation when research interests divided political communication from mass communication. The result was a predictable but unfortunate power struggle among expert groupings seeking recognition of their narrow specializations from within and reinforcement through financial rewards from outside the academy. Such a development was certainly not in the interest of an interdisciplinary approach toward a social theory of communication.

After the Second World War, however, American society came under renewed scrutiny from a number of disciplines, emanating from postwar changes, like the rapid expansion of a peacetime economy and the widespread prosperity of a growing white middle class. David Potter's *People of Plenty* (1954), Vance Packard's *The Hidden Persuaders* (1957), and William Whyte's *The Organization Man* (1957) were examples of popular and critical accounts of this period when mass culture became the target of an attack on the American public. There were others, like David Riesman and C. Wright Mills, whose critical characterizations of American society caught the imagination of social critics and caused a considerable debate among social scientists.

Riesman had been influenced by Erich Fromm and psycho-analytic analyses of culture. His book, *The Lonely Crowd*, co-authored by Nathan Glazer and Reuel Denney, and first published in 1950, dealt with the problem of historical change in industrial Middle America. The book became a basic document for the discussion of American culture during the 1950s; according to Hartshorne, "It was one of those rare books which, though intended primarily for a scholarly audience, enjoyed an enormous popular success" (1968: 173). It was an account of the American dream turned into a nightmare, according to Paul and Percival Goodman, demonstrating that "our beautiful American classlessness is degenerating into a static bureaucracy; our mass arts are beneath contempt; our prosperity breeds insecurity; our system of distribution has become huckstering and our system of production discourages enterprise and sabotages invention" (1960: 5).

Riesman and his colleagues were most interested in the problems of a changing society and pursued the discovery of social history by utilizing "previously neglected and underprivileged data" (1961: xiv), based on the insights of neo-Freudian analysis of cultural and historical change. They revealed a decisive shift of American society from "inner-direction" to "other-direction" in a study of culture and history that was mindful of a traditional, holistic approach, while taking advantage of newer research techniques. Thus, they relied on Lazarsfeld's findings about the two-step flow of information, while concentrating on questions about the long-run effects of communication and media on the emotional and private lives of Americans, since the exercise of control over the individual by peer groups was a characteristic of the "other-directed" individual. The authors suggested that since the media seem to be less effective than "the controllers of the media and their critics like to think," they are "much freer than they realize, to attend to the medium itself, rather than to the message it purveys or is believed to purvey" (1961: 205). In an atmosphere of conformity, they advocated allowing for more genuine escape, so that "Americans would become stronger psychically and more ready to undertake an awakening of political imagination and commitment" (1961: 204). Their concerns and criticisms remained differentiated and concentrated on the potential of the media as agents of human liberation from the delusion of self-determination, exploring the possibilities of moving between high and popular culture, to make a difference in the lives of people.

A few years later, in a new preface to the edition, however, Riesman voiced "gravest" concerns about the ethnocentricity of the media and the slanting of news in a misleading and self-serving manner (1961: xliii). He had produced a study that suggested to communication research the complexity of formulating meaningful research agendas and the need to supplement the range of social-psychological methodologies with historical considerations of individuals in communication.

The sociology of C. Wright Mills was enriched by his refusal to accept a social-scientific study of society that lacked a historical perspective and that refused to take a moral stand on the subject of its analysis. He railed against the "abstract empiricism" of the social sciences and the dogma of methodology and provided a scathing critique of advanced urban society in a series of books, from *The New Men of Power* (1948) and *White Collar* (1951) to *The Power Elite* (1956). His belief in the significance of an intellectual tradition of social thought became the rallying point of a "new" sociology which called for the consciousness of "basic premises and principles," suggesting that the sociology of "Pareto, Durkheim, Weber, Znaniecki, Simmel, and Marx" was important, because "it is to them that we owe the firm distinction between science as clarification and information as manipulation" (Horowitz, 1964: 18).

One of the goals was the reclamation of social history and its relationship to sociology; Mills demonstrated how the intellectual tradition of social thought could provide methodological guidance to questions of time and specificity. He has also been called an "American conscience" at a time when imperialism and nuclear war threatened total destruction, struggling "against the liberal rhetoric, Marxist dogma, and sociological dehumanization" (Casanova, 1964: 71). His sociological imagination called for the acquisition of a quality of mind which would enable individuals to "grasp history and biography and the relations between the two within society" (1959: 12).

Mills issued a pessimistic view of the media in *The Power Elite*, revealing a market orientation that facilitates "psychological illiteracy" rather than public discourse and enlightenment (1956: 311). Accordingly, he saw the media as presiding over a "pseudo-world," having provided external realities and internal experiences and destroying privacy by destroying "the chance for the reasonable and leisurely and human interchange of opinion" (1956: 314). But the media were not only a major cause of the emergence of a mass society in the United States, they were also a means of power elites. Because media play an important role in the execution of authority, they help create one of the major

problems of contemporary society, namely the denial of authority
to the people. Mills argued that "the power of initiation is in fact
held by small circles of men" whose "strategy of manipulation
is to make it appear that the people, or at least a large group
of them, 'really made the decision'" (1956: 317). The media
represent an aspect of this strategy, and *The Power Elite* was an
indictment of the American power structure. Its moral judgment
and intellectual integrity challenged liberal-pluralist arguments and
pointed the way toward a radical critique of society. It was also the
contribution of an intellectual whose moral obligation to oppose
the conditions of mass society resulted in an attack on the denial
of rationality and freedom.

Riesman and Mills recognized the importance of analyzing
power in society and sought to locate the basis for criticism in
the socioeconomic distribution of property or influence. They were
concerned with the structure of power and its consequences for
American society; although positioned quite differently – Mills
referred to Riesman's "romantic pluralism" (1956: 244), and
Riesman saw Mills searching for a "ruling class" (1961: 225) –
both observed a decline of political participation and the failure
of public opinion. These issues involved social communication and
the role of the media, and were central to communication research.
But their contributions seemed to have been of only peripheral
interest to the field, which had managed to retain a singularly
narrow theoretical and historical base in its endeavor as a social-
scientific enterprise.

Indeed, academic journals like *Journalism Quarterly*, *Public
Opinion Quarterly*, *Journal of Broadcasting* or *Journal of Communication*, in particular, did not seek theoretical controversy or
politicized participation in a critical assessment of American media
research, or question the premises of an implicit operating theory
of communication and society.

Since the late 1960s, the field of communication research
reflected the conditions of a society embroiled in controversies
over a war in Viet Nam and experienced the emergence of a
brand of social criticism strongly related to an earlier critique of
American society. This tradition has spanned the socialist writings
of political economists and sociologists during the turn of the
century, the populist criticism of political and economic authority
by publicists and muckraking journalists in the late 1920s, and the
social criticism of social scientists since the 1950s.

Among the first contributors to a critical literature of media and communication was Herbert Schiller, whose *Mass Communications and American Empire* (1969) supplied readers with a critical approach to the political and economic functions of American mass communication structures and policies. According to Dallas Smythe's introduction, the book supplanted the tangential and often outdated work of Mills, Robert A. Brady, Thurman Arnold, or Robert S. Lynd (Schiller, 1969: viii), and was an effort that critically addressed communication issues. The book helped establish Schiller's reputation as a social critic and humanist who challenged the desirability of an industrialization of communication, calling "ownership, control, financial support, national sovereignty and the character of programming" the "unsettled agenda" of society (1969: 149). In a series of small books (*The Mind Managers*, 1973; *Communication and Cultural Domination*, 1976; *Who Knows: Information in the Age of the Fortune 500*, 1981; *Information and the Crisis Economy*, 1984; and *Culture Inc.: The Corporate Takeover of Public Expression*, 1989) Schiller continued to expose the manipulation of information and the problems of cultural domination from a political economy perspective of communication and media. His analyses of power, however, were not without hope for the betterment of society, since they were based upon a belief in the ability of individuals to participate in the life of society, despite the increasing controls of the communication system. His work has been the crusade of a humanist who always seemed to feel that a "heightened consciousness" may eventually "develop its own means to force the social changes so desperately needed in this country today" (1973: 191). In this sense, Schiller has been an interventionist, helping to provide a critical balance in a debate that celebrated information societies and dehumanizing technological progress in the name of freedom and democracy.

His ideas were enhanced and supported by the work of Dallas Smythe, whose critical historical materialism offered a political-economic perspective on the control of information, the invention of the media by monopoly capitalism to produce an audience commodity, and the consequences of a "mass communication theory [that] begins and ends with audiences, prospective and produced [and consumed]" (1981: xv). Together with Schiller he offered probably the most radical and steadfast economic critique in the field; but more importantly, both demonstrated through their

work the possibility and the potential for Marxist criticism beyond
the 1960s.

The introduction of Critical Theory since the 1940s as a
competing social (and political) theory of society constituted a
significant development in American social thought. It rekindled
a Marxist debate, promoted radical criticism, and signaled the
beginning of substantial Marxist scholarship which continued after
the war and into the 1970s. The ensuing critique of contemporary
American social theory and research practice also established
the intellectual leadership of British, French and German social
theorists, when the center of theoretical innovations and reconsiderations shifted to the intellectual milieu of postwar Europe.

Thus, the encounter with critical theorists provided a solid
opportunity to examine form and substance of an ideological
critique of society. Specifically, the cultural pessimism of Adorno
and Horkheimer, together with the political critique of Herbert
Marcuse, the popular culture critique of Leo Lowenthal and, later,
the theoretical inquiries of Jürgen Habermas concerning the role of
communication in the struggle against bureaucracies and authority,
provided American social theorists with alternatives to questions
of power, change, and the future of society.

In his response to the influence of the Frankfurt School on
intellectual life in the United States, Shils attributed its critique
of mass society to the conditions of exile rather than to the
European experience. He suggested that "their anti-capitalistic
and by multiplication, anti-American attitude found a traumatic
and seemingly ineluctable confirmation in the popular culture of
the United States" (1972: 263). In fact, their critical writings
exemplified an abiding commitment to the study of culture –
including the complicity of the media industry in the ideological
struggle – and to an analysis of the cultural process. They were
also the result of recognizing attempts throughout this century to
merge the interests of science and industry under the auspices of
various institutions, including universities.

According to Schroyer, the Marxist cultural critique of contemporary society stressed the "sociocultural consequences of
stimulated economic growth." Consequently, it "transforms the
human milieu into a technologically determined system, and
systematically blocks symbolic communication by the superim-
position of more and more technical rules and constraints deriving
from rationalizing processes" (1975a: 223). These were continuing

concerns among cultural critics, and Alvin Gouldner, in particular, has traced similarities and differences between the Pragmatism of the Chicago School and Critical Theory in their analysis of the "cultural apparatus" and the "consciousness industry," respectively (1976: 167–78). He proposed that the common interest in public discourse manifested in the role of news in everyday life and the conditions of the public sphere were treated in a "taxonomic and positivistic" way by the Chicago School, while such interest received a historically specific treatment particularly by Habermas, who linked the deterioration of the public sphere with the development of a bourgeois economy (1976: 138–40).

When the debates over Critical Theory reached mainstream (mass) communication research in the 1970s, it had been a major theoretical event for over four decades, constituting a considerable body of theoretical literature which reflected the extent and quality of the modernist debate in a number of disciplines. Beginning with Martin Jay's *The Dialectical Imagination: A History of the Frankfurt School and the Institute of Social Research, 1923–1950* (1973), the volume of original works by Adorno, Horkheimer, Marcuse and Habermas, together with translations of German contemporaries and other secondary sources about the Frankfurt School increased dramatically,[1] although the subsequent readings and interpretations of Critical Theory by (mass) communication research remained a peripheral intellectual enterprise.

For instance, the marginal role of Critical Theory, or any other radical challenge of traditional social theories, had been revealed in the frequently cited 1959 *Public Opinion Quarterly* review of communication research. Berelson's pessimistic statement included no reference to Critical Theory as a potential source of theoretical stimulation (1959: 4), although in the same issue Riesman referred to a critique of society with the publication of *The Authoritarian Personality* (Adorno *et al.*) in 1950 and raised some questions concerning needed research on broader cultural and societal issues. He also mentioned the creative work of Leo Lowenthal, who had established himself as an early member of the Frankfurt School with his interest in the sociology of literature (Hardt, 1991).

Lowenthal was the most visible representative of Critical Theory in American communication research circles, having collaborated with Joseph Klapper (opinion research and psychological warfare) and Marjorie Fiske (popular culture), and having been included in a number of collected works edited by Lazarsfeld and Stanton, Schramm, and Jacobs.

He had understood better than some of his German colleagues how to bridge the differences between the methodological demands of a social-scientific analysis of media and society in the United States and the necessity of a historical dimension for inquiries into the nature of culture or cultural productions. He had gained acceptance (and respectability as a social scientist) with his widely quoted "Biographies in Popular Magazines" (1944) that was based on his earlier work in Germany and had appeared with Lazarsfeld's encouragement. In his recollections, Lowenthal remembered Robert Merton's favorable response as well as Lazarsfeld's complete misunderstanding of the "political and analytical meaning" of this study (1989: 234).

Underlying Lowenthal's contributions to the field was a deep-seated, European concern with the humanistic aspects of social theory and an active involvement in the promotion of theoretical and methodological traditions that had their origins in classic conceptualizations of culture. He became a mediator between the social and behavioral sciences and the humanities in their struggle for dominating the debate concerning the definition of fields of knowledge. In particular, his work on popular culture was influenced by a shared critical understanding of a pervasive attitude in society toward entertainment. According to Jay, members of the Frankfurt School argued that the notion of popular culture was ideological; in fact, "the culture industry administered a non-spontaneous reified, phony culture rather than the real thing" (1973: 216).

In a series of essays that he more recently combined under the title "Contributions to the Philosophy of Communication," Lowenthal produced a vision of the field through a discussion of the sociology of literature, the critique of mass culture and popular culture, and their proximity to communication research (1984).

He had established his own interest in the historical and sociological dimensions of literature early during his career and thought it essential in his approach to a sociology of literature and proceeded to argue for a materialistic explanation of literary history, but refused to place literature within a strictly economic explanation of culture. Instead, literature as a means of making culture transparent becomes also a reflection of ideology, while literary studies are "largely an investigation of ideologies" (1984: 248). His understanding of social theory as tentative and open to changes provided the necessary flexibility for incorporating new insights and meeting methodological demands in light of sociological criticism.

Lowenthal had recognized that the products of mass literature as increasingly popular objects of communication research had been neglected by literary studies. Academic disciplines which saw themselves in charge of accounting for literature had been "caught unaware by the impact of mass literature, the best seller, the popular magazine, the comics and the like, and they have maintained an attitude of haughty indifference to the lower depths of imagination in print" (1984: 257). He outlined a course of sociological action which included a number of suggestions related to communication research in an essay which reflected his unpublished remarks during the 1947 opening of the Institute for Communication Research at the University of Illinois, where he specifically addressed the requirements of critical communication research (1948).

Thus, it is necessary to place literature – and one could also include journalism as popular culture – within a "functional frame" within society, suggesting the location of literary material within a culture and its specific class stratifications, to gain an understanding of its social relevance. Such a positioning of literature or journalism in terms of their escapist or ideological functions would be supplemented with an analysis of specific forms. Lowenthal singled out his own work on popular biographies in mass circulation magazines to provide an example of how media succeed in constructing a topical environment in which the reader

> can experience the gratification of being confirmed in his own pleasures and discomforts by participating in the pleasures and discomforts of the great. The large confusing issues in the political and economic realm and the antagonisms and controversies in the social realm are submerged in the experience of being at one with the powerful and great in the sphere of consumption.
> (1984: 258–9)

Lowenthal would argue that the analysis of society from a literary (or journalistic) perspective must also include a discussion of the position of writers or journalists as intellectuals within the cultural milieu. Thus, the study of their political and economic standing and their own view of their function, including their treatment of social or political problems, is as important as seeking insights into conditions of production.

More significantly, Lowenthal felt that scholarly investigations should relate to the impact of the media. This had been a major area of traditional communication research, but Lowenthal argued that the question of effects involved more than the empirical analysis of consumption, but was destined to provoke theoretical explorations that would help define its "social determinants," including specific knowledge about the influence of "all-embracing social constellations on writing and the reading public," an understanding of "the influence of formal [and informal] controls of production and reading," and an assessment of "technological change and its economic and social consequences" (1984: 264–5).

Lowenthal urged sociologists of literature to join in the experiences of communication research, and he proposed a series of research projects that would enhance the standing of the discipline and add to its knowledge about culture and communication. He also offered a number of appropriate examples of critical research, including references to Walter Benjamin's "The Work of Art in the Age of Reproduction," Siegfried Kracauer's "From Caligari to Hitler," Adorno's "On Popular Music," and Horkheimer's "Art and Mass Culture."

His essay remains a remarkable, albeit incomplete, statement about critical communication research that has been virtually ignored since its publication in 1948. In fact, Lowenthal's analytical scheme, his themes and methodological suggestions, could be considered the beginning of a theoretical foundation of critical communication research in the United States.

The social and political movements of the time had been captured in Lowenthal's exposure of questionable communication practices, revealing the sensitivity of the foreign observer to the potential of aggression in society. Together with Norbert Guterman, he published *Prophets of Deceit: A Study of the Techniques of the American Agitator* in 1949, which appeared in the series on *Studies in Prejudice*. It became a significant contribution to the study of mass society, concentrating on the meaning of demagogy, its techniques and appeals, and served as a popular resource in the field of mass communication research. The volume also confirmed Lowenthal's own position among Critical Theorists; it remains a remarkable document of participation in the surveillance of the political and social environment of the United States. Lowenthal engaged in an analysis of the techniques of agitation, "turning psychoanalysis on its head," by suggesting that public agitation would result in neurotic and psychotic behavior and create a dependency on leadership. His purpose was the unmasking of "aggressive and destructive impulses hidden behind that rhetoric" on the basis of textual analyses which would reveal unconscious mechanisms of agitation (1989: 234).

The serious political engagement of Horkheimer, Lowenthal and others and the potential role of their work in the enlightenment process of American society were perhaps best illustrated by Lowenthal's revelation that Horkheimer intended to reproduce each book in the *Studies in Prejudice* series as a pamphlet for distribution to "so-called multiplicators," that is, journalists and opinion leaders, in a "given situation of anti-Semitic political outbreaks." He added that in the spirit of Critical Theory they wanted "to accomplish scientifically meaningful work in a manner that would allow its application to political praxis" (1989: 235). The series offered insightful analyses of power and authority in modern society, and *The Authoritarian Personality* (Adorno *et al.*, 1950) remains one of the seminal contributions from this era.

During the early 1960s Lowenthal continued to argue for a critical approach to (popular) culture and insisted on the recognition of the historical process in the definition of the cultural stimulus, since the relationship between stimulus and response has been "pre-formed and pre-structured" by their "historical and social fate" (1961: 13). In this context, he recognized the contributions of Park and Wirth who had "kept alive the conscience of a historical civilization" (1961: 8), and he concluded his assessment of American sociology with the observation that "expediency and the lack of a historical or philosophical frame of reference make a sorry marriage of convenience" (1961: 10).

Lowenthal's commitment to the exploration of mass culture was also confirmed in his reaction to Riesman's work about American mass culture with the publication of *The Lonely Crowd*. He praised the humanistic orientation of the book and used the opportunity to engage the field in a debate about the position of what he called "the scientific and the intellectual universe" (1984: 276). He credited the authors with helping reverse the dominant pattern of the social sciences, which had consisted of "a preeminent concern with methodology and with the construction of theoretical models" (1984: 279). Lowenthal acknowledged the difficulty of "interpreting within one conceptual framework the uniqueness of a historical period and the general features of human behavior prevailing in it" as a dilemma that must be faced "if one wants to understand *uno actu* individuals both in their social roles and in their personal imagery" (1984: 280). In addressing this dualism, Lowenthal also pointed to the failures of communication research which had usually remained closed to creative, intellectual risk-taking by relying solely on the promises of empiricism as an established social-scientific practice.

Lowenthal criticized this one-sidedness of communication research and suggested that, because the discussion of communication had deteriorated into discussion of the media, it had "seriously jeopardized productive discourse between social scientists and humanists" (1967: 335). He recounted how communication "has been almost completely divested of its human content" and projected the dehumanization of communication in a media culture that relied "on the ideological sanction of individual autonomy in the very process of exploiting individuality to serve mass culture" (1967: 336).

Earlier he had criticized the "splendid isolation" of social research and proposed that such a position may reinforce the suspicion that social research is "nothing but market research, an instrument of expedient manipulation, a tool with which to prepare reluctant customers for enthusiastic spending" (1961: 9).

In particular, Lowenthal accused social scientists of having evaded their moral commitment "by pretending to engage in value-free research – something that exists neither in logic nor in history." And he insisted, in the spirit of an applied and active Critical Theory, that in "an era of increasing positivistic infatuation . . . the inalienable birthright of the intellectual as a critic, trivial as it may sound, must be energetically asserted" (1967: 337).

Lowenthal turned to the experience of literature, philosophy and art to promote a humanistic meaning of communication that referred to genuinely productive imagination, free from instrumental concepts of language and communication as information technologies, and requiring intellectual effort and participation.

He reminded his readers of the human dimension of communication by citing Dewey's definition at a time when communication was becoming part of a culture which hardly distinguished between consumers and producers "because they are both the serfs of a life style of conformity and regulation" (1967: 344). And he reproached communication research for its failure to acknowledge the potential of a humanistic vision of culture and communication, based on his assessment of modern society and the problems of a displaced sense of participation.

From the beginning, Lowenthal's interest in popular culture and his recognition of media content demonstrated the effectiveness of historical analyses in a series of differentiated and time-bound observations about the role of escapism, ideology and information in the production of mass culture. Furthermore, he recognized the importance of levels of social stratification and, therefore, different bourgeois interests concerning media form and content, and suggested the need for investigating the relationship between class and media use. Thus, problems of consumption of mass culture are tied into the history of a dominant technological bureaucracy and the deteriorating psychological condition of individuals, like the loss of self-confidence and trust. Similarly, inquiries into the production of media content, in the form of a sociology of writers or news workers for instance, were bound to include questions about the impact of the cultural and political environment, economic decision-making, and the effects of role consciousness on the performances of these producers of mass culture.

Throughout his writings, but especially in his contributions to the sociology of literature, Lowenthal proposed a genuine interdisciplinary approach to critical communication research from a perspective of Critical Theory, which he defined as a "perspective, based on a shared critical fundamental attitude, that applies to all cultural phenomena without ever claiming to be a system" (1989: 112). This was a positioning of a critique of society in the tradition of Hegel's form of negation, on the periphery of the establishment and as an expression of marginality. For Lowenthal this meant a "critique of the production of commodities and words for a manipulated and manipulable mass market" (1989: 112).

Lowenthal's approach rested on the recognition of the separate roles of art and popular culture and incorporated the intellectual interests of a classic European tradition of social thought and the insights of a new American social science. Thus, an explanation of the uses of art and mass culture were dependent on the history of social and psychological conditions of society and individuals, respectively. His early work indicates the formulation of ideas toward a theory of reception and effects that were immersed in a critique of ideology. He rejected the behavioristic sociology of literature in the United States as ahistorical and limited in its scope to commercial and political propaganda and disapproved of a narrow Marxist interpretation of art as an ideological manifestation. According to Lowenthal,

> art teaches, and mass culture is learned; therefore, a sociological analysis of art must be cautious, supplementary, and selective, whereas a sociological analysis of mass culture must be all-inclusive, for its products are nothing more than the phenomena and symptoms of the process of the individual's self-resignation in a wholly administered society.
>
> (1989: 113)

Lowenthal's work was about the suppression of the imagination and the results of a mass culture that "reinforces and signals the instruction in the late-capitalist world that promotes a false collective" (1989: 119). Although his contributions turned out to be politically relevant and culturally instructive, they failed to impress the institutional forces of communication research enough to become a major theoretical and methodological resource. Nevertheless, in his analyses of literature and mass culture, Lowenthal demonstrated the richness of the material as a source of insights about the social and political conditions of a culture. His work also reminded the reader of his intellectual proximity to Walter Benjamin, whose work influenced the later period of cultural studies in the United States and elsewhere.

Lowenthal's self-defined position at the margins of an intellectual enterprise that dealt with questions of literature, culture and communication made him aware of the proximity of Burke and Duncan, for instance, but he was particularly attracted to the communication research of Paul Lazarsfeld. This may have been an indication that Lowenthal saw real possibilities for his work in the area of communication studies; it may also reflect the specific social and political conditions of the time, when Lowenthal, like other *émigrés*, depended on the influence and generosity of established individuals and their organizations. But more importantly, Lowenthal came to appreciate the concerns of interactionism with mediation as an aspect that was missing in Marxist theory, namely "the mediation between the fundamental economic and social forces and actual human needs," as well as the materialistic character of functionalism (1987: 142), although he distanced himself from both theoretical trends. In his autobiographical reflections he concluded that he had been most disturbed about "the so-called empirical research enterprise, where one had the feeling that the research was actually being done only for the sake of the method and not for the sake of the objects of research" (1987: 143).

The discussion of mass society and the effects of technocratic rule as an underlying theme of Critical Theory of these years also characterized the work of Herbert Marcuse, who emerged as the most popular (e.g. most frequently cited) member of the Frankfurt School in the United States. In fact, Clecak has suggested that

> Marcuse made especially good copy because his association with New Left figures suggested such easy and satisfying interpretations. Journalists and critics accounted for the unlikely alliance in pop Freudian terms characterizing Marcuse as a surrogate father who encouraged and sanctioned political and sexual rebellion.
>
> (1973: 212)

He responded to his popularity with an assertion that affirmative culture means "a world brought about not through the overthrow of the material order of life but through events in the individual's soul. Humanity becomes an inner state" (1968: 103).

His position against the empirical sociology of communication emerged from a number of contributions to the critique of mass society. Marcuse felt that contemporary sociology, "freed from all theoretical guidance except a methodological one, succumbs to the fallacies of misplaced concreteness, thus performing an ideological service while proclaiming the elimination of value judgments," and demanded the intervention of Critical Theory (1964: 254).

His particular interests in the mass culture phenomenon were the result of two major themes in his understanding of the history of modern culture: the transition from a period of affirmation, when distinctions between the spiritual and the material world emerged, to a period of resignation; and the relationship between happiness and freedom under the conditions of a bourgeois society.

The developing tensions between the needs of the inner world and the conditions of the outer world could no longer be reconciled and individual desires had to give in to the demands of a dominant society. As a result, the preservation of the economic and political order threatened the spiritual or cultural repositories of the individual. Likewise, the notion of happiness had become defined as freedom from work and remained attached to the idea of leisure. For Marcuse, happiness was more than a feeling of satisfaction; it was found in "the reality of freedom and satisfaction." He added, "Happiness involves knowledge: it is the prerogative of the *animal rationale*. With the decline in consciousness, with the control of information, with the absorption of individual into mass communication, knowledge is administered and confined" (1955: 94).

The result of mass society is an atmosphere of collective anaesthesia, in which the repressed individual shares a reality shaped by the alienation of labor and his reduction to an exchangeable object. Marcuse followed Freud's explanation of the history of culture and argued from a socio-historical perspective that the differences between freedom and happiness and between sexuality and culture were the result of institutional domination and not the outcome of human nature. He based his argument on the workings of "surplus repression" as a restrictive means of maintaining social domination and the "performance principle" under which individuals "do not live their own lives, but perform pre-established functions," working in alienation (1955: 41).

For Marcuse, the history of Western civilization was the development of the performance principle, which was perfected in the process of industrialization, and achieved when society gained total control of the individual by working conditions of alienated labor. Most recently, the concomitant reduction of leisure time to phases of passivity and "re-creation of energy for work" was redefined when "the technique of mass manipulation developed an entertainment industry which directly controls leisure time" (1955: 43).

Marcuse confirmed his understanding of the task of Critical Theory "to analyze society in the light of its used and unused or abused capabilities for improving the human condition" (1964: x) with the publication of *One-Dimensional Man* (1964).

Accordingly, such critical analysis must be based on value judgments, and Marcuse proceeded from a position of affirmation, suggesting that the foundation of social theory is based on "the judgment that human life is worth living, or rather can be and ought to be made worth living," and on a belief in the existence of specific possibilities "for the amelioration of human life" and the availability of "specific means and ways of realizing these possibilities" (1964: x–xi). For Marcuse, social theory is historical theory and since it is concerned with alternatives, it must "haunt the established society as subversive tendencies and forces" (1964: xii). Although his book is about these counterforces in modern society, which must act to realize the possibilities of a better life, Marcuse's efforts were devoted to showing that

> Technical progress, extended to a whole system of domination and coordination, creates forms of life [and of power] which appear to reconcile the forces opposing the system and to defeat or refute all protest in the name of the historical prospects of freedom from toil and domination.
>
> (1964: xii)

He envisioned a totalitarian society, that is, one in which forms of social control and social cohesion erase the differences between the private and public existence, while incorporating technology into systems of domination.

The role of mass culture and the use of media are crucial aspects of this vision of modern society in which consumption becomes a strategy of power. Rejecting charges that he possibly overrated the potential of the media as instruments of indoctrination, Marcuse suggested that individuals encounter media as "preconditioned receptacles of long standing," long before the impact of mass media technologies and their control. In fact, "the decisive difference is in the flattening out of the contrast [or conflict] between the given and the possible, between the satisfied and the unsatisfied needs" (1964: 8). Accordingly, media use by individuals regardless of their class differences does not indicate the dissolution of classes but "the extent to which the needs and satisfactions that serve the preservation of the Establishment are shared by the underlying population" (1964: 8). This is the emergence of the one-dimensional society, in which "Domination has its own aesthetics, and democratic domination has its democratic aesthetics." Marcuse recognized the benefits of a society in which people have instant access to culture, but he warned that "In this diffusion, however, they become cogs in a culture-machine which remakes their content" (1964: 65).

In *The Aesthetic Dimension* (1978) Marcuse placed art and aesthetics in a pivotal role within Critical Theory by developing dialectical aesthetics in which literature, in particular, functions as the conscience of society. He pronounced that "The truth of art lies in this: that the world really is as it appears in the work of art," and "the political potential of art lies only in its own aesthetic dimension. Its relation to praxis is inexorably indirect, mediated, and frustrating" (1978: xii).

His suggestions could have helped redirect (mass) communication research to explore alternative ways of social communication. One of them was the focus on the role of art in the process of revealing its own truth about reality and, therefore, sharing the experience of autonomy and freedom and providing a measure of the role of media in society.

Many issues pertaining to the consequences of mass society had been presented earlier by Lowenthal, Mills, Riesman and others; they now found support and one kind of theoretical unity in Marcuse's critique of contemporary society. It was character- ized by a deeply pessimistic vision, painfully without solutions, except a commitment to remain firm under what seemed to be the hopeless condition of the One-Dimensional Man. Marcuse concluded that "the critical theory of society possesses no concepts which could bridge the gap between the present and its future; holding no promise and showing no success, it remains negative" (1964: 257).

Yet it is equally clear that the theorizing of Marcuse and his *émigré* colleagues did not replace praxis; instead, it was the beginning of a project that would liberate the individual from the abstraction of contemporary social sciences. Jay has concluded that "the Frankfurt School preserved the hope of a more truly humane society inhabited by concrete men rather than by the abstract subjects of the humanists, with whom they have so often been confused" (1972: 305).

Marcuse also produced a different kind of Marxism, according to Kolakowski, who has charged that Marcuse offered a

Marxism without the proletariat [irrevocably corrupted by the welfare state], without history (as the vision of the future is not derived from a study of historical changes but from an intuition of true human nature), and without the cult of science, a Marxism furthermore in which the value of liberated society resides in pleasure and not creative work.

(1978: 413)

Nevertheless, in the context of leveling dimensions of thought and action, Marcuse raised the problem of functional and manipulated communication in which the use of language of government public relations, advertising, or journalism becomes an agency of domination, linking individuals to the functions they perform in society. In fact, throughout most of his writings Marcuse posed the picture of individuals trapped by a consumer economy and the politics of corporate capitalism that have resulted in material dependency and need fulfillment and served to stabilize the system.

Communication research, stuck in the fallibility of empirical concreteness and constrained by the institutional demands in support of the market, failed to respond to a critique of society. It was caught in the demands for services by those who created the public and also controlled its needs. Communication research expressed itself in the creation of methodological instruments and asserted itself in the application of such methodologies to series of problems defined by organized capitalism. Thus, it participated in the defense of entrenched institutional interests and their media system, affirming the power of communication in the reproduction of capitalism, that is, in the improvement of its means of manipulation. But communication research, like other academic pursuits, also suffered under the consequences of a repressive society, when intellectual autonomy remained buried under authority relationships that fail to provide mental and social space for reflection and negation.

The writings of first-generation critical theorists, like Horkheimer, Adorno, Lowenthal and Marcuse, offered the basis for an intensive examination of the critique of modern society, including a discussion of its philosophical (and political) consequences for (mass) communication research. They were enriched by the work of Jürgen Habermas (1981), who offered an epistemological justification for human emancipation. Indeed, taken as a critical position rather than as a theory, Critical Theory embarked upon a critique of the present and pointed to the potential of the future. For Habermas it involved an emancipatory interest, with the potentiality of the human being at its center.

Specifically, communication is a central idea in Habermas' theoretical project. It surfaced with *Knowledge and Human Interest* (1971), in which he presented his approach to language in the context of the development of a critical social science, and culminated with the publication of *The Theory of Communicative*

Action (1984a), which contains the normative basis of his social theory. In it he asserted,

> If we assume that the human species maintains itself through the socially coordinated activities of its members and that this coordination has to be established through communication – and in certain central spheres through communication aimed at reaching agreement – then the reproduction of the species *also* requires satisfying the conditions of a rationality that is inherent in communicative action.
>
> (1984a: 397)

Specifically, Habermas constructed the concept of communicative action from three "intertwined topic complexes": a communicative rationality freed from the limitations of individualistic approaches of social theory, a two-level concept that "connects the lifeworld and systems" paradigms, and a theory of modernity which accounts for "social pathologies." He added that "the theory of communicative action is intended to make possible a conceptualization of the social-life context that is tailored to the paradoxes of modernity" (1984a: xl).

The route toward such a theoretical position leads through the application of a reconstructive science. In *Communication and the Evolution of Society* (1979) Habermas already stressed the importance of understanding and asserted that the "task of universal pragmatics is to identify and reconstruct universal conditions of possible understanding [*Verständigung*]," arriving at "general presuppositions of communicative action" because he considered "the type of action aimed at reaching understanding to be fundamental" (1979: 1). Indeed, for Habermas, understanding meant to achieve an agreement that ends in mutuality and intersubjectivity, "shared knowledge, mutual trust, and accord with each other." Such an agreement rests on "recognition of the corresponding validity claims of comprehensibility, truth, truthfulness, and rightness" (1979: 3). The conditions underlying such a communicative practice are based upon a rationality which is determined by whether the participants "could, *under suitable circumstances*, provide reasons for their expressions." Habermas explained that "the rationality proper to the communicative practice of everyday life points to the practice of argumentation as a court of appeal" which will enable the continuation of communicative action under circumstances that would not allow for the "repair" of disagreements by "everyday routines," or the "use of force" (1984a: 17–18).

Since communicative practice occurs in the context of social and cultural structures, Habermas directed attention to the importance of the "lifeworld" as the context for symbolic reproduction. He identified and described three structural components that assist in creating favorable conditions for understanding. Individuals define themselves in terms of acting within their cultural tradition; they rely on their membership in social groups for the coordination of their actions "via intersubjective recognition of criticizable validity claims"; and they participate with younger generations which internalize "the value orientations of their social groups and acquire generalized capabilities for action" (1984a: xxlv). Thus, under these conditions communicative action serves to facilitate transmission and renewal of cultural knowledge, social integration and group solidarity, and personal identification.

The cultural context of the participants in communication, according to Habermas, consists of the objective, social and subjective worlds of the actors, which represent the totalities "of all entities about which true statements are possible," "of all legitimately regulated interpersonal relations," and "of the experiences of the speaker to which he has privileged access," respectively (1984a: 100).

Under these circumstances communication becomes a process of negotiation against the background of a shared culture, or a "lifeworld" which offers the presuppositional condition for any meaningful participation. Indeed, culture, society, and the individual are structural components of the "lifeworld" in which communicative action serves to reproduce cultural knowledge, to integrate individuals, and to shape personalities. Habermas sees *culture* as the reservoir of knowledge, from which participants in communication about the world take their interpretations; *society* represents the legitimate order, through which participants secure their membership in social groups and affirm their solidarity; and *personality* refers to the competencies which enable a subject to participate in the processes of understanding while maintaining its own identity. The semantic field of symbolic contents, the social space and historical time, form the *dimensions* in which communicative actions take place (1984b: 594–5).

The media as part of the everyday activities of the "lifeworld" function as generalized forms of communication. Thus the press, radio and television, for instance, have an enabling function. They free participants from their spatial–temporal limitations, provide availability of multiple contexts, and become instrumental in the creation of public spheres capable of serving authoritarian or emancipatory interests (1984a: 406).

Such perspective on communication and media suggests that (mass) communication theory and research are invariably tied to the analysis of communicative practices, that is, to issues of communicative competence, understanding, and participation of individuals in their lifeworld. In fact, Daniel Hallin has observed, that for Habermas, "all forms of human communication, even under conditions of mass dissemination, are essentially relationships between human subjects, derived ultimately from the elementary structure of dialogue" (1985: 142).

Habermas proposed that the study of the media must be a study of culture, the conditions of the lifeworld, and, indeed, the prospects of a public sphere that serves the emancipatory interests. For this purpose it must be based on a perspective of knowledge that is committed to openness (truth) and to the process of self-reflection. Richard Bernstein has argued that "an emancipatory interest is basic in the sense that the interest of reason is in furthering the conditions for its full development; the demand for non-distorted communication becomes fully explicit" since it "cannot exist unless we realize and institute the material social conditions that are required for mutual communication" (1985: 11).

With his latest work, Habermas has outlined a broad theoretical framework and provided a formidable agenda for communication research. The complexity of his work and the encyclopedic range of his intellectual effort offer a major challenge to the practitioners of communication theory and research in the United States. Indeed, problems of theoretical complexity and intellectual accessibility may have contributed to the failure of the field to participate actively in the critical assessment of Habermas' work. More likely, however, is the (intuitive) rejection of a theory of communicative action that seemed to interfere with the business of getting results. Such a practice is supported by Richard Rorty's conclusion that,

desire for communication, harmony, interchange, conversation, social solidarity, and the merely beautiful wants to bring the philosophical tradition to an end because it sees the attempt to provide metanarratives, even metanarratives of emancipation, as an unhelpful distraction from what Dewey calls "the meaning of the daily detail."

(1985: 175)

In fact, the field of communication theory and research is most likely to follow Rorty, whose criticism of Habermas reveals a strong commitment to the writings of Pragmatism. His argument is based on the notion that the "progressive changes" in society may tell the story, "without much reference to the kinds of theoretical backup which philosophers have provided for such politics." Rorty claimed that

things like the formation of trade unions, the meritocratization of education, the expansion of the franchise, and cheap news-papers . . . have figured most largely in the willingness of the citizens of the democracies to see themselves as part of a "communicative community" – their continued willingness to say "us" rather than "them" when they speak of their respective countries.

(1985: 169)

Such perspective reflects not only the compelling influence of the Pragmatist tradition, but also reveals its continuing theoretical appeal. Habermas has concluded that Rorty "wants to destroy the tradition of the philosophy of consciousness, from its Cartesian beginnings, with the aim of showing the pointlessness of the entire discussion of the foundations and limits of knowledge." He also suggested that the

stubbornness with which philosophy clings to the role of the "guardian of reason" can hardly be dismissed as an idiosyncrasy of self-absorbed intellectuals, especially in a period in which basic irrationalist undercurrents are transmuted once again into a dubious form of politics,

and he charged that "it is precisely the neoconservatives who articulate, intensify and spread this mood via the mass media" (1985: 193, 195).

For Alvin Gouldner, however, the work of the Chicago School and the earlier work of Habermas revealed both "continuity and basic discontinuity," especially since "The Chicago School view of the 'public' had been largely taxonomic and positivistic, liberal in its political assumptions and therefore both optimistic and lacking in historical perspective." Gouldner claimed that "It manifested an almost total inability to analyze the public in relation to the emergence and transformation of bourgeois society" (1976: 138).

His work also reflects a belief in the centrality of critical interaction as a source of societal unity and the essence of public rationality. He stressed that "people's talk" was the most powerful mechanism in social change (1976: 149) and acknowledged the role of the media operating as major agencies in the public sphere. For this reason they were primary targets of a critique of modern society. Gouldner suggested that Habermas "used analysis of the public sphere as a decisive occasion to explore the prospects of a politics based upon critical and reflective discourse. His central aim was to begin clarifying the possibility and requisites of rational discourse in modern society" (1976: 138). In this context, the study of interpersonal communication, as well as media freedom, become crucial tasks for Critical Theory. Gouldner asked "how can persons *speak* to one another so as to strengthen their capacity for rational judgment and free them from the control of external or built-in censors, *without* the prior institution of an already ideal speech situation?" (1976: 150). He also suggested that Critical Theory address the issue of media freedom, because only media offer the possibility of mass enlightenment "that might go beyond what universities may elicit" (1976: 160).

For these reasons Gouldner concluded that

> the path from critical theory to the long march through the institutions must go over the bridge of the mass media, and undertake the struggle for and critique of these media for what they are: a complex system of property interests, technologies, professional skills, strivings for domination and for autonomy, all swarming with the most profound inner contradictions.
>
> (1976: 160)

In recent years communication research in the United States has acknowledged the existence of alternative explanations of society and embarked on a debate of Critical Theory as the foundation of a theory of communication, although quite late and less consistent or vigorous than the reaction to Critical Theory in the literature of social theory.

Until the 1980s, however, theoretical concerns of the field had remained within the narrow, administrative research tradition of earlier years. For instance, in their assessment of theoretical influences during the last decades Davison and Yu regretted the general "lack of broad theorizing," wondered about the "elder statesmen, the philosophers of the communication field" and asked why no names besides "Innis, McLuhan, Lasswell and a few others" had been added to the roster (1974: 200–1).

A few years later, Lerner and Nelson in their half-century appraisal of the field proposed that the "story of communication research begins with the 1927 publication of Lasswell's *Propaganda Technique in the World War*" and proceeded with a series of contributions by communication researchers who represent a traditional approach to the field (1977: 1). They failed to provide a wider social theoretical context or to offer a historical account of the place of theory.

A rather abbreviated and incomplete acknowledgment of Critical Theory by Rogers only obscured the differences between Lazarsfeld's use of critical research (with which he seemed to sympathize) and the concept of critical research in the spirit of the Frankfurt School and other Marxist positions (Rogers and Balle, 1985). Indeed, his assertion that the "Critical School" had Marxist beginnings in 1930s Germany and that "critical scholars" were those who "set themselves off from empirical scholars by objecting to the effects-oriented, empirically minded nature of most communication research" (1986: 115), also failed to distinguish between Marxist and non-Marxist critiques of positivism.

But at issue is not a dangerous polarization of "schools," but the ability to engage in a necessary, critical reexamination of communication research. The emergence of critical scholarship is the result of such self-reflection about the conditions of a theoretical premise that does not reflect the social and political tensions of everyday life. The problem of empirical research, at least in this context, remains a secondary issue. Indeed, George Gerbner asked in 1958 that mass communication research respond to the challenge of combining "empirical methods with the critical aims of social science" and to "join rigorous practice with value-conscious theory" (1958: 106); Kurt Lang (1979) has also addressed the compatibility of empirical research and critical scholarship, and years ago Siegfried Kracauer also suggested that "qualitative analysis proper often requires quantification in the interest of exhaustive treatment. Far from being strict alternatives the two approaches actually overlap, and have in fact complemented and interpenetrated each other in several investigations" (1952–3: 637).

In fact, the reaction to quantitative analyses can be traced to an epistemological issue of Pragmatism which understood the importance of measurement but indicated a reluctance to have "things qualitative unlike and individual to be treated as if they were members of a comprehensive, homogeneous, or non-qualitative system" (Dewey, 1960: 241). According to Shalin, such a position is the reflection of an epistemology which "diverged from the traditional one in its deliberate blurring of the borderline between scientific and common sense knowledge" (1986: 18); or as William James once proposed, there is "theoretic knowledge about things, as distinguished from living or sympathetic acquaintance with them" (1967: 249–50).

The issue of critical research emerged more substantively with the most recent debates concerning Critical Theory and other Marxist approaches to communication research in "Ferment in the Field," a special issue of the *Journal of Communication* (1983). However, despite its ambitious goals, the publication barely moved beyond an acknowledgment of Critical Theory or neo-Marxist perspectives on communication to engage the field in an epistemological debate of any significance. Instead, it became a statement of positions and intentions with rare insights into an understanding of the epistemological forces that had surrounded communication research for several decades. Nevertheless, Jennifer Daryl Slack and Martin Allor acknowledged "a range of developing alternative approaches to the study of communication," and they provided a description of the "critical" as an "appropriation of the term" from the Frankfurt School (1983: 208–9). Other authors were vague in their use of the term "critical research" or "European-style" research (Haight, 1983: 232; Schiller, 1983: 255; Mosco, 1983: 237; Stevenson, 1983: 262), although the implications were that such research activities involve questions of power and control. Slack and Allor offered the explanation that the "central concern of all critical positions is the effectivity of communication in the exercise of social power" (1983: 215). Dallas Smythe and Tran Van Dinh, while commenting upon the conditions of Marxist scholarship in communication studies, advanced a definition of Critical Theory which "requires that there be criticism of the contradictory aspects of the phenomena in their systems context" (1983: 123).

The range of Marxist and non-Marxist views on communication

research was ultimately collapsed by George Gerbner into an extended notion of "critical scholar" which included those "who search and struggle" in order "to address the terms of discourse and the structure of knowledge and power in its domain and thus to make its contribution to human and social development" (1983: 362).

The presentation of critical alternatives to the traditional approach to communication research revealed that the choice is not between ideology and social science, but that social science practice remains imbedded in an ideological context. Although the language of orthodox Marxism, Critical Theory, or Cultural Studies is reflected throughout the discussion of the "ferment in the field," providing a vocabulary and a focus for a critique of contemporary societal practices, it was reproduced by many authors without further discussion of the consequences for the ideological perspective of mainstream American mass communication research.

It reveals a practice of collecting and adapting theoretical propositions and practical applications for the betterment of society which disregards cultural or political origins and ideological foundations. Such a practice also reflects an intellectual tradition of Americanizing foreign ideas. It occurred in the social sciences with the influence of European knowledge on American scholarship and is most clearly visible since Pragmatism, which seemed to acquire and apply suitable theoretical propositions according to the interests they served at the time. In this context, Novack's confrontation of Dewey's liberal position *vis-à-vis* the political reality of his days is an appropriate example of a Marxist critique of Pragmatism as a philosophical and political power in American society (1975).

Thus, to realize the potential contribution of Critical Theory to a critique of contemporary society, (mass) communication research needed to explore the rise of Critical Theory in the cultural and political context of Weimar Germany and its criticism of mass society in the United States. The decisive elements for this analysis were the attempts of Critical Theory to replace the preoccupation of traditional philosophy with science and nature by shifting to an emphasis on history and culture, and its acute awareness of the relationship between epistemology and politics.

The encounter with Critical Theory during the 1940s also came at the time when American (mass) communication research could have acted upon the fundamental difference between the ideas of culture and cultural critique offered by Critical Theory and traditional studies of culture and media, respectively. Critical Theory (and particularly Horkheimer and Adorno) insisted upon a holistic treatment of culture based upon the realization of the irreducible contradiction between elitist notions of culture and culture as a way of life. Indeed, Adorno felt that

> the greatest fetish of cultural criticism is the notion of culture as such. For no authentic work of art and no true philosophy, according to their very meaning, has ever exhausted itself in itself alone, in its being-in-itself. They have always stood in relation to the actual life-process of society from which they distinguished themselves.
>
> (1981: 23)

The media represent a major aspect of modern culture. They were identified by Horkheimer and his colleagues as part of the culture industry, and remained suspect when they became the "irrefutable prophet of the prevailing order" (1972: 147). On the other hand, the analysis of culture in the context of American (mass) communication research tried to resolve the operating contradictions between elitist and anthropological notions of culture; as a result, such critique of culture tended to be reduced to technological aspects of the media, for instance, the production and reproduction of messages, the size and demographic characteristics of audiences, and the transmission of symbols. These were irreducible differences, and, as Jay has observed, "Adorno was determined to preserve a critical vantage point towards cultural issues, which he felt was severely jeopardized by the empirical approach of mainstream sociologists of culture." He noted that Adorno "always contended that 'Culture is the condition that excludes the attempt to measure it'" (1984: 118).

The problematic of mass culture had been one of the major intellectual issues of the 1960s and 1970s. Fueled by the contributions of progressive Marxist and non-Marxist scholarship, including Critical Theory, American concerns over the cultural climate in society, caused by the uses of technology and reinforced by educational and cultural institutions, emerged from the social science literature and became a significant intellectual endeavor inside and outside of the academy. In these discussions it had become clear that the partisan nature of knowledge must lead to explorations and challenges of the dominant views of society and connect with visions of a different social environment. In this context social theorists must find appropriate links to the demands of their own times. Gouldner has expressed such a sentiment when he urged that "social scientists need to find a place for themselves beyond academic purism and cynical opportunism. With the understanding and the cooperation of informed laymen, they must edge out across the gap between what they know and what the times need" (1981: 82).

In addition, Critical Theory supported the possibilities of negation and introduced a political dimension to the discussion of mass culture and the prospects of mass society. It raised the specter of totalitarian rule and insisted on the investigation of authoritarianism as a way of learning about the psychological conditions of American society. Critical Theory enriched the theoretical discourse and demonstrated the need to question the vocabulary of political and social realities in the pursuit of exposing the suppression of history. The major thrust of Critical Theory against the undemocratic spirit of popular culture offered American communication research an opportunity to search for its own failures in the service of the dominant political and economic system, and to participate in a radical critique of society.

Instead, the field of communication theory and research maintained its posture of a traditional social science until the 1980s, when individual contributions to the literature revealed the presence of resistance and the possibilities of alternative perspectives on communication research with the emergence of Cultural Studies and a renewed effort to assess the conditions of society. They involved new journals, like *Critical Studies in Mass Communication*, discussions of paradigm changes, an increasing rate of "critical" research published in a variety of journals, and curriculum development in the area of critical media studies at a number of universities.

At the same time, however, the cultural pessimism of Horkheimer and his colleagues in the United States had been rejected, while the Habermasian struggle to forge a path for the position of an emancipatory social science in a world in which the problems of cultural reproduction create tensions and social conflicts, remained a solitary effort. By the end of this period communication research encountered a new challenge when the American exponents of British Cultural Studies popularized and revitalized the idea of culture as a necessary context for the study of communication and society.

Chapter 5

On understanding hegemony
Cultural Studies and the recovery of the critical

> The new sociology of culture can be seen as the convergence, and at a certain point the transformation, of two clear tendencies: one within general social thought and then specifically sociology; the other one within cultural history and analysis.
>
> Raymond Williams

Not unlike Critical Theory a few years earlier, the introduction of British Cultural Studies as a European critique of contemporary society has remained a theoretical confrontation and political challenge of traditional American communication research and its ideological context. It continues to question the liberal-pluralist aura surrounding communication studies and proposes a Marxist alternative as a viable theory of society. Cultural Studies is a specifically British critique of contemporary culture within Western Marxism; reminiscent of the Frankfurt School in the United States more than thirty years ago, it represents the quality and intensity of an intellectual commitment to a critique of ideological domination and political power.

After the end of the Second World War there were similar observations in the United States and Britain about the return to a peacetime economy and the resulting expansion of society. An active and sufficiently diverse political environment helped create the necessary conditions for a correspondingly vibrant public discussion in Britain. At that time, socialism was not only a historically grounded and accepted way of looking at the world, but it also exerted a strong influence on these debates about the future of society, particularly among those whose political interests and academic pursuits merged into questions dealing with the lives of people, their social conditions or their economic aspirations. Concurrently, there was a sense of national recovery and consolidation amidst an atmosphere of conformity in which "the forces of commercialism were redoubling their efforts to make the ordinary man accept unquestioningly the feelings of his rightful cultural heritage, [while] he was also being given a far greater opportunity than ever before of enjoying its fruits" (Marwick, 1962: 121). Perry Anderson has observed the difficulty of proceeding in the struggle for socialism in a country where "Keynesian capitalism [had] eliminated mass unemployment and allowed a steady increase in the material standard of living of the working classes" (1965: 4).

But in the 1950s and early 1960s Britain also experienced the rise of radicalism, aggravated by immigration and racial tensions, a myriad of related social problems, including reactions to the threat of nuclear war, and the centralizing effects of the media industry. Britain also witnessed the emergence of the New Left, which Anderson described as "a distinctly British phenomenon, beyond its economic context or its cultural antecedents" (1965: 15), which made its political entrance as a cogent, recognizable voice of criticism in an atmosphere of revolt against a realization, particularly among working-class and lower middle-class youth of lacking control over their own lives. Anderson has suggested that the "most valuable work" of the New Left "continued to be a moral critique of capitalism, and as time went on, this in turn tended to become more and more concerned with cultural problems – precisely those which most immediately and intimately affected its audience of teachers, writers, students" (1965: 17).

Therefore, the rediscovery of ordinary people as consumer-participants in a postwar industrial culture was accompanied by a growing literature of critical attempts to recover the everyday life of individuals in their local or regional conditions. These endeavors to broaden an understanding of society in order to learn more about the self resulted in the questioning of the past and in activities which Raphael Samuel has described as a "thrust of people's history." He called it a "major effort to present historical issues as they appeared to the actors of the time; to personalize the workings of large historical forces; to draw on contemporary vocabularies; to identify the faces in the crowd" (1981: xviii). The result was a range of significant texts which have come to represent the intellectual preoccupation of this era, beginning with Richard Hoggart's *The Uses of Literacy* in 1957, Raymond Williams and *The Long Revolution* in 1961, and E. P. Thompson's *The Making of the English Working Class* in 1963.

The leading role of literary studies in the initial phases of Cultural Studies, as opposed to sociology or political science, was exemplified in the works of Hoggart and Williams, who also acknowledged the importance of a critique of history with their explorations of everyday life. The matrix of literature, literary criticism and Marxism produced a necessary and convenient context for questioning cultural activities, including social communication. Such contextualization and the location of the problematic in the cultural process, specifically among cultural, political and economic phenomena, restored theoretical complexity and descriptive power to the analysis of communication and media practice. Notably, the field of literary studies, with its curiosity about the process of social communication, including the role of the media, had moved freely among leading intellectual currents and was able to create an awareness of British and Continental European thought and its contribution to the modernist and postmodernist debates.

Authors like Williams, Hoggart and Thompson shared an intellectual commitment to studying British culture in a concrete manner and provided an ideological focus for a debate about the need for cultural analysis. They also introduced preliminary understandings of culture, which emerged, for instance, from Thompson's polemic against orthodox economic history and against "abbreviated economistic notations of Marxism" to demonstrate how a "transformed consciousness" of people was the result of cultural processes (1976: 6–7); Williams was equally oppositional in his approach "to counter the appropriation of culture" by recovering the "true complexity of the tradition" from reactionary claims and to establish its centrality in lived experience (1989a: 97–8).

A major concept in these cultural debates was "working-class culture." It appeared with Hoggart, for example, who replaced the notion of economic class power with cultural domination, and Williams, who defined it as the "basic collective idea, and the institutions, manners, habits of thought and intentions which proceed from this" in contrast to bourgeois culture which is based on the "individualist idea" (1958: 327). Both authors rejected the idea of culture as ideology and proceeded, instead, to pursue definitions of culture that concentrated on its living and collaborative nature. According to Swingewood's evaluation of this debate, the results were hardly satisfactory. Hoggart showed no awareness of "the role of ideology in the formation of popular consciousness" and his concept of culture remained "static and passive," while Williams produced a "subjectivist concept of culture" that lacked the "complex synthesis of specific determinations" of a Marxist orientation (1977: 41–3). Hoggart's vision of socialism, in fact, is described in his autobiographical writings; it focuses on the human possibilities of people and becomes operant in his work with adult education (1990).

When Hoggart offered an assessment of the media and their influence on working-class people in Britain, he presented a detailed view of how a concerted effort to reach the sensibilities of individuals by mass entertainment media may have contributed to cultural changes. His study involved working-class individuals and noted their resilience and strength in an active media environment. He concluded that "The strongest objection to the more trivial popular entertainments is not that they prevent their readers from becoming highbrow, but that they make it harder for people without an intellectual bent to become wise in their own way" (1970: 276). The greatest danger seemed the invitation by the media to join others in order to be like others, or as Hoggart said, the power of "encouragements towards an unconscious uniformity" (1970: 278).

Hoggart rejected distinctions between high culture and mass culture to proceed with an analysis by social class. However, he proposed a differentiation between "synthetic" or "processed" culture, and "living" culture and explained that while processed culture concentrates on audiences, consumers and customers, living culture concentrates on the subject or the material. He added, "Processed culture asks: 'What will they take? Will this get most of them?' Living culture asks: 'What is the truth of this experience and how can I capture it?'" (1973: 130–1).

Equally important, however, were Hoggart's admonitions of those whose claims of authoritative knowledge of mass culture phenomena may have given rise to paternalistic attitudes toward mass culture practices, inspiring regulatory or even censorial activities. He felt that such a position may actually reveal the ignorance of experts who "live in a sort of clever man's paradise, without any real notion of the force of the assault outside" (1970: 281).

Indeed, Hoggart alluded to one of the major problems of

contemporary communication research, and cultural studies for that matter, which remains the need to overcome stereotypical attitudes toward mass-produced tastes and media-induced uniformities of existence. There is a continuing need to weigh questions of freedom of choice and abilities of participation in society under vastly different social conditions against technological tendencies of centralization and political or commercial manipulation of media content.

The considerations of working-class culture which dominated British social thought during these years resulted in what Richard Johnson has called a "break with Leavis and with elitist conceptions of 'culture' in a 'literary sociology,' the rediscovery of 'class' by an empirical social democratic sociology and the break with positivism and theoretical functionalism in the new sociologies of the 1960s" (1981: 392).

Actually, the Cultural Studies debate may have begun in 1961 with the struggle over a direction of cultural history and Thompson's review of *The Long Revolution* in the *New Left Review* which had been under the editorship of Stuart Hall. Thompson's criticism reveals the importance of understanding the role of history in the creation of a theoretical foundation of Cultural Studies. Arguing against Williams and his idea of a cultural history, however, Thompson insisted that "any theory of culture must include the concept of the dialectical interaction between culture and something that is not culture." His counter-proposal to regard the class struggle as "a whole way of struggle" (1981: 398) was not only a defense of his Marxist position, but also helped focus attention on the complexity of the notion of culture after its liberation from narrow, elitist appropriations.

The analysis of real-life experiences and the exploration of personal narratives in the context of probing social formations and reconstructing social relations produced working definitions of culture that became the foundation of later projects. Scholarly considerations of relationships between individuals, classes, media and the state supplied important lines of questioning for a critique of contemporary society, and issues of state and commercial power determined research agendas, frequently with the encouragement of the left. Ralph Miliband's analysis of media–state relations is an example of such a critique of mass society. He concluded that media contribute to the fostering of a climate of conformity not by the total suppression of dissent, but by the presentation of views which fall outside the consensus as curious heresies, or, even more effectively, by treating them as irrelevant eccentricities, which serious and reasonable people may dismiss as of no consequence. This is very "functional."

(1969: 213)

Indeed, power and problems of destroying and reconstituting cultural relations between dominant and dominated segments of society have remained a major concern of structuralism and culturalism. According to Bennett *et al.*, both represented "the 'imported' and the 'home-grown' varieties of cultural studies"; the former equated concepts like "popular culture," "mass culture," and "dominant ideology" through "a series of sliding definitions," and the latter equated popular culture with "the 'autochthonous' culture of subordinate classes" (1986: xii–xiv). Both shared an understanding of the division of the cultural and ideological worlds of bourgeois and working classes.

Cultural Studies was located within an intellectual environment that promoted the making of a bottom-up history of British society in its desire to understand the formation of classes and class consciousness within a literary rather than social science tradition. These activities were not specifically directed at an academic audience. While Thompson was addressing the kind of readers he had encountered in his work as a tutor in adult education, such as working-class individuals and trade unionists (1976: 7), Williams had likewise begun thinking about the notion of culture in his own work with adult education (1979: 97).

Cultural Studies had its roots in a Marxist interpretation of society and prospered through its access to literary/historical and anthropological interpretations. Its rise was evidence of an ongoing postwar debate about Marxism during a politically charged period of British Marxism which revealed the dilemma of Marxist theory in the presence of Stalinism and the political practices of an authoritarian state orthodoxy. It also gained from external influences and challenges of postwar Marxism and the increasing significance of Central European thought, particularly through the works of Lukács, Gramsci, Benjamin and the intervention of the structuralisms of Lévi-Strauss and Althusser.

Thus, Cultural Studies must also be identified with a strong

theoretical interest which is based on the philosophical predispositions of its practitioners and the spirit of socialism in its critique
of society. These interests constituted an oppositional context for
Cultural Studies and challenged the conventional approach to the
exploration of working-class culture. Stuart Laing has noted that
"By the early 1960s the 'novelistic' quality of social exploration
and some sociological writing was on par with the 'sociological'
qualities of working-class fiction in their mutual transgression
of dominant categories" (1986: 57). It followed a tradition of
empirical sociology that typically identified working-class analyses
with the study of poverty and unemployment, the experiences with
Mass Observation as a social research tool in the hands of "ordinary
people" notwithstanding (Pickering and Chaney, 1986: 53).

Consequently, the critique of mass society, attacks on state
power and the domination of elites were topics of a renewed
European concern about the future of modern society; they
incorporated a number of developments in Marxist thought and
surfaced with the development of a new literature of social criticism
which made its way to the United States.

The rise of Cultural Studies in Britain within a social and political
environment that was undergoing significant changes enabled
its proponents to respond effectively to state authority and to
the particular developments of society. Although its beginning
is customarily identified with the activities of the Centre for
Contemporary Cultural Studies at the University of Birmingham,[1]
there is reason to argue that it gathered intellectual strength and
academic significance from a larger political culture throughout
Britain. This included the presence of feminist studies, which has
become a vital theoretical force inside Cultural Studies but has
rarely received credit for its role in the rise of a new perspective
on society.

More generally, Cultural Studies was aided by the political
predisposition toward alternative explanations of society and the
mood for change, which were sufficiently widespread and perhaps best demonstrated by dramatic modifications in Britain's
educational system, when advanced university-level training in
the sciences and humanities became available to large segments
of society. Access to education had been important for the
growth of Cultural Studies, which also claimed some credit for
this development. Years later, Johnson called for a defense of
"real spaces" occupied by Cultural Studies and the clarification

of teaching and research activities of the Centre amidst a struggle against "the disconnection that occurs when cultural studies is inhabited for merely academic purposes or when enthusiasm for (say) popular culture forms is divorced from the analysis of power and of social possibilities" (1983: 9). These statements were made almost two decades after Perry Anderson had observed that the New Left had "gained a certain-minority-middle-class audience: it never touched any section of the working-class, however" (1965: 16), and therefore failed as a large-scale political movement.

On the other hand, analysis and critique of the social and political structures in the United States were largely determined by practitioners of well-established social science paradigms. The explorations of power or the functions of communities in the United States were conducted in the tradition of a liberal-pluralist theory of society which had influenced not only communication research and media studies in the United States, but had also reached a number of European countries, including Britain, and contributed significantly to the Americanization of the social sciences after the Second World War. The recognition of Lazarsfeld's work and the reception of Schramm's initial publications in Western Europe are typical examples of the widespread use of American communication research. As a result, problems of cultural production and media use which had surfaced in the internal debates among leftist intellectuals, historians and literary critics also occupied traditional British media sociologists whose work offered models of analysis that had its roots in the empirical research tradition of US sociology and typically focused on questions of effects.

Consequently, the discussions of culture and communication in Britain, which had been fueled and stimulated by an extended analysis of working-class cultures and by a quest for a total history of British society, offered a genuine alternative to those dominant interpretations of social and political culture that originated in the postwar influence of American social research.

In contrast, communication research and media scholarship in the United States lacked the force of a similar opposition, with an intellectual commitment to a Marxist perspective offering alternative visions of culture and the study of communication. The existence of radical history or sociology, for instance, did not effectively reach communication research; the work of C. Wright Mills, which was much admired in Britain, had hardly inspired the kind of radical media analysis of capitalist societies that had become a major feature of the British intellectual scene and a prominent aspect of Williams' project. Likewise, it is debatable to what extent Herbert Schiller's contributions during the late 1960s, or the contemporary social criticism of Noam Chomsky or Edward Said, whose oppositional views are also an intellectual and political enrichment of American media studies, have influenced current work in the field. They reinforce an existing, marginalized media critique and survive only as deviant perspectives of a dominant communication research position, which has rejected theoretical alternatives and possibilities of radical dissent, frequently on the grounds of methodological unorthodoxy. The idea of a Cultural Studies perspective on communication research remained theoretically and practically exclusive. In fact, Eileen Meehan has argued that in the United States "cultural studies has been largely in the hands of neo-Boasian idealists," citing James Carey, Asa Berger, John Cawelti and Horace Newcomb (1986: 86).

However, the writings of Raymond Williams have been found to be compelling sources for helping to emphasize the importance of culture in the study of communication, for instance, and have attracted considerable attention among American communication scholars. Such attention to his work is accompanied by a benign neglect of its theoretical/ideological aspects and a desire to combine his considerations of culture with latent cultural concerns that grew out of Pragmatism. Consequently, Williams has become strongly identified with the *cultural* component in Cultural Studies, while Hall and others are seen as Marxist theorists preoccupied with the exploration of *ideological* aspects of social existence.

Williams addressed the complexity and problematic of studying communication through the linguistic practices of individuals to media institutions, suggesting that its openness invited the study of "whatever can be learned of the basis of this practice" ranging from "processes of language" to the effects of "particular technologies" (1974: 18). Thus, communication falls within culture, because it is "concerned with practice and with the relations between practices" (1974: 20). He also deplored the "deep" and "disastrous" deformation of communication studies by having been "confidently named as the study of mass-communications" (1974: 22). This label effectively limits the scope of inquiry to media activities while disregarding more fundamental aspects, like rhetoric and writing. In addition, Williams argued that the "'mass' metaphor overtook us in its weakest meaning, of the large ultimate audience, and then positively prevented the analysis of most specific modern communication situations and of most specific modern communication conventions and forms" (1974: 22). As a result, the sociology of media turned to investigations of communication that followed a Lasswellian course of questioning specific aspects of the process without raising the issue of intentions.

Williams called for a radical change in communication studies, announcing "an open conspiracy" against the "defences of vested interests, the general drizzle of discouragement, and even the more deeply-rooted inertia of contemporary orthodox culture" to engage in an analysis of communication, "because it needs to be done" (1974: 25).

In this context of promoting a cultural perspective on communication studies and of weighing the potential of Cultural Studies as a source of alternative thinking about communication research, Williams offered a wide-ranging and appropriately concrete discussion. His work is not only perceived as being dedicated to an understanding and appreciation of the role of culture, but also engages in the uses of cultural history and may serve as an example of the application of historical consciousness and its power of explanation and clarification of contemporary conditions of society. Alan O'Connor has recently demonstrated the breadth and diversity of Williams as Britain's most influential contemporary cultural theorist (1989a).

Williams set out to restore the notion of culture to its central place in the analysis of society; thus, when he suggested that "culture is ordinary," he meant that the "making of a society is the finding of common meanings and directions," and that the growth of a society rests in "active debate and amendment under the pressures of experience, contact, and discovery, writing themselves into the land" (1989a: 4). He introduced a usage of culture "to mean a whole way of life – the common meanings; to mean the arts and learning – the special processes of discovery and creative effort" (1989a: 6) that involved two essential and related aspects of describing society. His notion of culture had also produced a terrain on which to test competing definitions and to establish the priorities of a discourse about individuals relating to each other and to society. Williams helped draw its boundaries in a significant way by amending and reducing the base–superstructure argument in Marxist cultural theory (1980a).

Consequently, communication rises to become a crucial element in an analysis of culture; in fact, it represents a basic condition of being and, therefore, assumes an important role in the study of society. Elsewhere, Williams had noted that "a definition of language is always, implicitly and explicitly, a definition of human beings in the world." His phrase identifies the individual as a creator of culture and captures the essential element for a conceptualization of a theory of culture (1977: 21). It also implies the historical, material nature of language, which is a major argument of *Marxism and Literature* (1977), in which Williams insisted that culture be restored to its place among economic or political considerations. His discussion of literature provided the context for elaborating on the idea of linguistic practice outside of class relations or institutional uses and related to a process of human experience within social, political or economic transformations.

Similarly, the discussion of communication in society is related to a variety of experiences and feelings of individuals in and about society; it ranges from realizing the meaning of life as it is expressed through the physical environment to sharing the conditions of language and community and its institutions. Williams insisted that a theory of communication is a necessary development in an attempt to gain some understanding of the relationship between individuals, communication and society. As a result, communication constitutes a primary process for Williams, who had observed that "it is through the communication systems that the reality of ourselves, the reality of our society, forms and is interpreted" (1989a: 23).

He had also concluded in *Culture and Society* (1958) that "the human crisis is always a crisis of understanding: what we genuinely understand we can do" (1958: 338). And he proposed that an examination of society from the perspective of communication and its societal institutions, like the media, may result in discoveries which older political or economic descriptions were unable to make, because "How people speak to each other, what conventions they have as to what is important and what is not, how they express these in institutions by which they keep in touch: these things are central" (1989a: 23).

Williams was disturbed by the emergence of a widely accepted view of people as consumers located within a capitalist culture and "massed as 'public opinion,' with internal sectors designated as areas of a market." In fact, he found that the sale of "political opinions and definitions of politics" had resulted in a political assessment of people as "primarily possessing and consuming individuals" (1989a: 147), suggesting the ascendence of a sphere of consumption as an economic reality and a source of social-scientific exploration that obscured the complexity of society. At the same time, he attacked the production of mass culture and the control of the means of production by a capitalist system that was determined to perpetuate its domination of communication in society. Williams developed an extensive argument for a theoretical consideration of the means of communication as means of production, advocating a "sustained historical inquiry into the general history of the development of means of communication," and lamenting the "popularity of shallowly-rooted and ideological applications of other histories and other analytic methods and terms" based on a deficient understanding of history (1980b: 54).

Williams also felt that "the organization of our present mass culture is so closely involved with the organization of capitalist society that the future of one cannot be considered except in terms of the future of the other" (1989a: 17). Such a view clearly marked the target of criticism and helped identify the need for an analysis of the means of communication. Under these circumstances, communication theory assumes a critical position, because understanding communication and media involves a critique of their present conditions with the goal of transcendence and improvement. It is part of a process of liberation which begins with the desire for a recognition of the complexity of culture, its inherent potential as an arena of participation and the rise of a democratic society through universal access to learning and participation in the means of production. Such a critique is aimed at institutions and social processes which resist the concrete development of communication as a cultural activity and the growth of an equitable, participant-oriented communication system. In other words, communication theory becomes part of a theory of socialism and, to paraphrase Williams, serves to facilitate a critique of the definition of human beings in capitalist societies.

In this context, Williams' definition of language as "once individual and social – as historically and socially constituting" (1977: 43) provides the basis for thinking about society and a democratic system of communication which, in turn, "depends on maximum participation by the individuals in society" (1989a: 29).

Disappointed by the failure of socialism to develop an alternative understanding of communication and media, or communications as Williams preferred to call it, he urged that "the stifling orthodoxy which continues to produce its 'correct' definitions of cultural production and communications practice" be ended. Instead, he suggested that "Only the positive recovery, development and open exploratory use of the new forms and technologies by actual societies, for their own diverse purposes, can make new socialist cultures." And he recommended that "socialists everywhere must support the demand for a new international information order, beyond the controls and influences of Western capital" (1989a: 310–11).

Williams' theory of culture and communication was translated into a concrete approach to the contemporary problems of the cultural sphere with the publication of *Communications* in 1962. The book became a major force in an ongoing discussion about the nature of the media and the state of education with its concrete proposals pertaining to the public management of the media, as well as to the cultural policies in the arts and education. The book also testified to the necessary proximity between matters of communication and learning. By rejecting established structures of culture and communication, Williams embarked on teaching his readers about the importance of communications in society. He proceeded to outline a media system which would follow "a general policy of decentralization, within public ownership where necessary, and with the decision about what is to be produced resting firmly in the hands of the people who in any case have to produce it" (1989a: 30). He summarized his constructive proposals years later when he noted that "public ownership of the basic means of production should be combined with leasing of their use to self-managing groups, to secure maximum variety of style and political opinion and to ensure against any bureaucratic control" (1979: 370).

While Williams emphasized the notion of culture throughout his work, others, like Stuart Hall, have concentrated on the importance of ideology in the production of culture. In either case, there is a conscious awareness of the path of Cultural Studies as an integrative field of study through the interpretative branch of sociology (Max Weber), the ethnographic discourse of subcultural theory (Howard Becker), and the experience of Western Marxism, which includes the contributions of Lukács, Goldmann, Benjamin, Horkheimer, Adorno and Marcuse, in particular.

According to Hall, these texts "restored to the debate about culture a set of theorizations around the classical problem of ideologies. They returned to the agenda the key question of the determinate character of culture and ideologies – their material, social and historical conditions of existence" (1980a: 25). They also reaffirmed the importance of a holistic perspective and confirmed the criticism of empiricism and its insistence upon isolated facts. Louis Althusser's notion of ideological state apparatuses (1971) and Antonio Gramsci's concept of hegemony (1971) have helped Cultural Studies build a rationale for the study of social practices within societies "as complex formations, necessarily contradictory, always historically specific" (Hall,1980a: 36).

Hall's consideration of media studies provides a useful context for the application of Marxist thought, including the contributions of French structuralism, to the study of social practices. He recounted the process of media studies at the Birmingham Centre as a direct reaction against the Americanized, effects-centered study of mass communication. Studies at the Centre proceeded, instead, from an ideological perspective, assigning the role of a "major cultural and ideological force" to the media. In fact, he concluded that the "'return' to the concern with the media and ideologies" had been "the most significant and consistent thread in Centre media work" (1980b: 117). Such a redefinition of media also resulted in the rejection of traditional analyses of messages in favor of an analysis of the "linguistic and ideological structuration" of media texts (1980b: 118). In addition, Hall stressed the reconceptualization of audiences as active participants in the process of communication. Throughout the reorganization of traditional notions of communication or media research, the ideological dimension claimed a determining role in the formulation of questions about media, messages and audiences. The rapid expansion of television and film studies led to reconsiderations of the notion of ideology under the influence of French Marxist thought and to additional theoretical work as a response to activities in feminism. In particular, Althusser's understanding of society as an interrelated network of social and intellectual activities, and the location of the individual through economic, political and ideological practices within the social formation (1971: 127–86), appealed to Cultural Studies, which proceeded to study the socially determined modes of representation as a way of understanding the production of meaning in the context of ideological practice.

Hall elaborated on the ideological aspects of media in several important ways. In "The Rediscovery of 'Ideology': Return of the Repressed in Media Studies" (1982) he developed a historical context for the rise of the "critical paradigm" in media studies which questioned the workings of the ideological process and its realization among other practices within a social formation (1982: 65). In particular, growing out of a critique of liberal-pluralism, Hall insisted upon the importance of the place of ideology in any theoretical considerations which try to explain "the monopoly of power and the diffusion of consent" (1982: 86).

Beginning with questions of language and discourse, Hall emphasized the integral role of structuralism in understanding the process of ideology in everyday life. Accordingly, a critique of traditional theories of language confirmed the importance of moving from intrinsic meanings or referential views of language to the power of signification and a position of meaning as social practice and language as a method of meaning production. When Hall insisted that "The world has to be *made to mean*" (1982: 67), he conferred status on the process of making meaning and raised questions about the emergence of dominant meanings or explanations and their survival in society. Such a break also acknowledged the polysemic nature of language, and focused on the consequences of thinking about meaning as a "struggle for mastery in discourse," and on the implications of meanings as potential fields of ideological struggle (1982: 77–9).

Media play a significant role in the creation and reinforcement of specific images of the world, the manufacture of consent, and the positioning of political and economic interests. Hall recognized that the process of signification as a production of discursive objects was the result of an organization of social practices within the realm of media institutions. By raising questions about the function of media in the production and reproduction of dominant ideologies, he also raised the issue of the ideological nature of such practices, which are perpetuated by a media system that continues to produce claims of independence from commercial or state interests.

The advantage of the "critical paradigm" was that it challenged the established *Weltanschauung* of communication research. Hall talked about the "profound theoretical revolution," and the new foundation of media studies in the presence of a breakdown of traditional analyses, "when the hard-nosed empirical positivism of the halcyon days of 'media research' has all but ground to a stuttering halt." At the center of this challenge was "the return of the repressed," that is, the "rediscovery of ideology and the social and political significance of language and the politics of sign and discourse" (1982: 88).

A few years later, Hall articulated the problem of ideology through a review of questions related to the rise of ideas, and, in particular, "the ways in which ideas of different kinds grip the minds of masses, and thereby become a 'material force'" (1986: 29). He emphasized a political perspective on ideology in which both the perpetuation of dominant ideas and the manner in which forms of domination are reinforced and maintained through symbols and language, as well as the processes and practices that lead to new visions of the world which move people to action and change, become a focus of theoretical concerns.

Offering a rereading of Marx, Hall introduced the potential and the challenge of openness or indeterminacy as a theoretical condition – moving theory from orthodoxy to operating on the terrain of social forces – which undergoes change and redefinition within the concrete existence of people in their specific historical moments. The result was an emphasis on the idea of process in the conceptualization of ideology and the accommodation of hegemonic struggle in an evolving theory of society. Hall argued for "the open horizon of marxist theorizing – determinacy without guaranteed closures" (1986: 43). The consequences of such a new understanding of theory implied an end of certainty.

At the center of Hall's project are individuals confronted by political and economic conditions which are not of their making and involved in communicative practices which are characterized as a struggle over meaning and making sense of the world. Ideology emerged as a major concern, since it involves the problematic of specific reality claims, using language as a means of articulation, and provides a terrain of contradictions and struggles with rising structures of domination and resistance. In fact, Hall relied on Gramsci's expression that ideologies organize the masses and "create the terrain on which men move, acquire consciousness of their position, struggle, etc." (1971: 377).

Colin Sparks has recounted the rise of Stuart Hall throughout the early phases of Cultural Studies with its strong "literary bent" and a "problematic" relationship to Marxism, to the encounter with French Marxism, which encouraged major activities of the Centre, to his latest theoretical affiliation with Laclau and French political theory. Indeed, Sparks observed that Hall is marginalizing economics and politics and is, in effect, on a "trajectory of thought which, over a long period of time, is moving consistently away from the classic Marxist problematic of trying to demonstrate the priority of the economic within the social reality" (1990: 87).

Cultural Studies employs but one of several strategies of cultural interpretation that have emerged from Marxist theory in recent times (Curran, Gurevitch and Woollacott, 1982; Grossberg, 1984). Accordingly, Curran and his colleagues have suggested that Cultural Studies has developed from a reaction to economic reductionism. They also proposed that "cultural studies incorporate a stress on experience as the 'authenticating' position and a humanist emphasis on the creative" seeking to place the media and other practices "within a society conceived of as a complex expressive totality" (1982: 27). This statement, in particular, reflects Williams' position, which had been identified throughout these years (and since the 1980s) with a rejection of the type of Marxism that exhausted itself in debates about the relationship of culture, ideology and economy which were characterized by supporting an extremely limiting form of economic reductionism. According to Tony Bennett and his colleagues, there is a decided emphasis in culturalism on "the *making* of culture rather than on its determined conditions" (1981: 10–11).

In his assessment of these inquiries into the complex relationships of individuals, media and society, Sparks also found that Cultural Studies used an "evaluative approach" to the media and had failed to develop its own analytical tools, "promiscuously borrowed methods and models from the most diverse of schools," and, generally speaking, developed along a critical orientation without formal political ties and in a position of marginality which was expressed in its actual distance from media institutions as objects of analysis (1987: 10). These observations were based on his earlier appraisal of Cultural Studies, which had "adopted a Marxism which systematically evaded the squalid concerns of political parties, trade unions, and all the rest of the baggage of Marxist orthodoxy and which elevated debates on culture, epistemology, etc. to the centre of theoretical concern" (1977: 22).

In fact, the activities of Cultural Studies have raised questions about the role of theory, including theoretical differences, and the position of intellectuals in an academic setting which was also committed to remain actively involved in the concrete political struggle for change. Hall wrote about the problematic of facing theoretical inclinations and practical demands in the context of Centre activities, suggesting that the error of assuming a unity of theory and practice has resulted in a "widespread inability to develop a proper understanding of the role of intellectuals and the place of intellectual work" (1980a: 287). He referred to the need to define the intellectual functions, in a Gramscian sense, of those who are committed to the critique of culture. These are issues that remain unresolved, particularly in the American attempts to re-create a Cultural Studies experience as a political confrontation.

Throughout the positioning of theoretical and practical interests, however, media of communication have provided the concrete reality for a critique of culture. In fact, the media constitute a major terrain for critical analysis and political or social action, since they dominate the cultural sphere of modern societies. They are important, because they help produce the understanding of a social totality by bringing together and, if necessary, reconciling conflicting and confusing fragments of reality. The study of media raises questions of power and ideology as necessary and significant issues of cultural practice.

Cultural Studies locates the media and media practices within "a complex expressive totality." That is to say, media studies are involved in the issue of human practice. Williams also stressed such a holistic perspective as the underlying condition of a sociology of culture, when he stated that

> the most basic task of the sociology of culture is analysis of the interrelationships within this complex unity: a task distinct from the reduced sociology of institutions, formations, and communicative relationships and yet, as a sociology, radically distinct also from the analysis of isolated forms.
>
> (1977: 139–40)

The media function in several ways to maintain their cultural and ideological position; according to Hall, they provide and selectively construct social knowledge, they classify and reflect upon the plurality of social life, and they construct a complex, acknowledged order (1979: 340–2). Similarly, David Sholle has talked about the fact that "media create a way of seeing, a method of ordering and judging, a means of selection and preference that constitutes the domain of the discussable," with the result of producing "an exclusive domain of knowledge and subject positions corresponding to that domain" (1988: 38). The implications of these perspectives for an analysis of cultural processes are two-fold: they suggest a return to the subject of experience and a struggle over the power of the text within a cultural and historical moment. They also infer a consideration of the ideological effect of the media as they necessarily and incessantly intersect with the social practices of groups and individuals in society.

John Fiske, whose work has been widely circulated in the United States, also offered a historical perspective on British Cultural Studies, tracing its development to the demands of an industrialized society to generate and circulate meanings. He recapitulated the influences of Althusser and Gramsci, primarily through the work of Stuart Hall. He also acknowledged the contributions of Williams and reinforced the evolving concept of "culture as a constant site of struggle between those with and those without power" (1987: 260). His vision of a cultural democracy is based on Hall's theory of "preferred reading" (dominated, negotiated and oppositional), which assumes a definition of audiences with active interests and intellectual capabilities to engage in such strategies, and utilizes ethnographic/meaning-centered and semiotic/structuralist methodologies. In fact, Fiske provided a view of the empowered individual and created a sense of participation in the social, political and economic experiences of everyday life which revises earlier notions of mass audiences as passive, unstable and impressionable. Instead, people "take mass-produced signifiers and, by a process of 'excorporation' use them to articulate and circulate subcultural meanings" (1987: 285). His work expresses not only confidence in the abilities of individuals, but also in the contribution that Cultural Studies can make to strengthen and perpetuate such a democratic process. He declared that

> Despite the cultural pessimism of the Frankfurt School, despite the power of ideology to reproduce itself in its subjects, despite the hegemonic force of the dominant classes, the people still manage to make their own meanings and to construct their own culture within, and often against, that which the industry provides for them. Cultural studies aims to understand and encourage this cultural democracy at work.
>
> (1987: 286)

Fiske presents a version of Cultural Studies which enables and transcends the subject of its study; it is attracted by the possibilities of intervention through preferred readings and becomes part of the process by empowering itself to engage in the construction of its culture, that is, to participate in the realization of its own vision of cultural democracy. As such, Fiske's work has become an ideologically attractive and politically relevant example of a Cultural Studies approach in the American context.

The intervention of Cultural Studies in the traditional approach to media studies may serve as a measure of the fundamental changes involved in turning from communication research to a cultural and critical perspective on media and society. Specifically, by the 1970s American communication research had shifted its focus to audiences with the uses and gratification approach (Katz *et al.*, 1974), which retained its functionalistic character regarding the presence of an active (consuming, need-fulfilling) audience, while struggling with the notion of the effects of texts and producers upon audiences under specific cultural, social or economic conditions. Similarly, the agenda-setting model (McCombs and Shaw, 1972, 1976) continued to perpetuate a powerful effects model of the media and identified itself with the traditional, theoretical assumptions of the uses and gratification approach (Shaw, 1979).

At about the same time Hall had observed that Cultural Studies had discarded models of direct influence and formulated an approach that addressed the ideological role of the media, which problematized theories of mass communication, including their definitions of reality; and he developed a sophisticated, albeit incomplete, theory of society in which media participate in securing dominant ideological representations.

This vision of Cultural Studies is based upon an understanding of communication as related to the historical process of which it is also an integral part. Such an approach is quite removed from conceptualizations of popular culture and mass society in the American communication literature, which has preferred to view the analysis of culture as an investigation of a series of empirical facts about media, content and their effect on audiences. Indeed, this position has provoked a Cultural Studies critique of the prevailing models of communication and the study of media by the field. Such a critique was consistent with the political tradition of British Cultural Studies which had emerged from an intellectual climate created and sustained by a political discourse that continues to operate on the assumption that Marxism as a social theory is capable of improving the social and economic conditions of present-day society.

The assumption of an oppositional stance against positivism, and in particular an established empirical social science tradition, have increased the popularity of Cultural Studies among progressive American communication researchers as an alternative, culturally expansive theory of society during the 1980s. An equally important factor has been the accessibility of Cultural Studies ideas through a direct and immediate transfer of contemporary writings and the availability of supporting sources. Thus, the spread of Cultural Studies in the United States is also a case study in international publishing and distribution practices, involving particular academic institutions and individuals as multipliers.

For instance, O'Connor addressed the question of selection and interpretation of British Cultural Studies as an intellectual source; he suggested that "Cultural Studies in the United States is discussed with particular reference to the work of Grossberg" (1989b: 405), while Sparks has talked about Grossberg as the "holder of the exclusive franchise for retailing Stuart Hall in the USA" (1990: 80). These comments are important because they are reminders of the cultural context of interpretation, the potential marginalization of ideas and the political posturing in the process of assimilating an intellectual tradition into an American method of inquiry about communication and society.

But the question of adapting Cultural Studies to an analysis of social and political conditions of American society is not only a commitment to reconsiderations of culture and, therefore, to the uses of history; it also requires an emphasis upon ideological practice in the review of those intentions, interests and actions of subjects which intersect in the spheres of cultural, economic and political power, thus rendering a fundamental critique of the dominant model of society. This means coming to an understanding of what Hall has described as "the 'subject' positioning himself in the specific complex, the objectivated field of discourses and codes which are available to him in language and culture at a particular historical conjuncture" (1979: 330).

Cultural Studies also stresses experience as the product of cultural practices which are imbedded in ideological contexts. According to Grossberg, a discursive approach to culture sees ideology as "the power of a particular system to represent its own representations as a direct reflection of the real, to produce its own meanings as experience" (1984: 409). Such a perspective indicates the importance of media environments and their major role in defining the social and political conditions of individuals, whose lives are determined and conducted within a media sphere. Grossberg suggested such a dependence on media, or cultural systems, by arguing that the "issue is not so much the particular knowledge of reality (true or false, mystified or utopian) which is made available, but the way in which the individual is given access to that knowledge and consequently, empowered or de-powered" (1984: 409). For him the "problematic of cultural studies is transformed, concerned with how a particular practice – signifying or social – is located in a network of other practices, at a particular point, in particular relations" (1984: 412).

Implicit in Grossberg's approach is the consideration of authority, that is, of people living and thinking an existence under specific conditions of domination which organize the ideas and beliefs of individuals through social institutions, including the media. It is this interpretation that has appealed to the critics of American communication research because it contains the potential of seeing the individual constituted by and in social discourse, of redefining social conflict, and of legitimizing a provocative confrontation with traditional investigations of social problems. In addition, there is a real sense of engagement between political practice and theoretical consideration within the public sphere. This is a qualitatively decisive difference from a system in which the nature and extent of social research depend upon the relationship between academic organizations, economic interests and the political system. Hence, the history of communication and media research in the United States, with its primary location within the organization of universities, is a series of encounters with the practical effects of politicizing research (for instance, through the policies of funding social-scientific inquiries). In seeking alternative paths, communication research in the United States may discover that the organizational aspects of the British Cultural Studies perspective in a climate of political engagement are equally appropriate and useful for producing its own answers to socially important and politically relevant problems.

At the same time, the adoption of a Cultural Studies stance within American university settings raises questions about the role of intellectuals and the separation of theory and practice as part of a social reality that Hall and others also recognized but addressed less successfully in conjunction with Centre activities many years ago. Gramsci's question about the relationship between intellectuals and the masses also directs attention to a growing problematic in the United States. He asked,

> is a philosophical movement properly so called when it is devoted to creating a specialised culture among restricted intellectual groups, or rather when, and only when, in the process of elaborating a form of thought superior to "common sense" and coherent on a scientific plane it never forgets to remain in contact with the "simple" and indeed finds in this contact the source of the problem it sets out to study and to resolve?
>
> (1971: 330)

Still, British Cultural Studies has been met in the United States by at least two distinct interests. The first is the academic pursuit of the idea of culture as an appropriate site for the explanation of communication and media; the second is the social and political critique of society with its distinct emphasis on questions of ideology, power and domination in the context of social communication. In both cases, there has been a major attraction to the concepts of an active audience and of resistance. Specifically, the appeal of theoretical claims concerning the liberation of individuals from the embrace of mass society theories which had condemned people to a robot-like existence under the conditions of mass production and consumption, and their ability to react, even in an oppositional fashion, to dominant social structures, restored visions of robust individuality and confirmed ideas about freedom and participation that had been threatened by the voices of cultural pessimism and technological determination. As a result, Cultural Studies has been effective in assembling a significantly large and receptive audience in (mass) communication studies, not to speak of other, related fields of scholarly inquiry. Indeed, the interdisciplinary activities generated by Cultural Studies represent an essential part of the general developments in the study of communication.

In her appraisal of critical communication research Meehan contrasted the activities of idealist culturalists like James Carey with the contributions of Schiller, Smythe and Guback, and concluded that "Hall and his colleagues have repatriated ideology from the metaphoric subconscious where it lay bedevilling our research." She concluded that by focusing on the notion of process and rejecting "paradigm dialogues," Cultural Studies had provided an important challenge to critical research (1986: 92).

The American Cultural Studies approach to communication research has its roots in American Pragmatism and progressive historians of that era; it also winds its way through the technological determinism of Harold Innis and Marshall McLuhan and refers to the anthropology of Clifford Geertz, with its emphasis on culture as a symbolic system and more recently, to the neo-Pragmatism of Richard Rorty. Its most prominent representative is James Carey.

In fact, the American Cultural Studies approach has been influenced by Carey's reconceptualization of the "transmission" view of communication which had dominated the construction of communication models with their sender–channel–receiver frame of reference for decades, although its origins are considerably older and related to nineteenth-century notions of transportation and technology. Carey offered a "ritual" perspective on communication for consideration as a culture-based, complex relationship between individuals and society and as an opportunity "to rebuild a model of and for communication of some restorative value in reshaping our common culture" (1975: 21).

His explanation documents a historical condition of the American social sciences which has been determined by a technological view of the world and preoccupied with problems of transmission. Carey revealed the potential of an alternative perspective, that is to say, the realization of a cultural concept of communication that has its roots in the American experience. His theoretical perspective is closely identified with Pragmatism and the contributions of the Chicago School, connecting ideas of community and participation with historically grounded notions of shared beliefs. Carey's approach to Cultural Studies involves a definition of communication which "constitutes a set of historically varying practices and reflections upon them. These practices bring together human conceptions and purposes with technological forms in sedimented social relations." He offered a meaning-centered approach to communication "to contrast it with versions of communication that search for laws and functions and to focus on the hermeneutic side of the task" (1982: 30).

Implicit in this view is a significant shift from a preoccupation with communication or media phenomena, characterized as mass communication research, to a concern with culture and the redefinition of the field to incorporate the interdisciplinary perspective of Cultural Studies. It is a change based on under-standing communication not as an assertion about the world, but as a conversation which structures and which is a structure of human action. Such a retreat from a rather narrow definition of "mass" communication research as part of a sociological effort to expand and incorporate other fields of inquiry like cultural anthropology or literary studies, in particular, also has political consequences for redrawing the map of institutionalized, academic scholarship. The reception and acknowledgment of Carey's work in "mass" communication research provides some evidence of a willingness to reconsider the potential benefits of diversity in the field and projects a modest redefinition of its boundaries.

An equally important and substantive change occurred when the potential contributions of Critical Theory, in particular the work of Leo Lowenthal on mass culture, if not the cultural critique of Benjamin, Adorno or Marcuse, were eclipsed by a widespread reliance on the discovery and application of Critical Theory and other Marxist perspectives by British Cultural Studies. As a result, intellectual guidance and support for a cultural and ideological rationale of communication studies evolved from the encounter with a neo-Marxist vision of culture that had its roots in specifically British concerns.

Carey's attraction to British Cultural Studies rests on the reali-zation that the works of Williams and Hall, for instance, contain a critique of culture that arises from people's experience with objects or media and the social environment in which they are produced. Carey also sees the need for cultural criticism, albeit from a phenomenological position that has taken its theoretical clues from symbolic interactionism and Pragmatism. As a result, he has advanced a theory of communication as a theory of culture that is based on a preoccupation with the notion of process, that is, "having conversations, giving instructions, imparting knowledge, sharing significant ideas, seeking information, entertaining and being entertained" (1989: 24), which reflects a phenomenological discourse. In it Carey raised questions about his own search for ways of reconstructing his world, reminding his readers of the importance of human activity. He proceeded along the lines of a neo-Kantian philosophy that assumes the symbolic nature of human knowledge and agreed with Cassirer, who had said that "instead of dealing with the things themselves, man is in a sense constantly conversing with himself" (1944: 27). Carey posits a functional definition of human beings, emphasizing the making of meaning as a central human practice; he would probably agree with Merleau-Ponty, who once declared that "Because we are in the world, we are *condemned to meaning*, and we cannot do or say anything without its acquiring a name in history" (1962: xix).

Similarly, when Carey talked about the daily "miracle of producing reality and then living within and under the fact of our own productions" (1989: 29), he could have alluded to Husserl's paradox of human subjectivity, that is, the fact that while individuals are free to create their cultural world, they are also determined by its very existence.

Thus, informed by symbolic interactionism of the Chicago School and the Pragmatism of John Dewey, Carey developed a way of talking about communication that focused on participation and creation. He involved a diversity of disciplines, and produced a sense of intellectual continuity and participation which reinforced a view of the world in which "reality is brought into existence, is produced by communication; that is, by the constructions, apprehensions, and utilization of symbolic forms" (1975: 12). A phenomenological perspective could have produced an introduction to Marxist concerns, particularly through the influential work of Merleau-Ponty on the postwar debates between Marxism and phenomenology in France, for instance, or through the contributions of Paul Ricoeur; but such points of contact, like history and lifeworld, tradition and ideology, or the constitution of meaning in communication and cooperation, remained unexplored.

In fact, the proximity of the American Cultural Studies perspective on communication research to Cultural Studies remained illusory in these discussions of communication theory, since Carey referred to an American intellectual tradition that hardly represented Marxist considerations. Instead, there are fleeting references in his work to individuals, as in his approach to communication as a text, when he reminds the reader that the

> task of the cultural scientist is closer to that of a literary critic or a scriptural scholar than it is to a behavioral scientist. Hence, the connection of this reading of the discipline with the work of critics like Kenneth Burke, Raymond Williams, Richard Hoggart, and the classical discipline of hermeneutics.
>
> (1977: 422)

Similarly, when Carey described texts as sequences of symbols, "speech, writing, gesture – that contain interpretations," he referred to the task of interpreting the interpretations (1977: 421), citing Geertz instead of providing a concrete discussion of the consequences for a Cultural Studies perspective.

For instance, Williams has been very clear on the need for concreteness and specificity when he suggested that "the exploration and specification of distinguishable cultural formations" is the "most central and practical element in cultural analysis," which also lends significance to cultural theory. And he warned that a failure to identify such specific formations can result in a "decline into such abstractions as 'state ideological apparatus,' or the still relatively loose 'traditional' and 'organic' intellectuals" (1989b: 174).

There is, then, an informed theoretical concern in Carey's work that fails to be imbedded in practice. And while it seems quite appropriate for an American Cultural Studies enterprise to begin addressing questions of contemporary culture (instead of problems of mass communication), there is a concomitant need to develop theoretical propositions and practical applications, which define Carey's reference to the idea of "culture as a total way of life" (1977: 424–5) in terms of discoveries of existing or changing formations and the nature of individual practice and collective action within them.

Carey has recognized the poverty of theoretical discourse in the field of mass communication. He has suggested that the field "unload" the "effects tradition" (1989: 89) and reorient communication research by advocating a position of rediscovery and appropriation. In the process of staking out a territory of American Cultural Studies, however, the recognition of British Cultural Studies as a competing and often contradictory source of theoretical discourse will remain problematic as long as a reassessment of the theoretical foundations of Pragmatism and the explication of ideas relating to culture and communication remain unresolved issues, particularly for those who sense a compatibility with American Pragmatism as a source of a comprehensive theory of society.

Carey has discussed the impact of these two traditions, sensing formidable resistance to a form of Cultural Studies that would reflect neo-Marxist considerations of power and ideology and a type of textual analysis that could endanger the potential of diversity of interpretations and, in the final analysis, could create a potential conflict in his own theoretical approach. Thus, he observed that American Cultural Studies remains in a ferment concerning "its ability to retain enough of the origins, insights, and tone of pragmatism while it squarely faces the fact that societies are structured not only in and by communications but also by its relations of power and dominance" (1983: 313). And he remains equally concerned not "to trade the well-known evils of the Skinner box for the less well-known, but just as real evils of the Althusser box" (1985: 36), reflecting on the virtues of a plurality of experiences.

Indeed, the discussion of power and domination, or considerations of process or change as important principles of a cultural theory are not a commitment to a Marxist theory, but rather a reflection of a distinctive tradition in social thought and its continuing usefulness for the analysis of contemporary culture. Marxist theories, on the other hand, may help stimulate a search for alternative theoretical positions within such a non-Marxist tradition of Cultural Studies and should serve to initiate a clarification of the relationship between Marxism and Pragmatism or any other theoretical foundation of American Cultural Studies.

In any case, the American Cultural Studies approach as represented by Carey must move beyond the expressed appeal of a cultural dimension and the pleas for a variety of diversity, including whatever can be carved out of the Cultural Studies approach, and the pleasure of conceptualization, to address the concrete conditions of the historical moment when the idea of the ritual turns into manifest forms. It seems appropriate to invoke Geertz, who observed that

> The danger that cultural analysis, in search of all-too-deep-lying turtles, will lose touch with the hard surfaces of life – with the political, economic, stratificatory realities within which men are everywhere contained – and with the biological and physical necessities on which those surfaces rest, is an ever-present one. The only defense against it, and against, thus, turning cultural analysis into a kind of sociological aestheticism, is to train such analysis on such realities and such necessities in the first place.

(1973: 30)

Carey's approach begins to subsume questions of ideology under the process of culture, attempting to avoid what Geertz has called the ideologization of the term ideology (1973: 193) and to consider ideology as standing to the social sciences in a system of critical considerations, which places ultimate trust in the reliability of science as a source of knowledge. After all, Dewey's Pragmatism championed scientific inquiry and advocated the application of scientific methods to the social sphere. Differently expressed, there is a tendency in this American Cultural Studies perspective to use the notion of ideology in the extended fashion of idealist cultural theories which ignores the processes and conditions under which ideology is produced.

Carey believes that American Cultural Studies can advance without reducing "culture to ideology, social conflict to class conflict, consent to compliance, action to reproduction, or communication to coercion" (1989: 109). He relies on the work of Raymond Williams, whose emphasis on the question of culture seems to provide more suitable linkages with the American tradition of cultural history. In fact, Carey's writings on culture and cultural history, in particular in connection with his critique of journalism history, coincide with an increasing interest in social history to "develop, or return to, a close relationship between social and cultural history," according to Peter Stearns (1982: 228), which also involves a turn to anthropology and what Geertz labeled "thick description" (1973: 9–10). Contemporary social history, while concerned with producing a bottom-up history, has dealt, however, with questions of development and social control without engaging an ideological perspective in the analysis of subcultures. (An exception is the work on slavery, which has made use of a Gramscian theory of hegemony.)

Indeed, since culture cannot be separated from individuals and social groups, questions of power and control, exhibited and exercised through communication and media, are essential aspects of a cultural history of communication that still needs to be written.

The current understanding of a cultural history of communication in the United States relies on the contributions of other disciplines, including anthropological and psychological interpretations of the individual, and recognizes the subjective nature of the historian's insights; in its outlook and approach, it is a version of a progressive history which aims to look at the total structure of society. The concept of culture offered a perspective which acknowledged the presence of ideological and institutional structures, but has been mostly involved in an institutional analysis and explanation of the impact of communication technologies, modeled on the work of Harold Innis rather than on the suggestions of Raymond Williams, for instance. This approach ignores the fact that a cultural history of communication must also be a political history. This is particularly relevant when individuals face shrinking private and public spheres and increasing bureaucratic and technological control of everyday life.

The field of journalism history, with its almost total neglect of subcultures and its failure to explore the role of newsworkers in the rise of media industries, provides an appropriate terrain of struggle over the meaning of cultural history. Carey's critique (1974) has remained an isolated attempt to provide a cultural perspective in the spirit of a progressive history, while neo-Marxist scholarship, which would explore the total culture through an analysis of the experiences of people as workers and consumers and their relationship to the dominating system of journalism and media, has yet to establish itself. Such a cultural history of journalism would expose the reigning ideology in society, raise questions about the exercise of freedom of the press and test its validity as a cherished and celebrated principle of society under current economic and political conditions.

There is no reason to doubt the future of a Cultural Studies approach in communication research, except to note that Carey's theory of communication appears to be mired in a celebration of communication as community that produces and reproduces society, offering opportunities for participation as inquirers, and reflecting on the process of sharing in a democratic experience. If Cultural Studies is "a thinly disguised moral and political vocabulary," his own writings exhibit a similar slant, as Carey is quick to remind the reader; in fact, he continued that one cannot "do intellectual work without adopting a language that simultaneously defines, describes, evaluates, and acts toward the phenomena in question" (1985: 33).

The return to Pragmatism, however, is fraught with problems. While certain conceptualizations of culture and cultural processes, like the treatment of language (Peirce) and the role of communication (Dewey) are useful elements in a theory of communication and media practice that evolved from an application of Pragmatism, other considerations, like the relationship among social, economic and cultural practices and the role of the media, the power of institutions and the concepts of freedom and participation, have become increasingly problematic, since they continue to be defined in terms of dominant social and economic interests.

As Bernstein has suggested in his sympathetic review of Pragmatism, Dewey failed to be genuinely radical, because "he underestimates the powerful social, political, and economic forces that distort and corrupt." And he concluded that, despite Dewey's intentions, "the consequence of his own philosophy is to perpetuate the social evils that it seeks to overcome" (1971: 228). Likewise, contemporary versions of Pragmatism tend to recognize the existence of a dominant power structure, but fail to act on it, thus helping to maintain its position. Also, these interpretations of society are apt to be grounded in an empirical-analytic approach to the social and natural environment, which is interested in technical control and which differs significantly from what Habermas has called hermeneutic or critical "knowledge-constitutive" interests (1971: 195–7).

American Cultural Studies, following Carey's argument in favor of Pragmatism as a useful theoretical context, needs to resurrect a theory of inquiry which develops and supports a notion of radical thinking linked to an understanding of the constitution of social life. Although it confidently separated its interests from "mass" communication by including the varied conversations of society, American Cultural Studies must acknowledge the potential of epistemological diversity in light of the recent assault on idealist notions of culture. A Cultural Studies perspective that continues to operate within the dominant system of meanings and values can only produce a nostalgic vision of the potential of communication and the power of the community. As long as it fails to generate a critique of its own tradition, including an alternative cultural perspective which overcomes the ideological conditions of the prevailing theory of democracy, a Cultural Studies approach to communication research is in danger of sliding into the type of "cheerful negative classicism" represented by McLuhan who, according to Brantlinger, offers "a prophetic and total reading of past and future according to which all will be well because all will be well" (1983: 270).

In fact, the rise of McLuhan must be considered an important episode in the history of communication research, since it became a vivid reminder of the humanities as a method of acquiring knowledge about society. McLuhan combined an appreciation of the (apolitical) aesthetic dimension of communication with strategies of self-promotion and offered what seemed to be an irresistible pop philosophy. He attracted as much criticism from academic scholars as public admiration for the fact that he almost single-handedly took on the media and defined their function in modern society. The appeal of his slogans ("the medium is the message"), and his visions of a shrinking world ("the global village"), contributed not only to a reflection about his theoretical assertions, but also exposed the isolation of a communication research establishment that was locked into its own social-scientific culture, unable or unwilling to deal with McLuhan's assertions about the potential effect of the medium itself and the structure of communication found in the realm of everyday experience in which information moved the mind. Although his optimistic notions concerning communication and technology would surface in debates concerning the technological challenges of the times, conveniently supportive of an American belief in the positive power of technology, communication studies never fully embraced McLuhanism. It may survive, instead, as a point of (re)discovery of communication in the conceptual apparatus of contemporary studies of literature and art.

Years later, the incorporation of Cultural Studies into an independent, if not oppositional Cultural Studies approach in the United States also remains a marginalized activity. It is handicapped by the lack of a strong neo-Marxist tradition of communication scholarship, which was evident already during the activities of Horkheimer and other Critical Theorists in the United States, when a Marxist critique of mass culture remained an isolated phenomenon within the boundaries of communication research.

Similarly, Walter Benjamin's reduced and thereby simplified work has been received more prominently since the arrival of Cultural Studies. But what has been featured in communication studies is Benjamin's materialist position on cultural phenomena. Wolin correctly observed that such a "view of the later Benjamin consequently accords programmatic status to the 1936 essay on 'The Work of Art in the Age of Mechanical Reproduction' and related studies" (1982: xiii). In it Benjamin (1969) argued that art could function in a society where it is produced and appropriated by the masses after the rise of technology enabled its reproduction while depriving it of its uniqueness (the loss of its aura). The essay offered not only a theoretical context for the study of the production and reception of art, it also helped support the idea of an oppositional function for an emancipated art in the social and political environments of contemporary society. Consequently, it appeared in one of the first Cultural Studies readers, edited by Curran, Gurevitch and Woollacott (1977), where it became a major contribution to the Marxist discourse on culture, which also aimed to produce a theoretical foundation for the critique of communication and media in the United States.

The advancement of Cultural Studies as a return to the study of ideological processes, and particularly the contributions of Stuart Hall, as an alternative to the American approach to communication studies, have been associated by O'Connor with the work of Lawrence Grossberg (1989b). Grossberg's association with Hall and the Birmingham Centre has led to a considerable effort on his part to demonstrate the need for theory *and* practice through his own research. He announced more recently the rapid advancement of Cultural Studies into "the mainstream of contemporary intellectual and academic life in the United States," jealously guarding its status against other marginalized individuals who seem to be less fortunate in their positions, or fail to see that "within the discipline of communications" it is "courted and even empowered – within limited parameters – by the discipline's ruling blocs" (1989: 413). While his observations are certainly correct, they raise serious questions not only about political accommodation and strategies of compromise, but also about a working definition of Cultural Studies.

Grossberg's version of Cultural Studies refuses to be identified with a completed, single theoretical position, but wants to be understood as open to challenge and change in its historical condition. He insists that it be located within the political and social reality in which it acts or reacts to social practices and structures in an interventionist manner, and surfaces as a collective activity within its interdisciplinary boundaries. It takes its definition from the intellectual and political potential of its practitioners who are

> concerned with describing and intervening in the ways "texts" and "discourses" [i.e., cultural practices] are produced within, inserted into, and operate in the everyday life of human beings and social formations, so as to reproduce, struggle against, and perhaps transform the existing structures of power.
>
> (1989: 415)

This is the militant language of a radical opposition, reminiscent of Gramsci's suggestion that ideology is the battleground of modern times, with its own traditions in the United States and abroad; but it remains first of all the organizing voice of contemporary feminist praxis. And it is primarily in this context that Grossberg's claims of a popular front and his hunch that Cultural Studies can never exhaust its theoretical and practical resources, are confirmed and validated.

Adapting Cultural Studies to the American environment is a process of rearticulation that has been more successfully effected by feminist scholarship and, therefore, has been given purpose and direction within a much broader feminist agenda. It provides the thrust of a radical break with traditional communication research and has emerged as a significant and powerful alternative perspective that may eclipse the original impact of Cultural Studies on American versions of a Marxist or non-Marxist study of culture.

The rise of Cultural Studies and its significant feminist component in Britain had helped support a rapidly growing field of Marxist feminism in the United States. The result has been a theoretical and political focus on the devaluation of women and on questions of gender, race and class from a variety of perspectives, ranging from economic explanations and the role of ideological expressions to psychoanalytic theories. Underlying these observations about the emergence of feminist theories as social theories and political practice in communication research is the understanding of the complexity, and perhaps the internal contradictions, of the definition of feminism.

According to Caroline Ramazanoglu, the acknowledgment of universal feminism as "cultural product of a particular historical period" (1989: 21) is merely a starting-point of varying and even conflicting experiences. Likewise, the opposition of versions of feminist theories, that is, radical and Marxist feminism as well as the inherent problematic of articulating Marxist feminism, also creates alliances and helps support the general idea of feminism as a theoretical and practical force in contemporary society. Thus, feminism offers substantially different political strategies.

The contribution by Nancy Fraser (1989) to the critique of American and European social theory, in particular the work of Richard Rorty, Michel Foucault and Jürgen Habermas, finally culminates in the integration of various notions of feminist theory,

Pragmatism, Critical Theory and poststructuralism into a socialist-feminist approach. Fraser emphasized the centrality of communication and interpretation in theory building; and her model of social discourse, or how talk about people's needs in society occurs, should be of particular interest to the field of communication studies and those who appreciate the attempt to provide a critical social theory.

Thus, feminist communication scholarship could benefit from these developments in other fields. It is difficult to identify the origins of contemporary feminist work either in the political conditions of society and the academy, or in the growth of a common interdisciplinary attack on the insufficiency, if not bankruptcy of the traditional theoretical enterprise. Nevertheless, the development of feminism as a social theory provides a major challenge to participate in the task of creating an understanding of society which, from a Marxist feminist perspective, would include the abolition of institutionalized gender differences.

In any event, beginning with the 1980s, it appears as a real and sustained effort to address issues of communication, gender and class in an active and highly productive way, although the history of feminist communication scholarship is older and needs to be rediscovered in an effort to trace the earlier considerations of a genuine alternative perspective on issues of media and society. Lana Rakow has described the progress of feminist scholarship in communication and media studies, including the institutional and professional environment, under intellectual conditions of working within a language and discourse that "means to disrupt" (1989: 211). And Pamela Creedon prefaced a recent collection of essays with an observation about the political dimension of feminist research and its ability to create controversy whenever it challenges orthodoxy (1989: 27).

In an earlier appraisal of feminist scholarship, Brenda Dervin had noted its absence from the "Ferment in the Field" discussion in the *Journal of Communication* (1983), which may have been indicative of its effect on communication research at that time. She also concluded four years later that feminist scholarship had yet to make a major contribution to the field (1987: 111), although it had grown significantly in the United States.

In fact, Leslie Steeves's topography of feminist theories during the same year details the extent of feminist perspectives on the study of communication and media in an attempt to introduce a hesitant, if not poorly informed, field of media research to the potential of a feminist framework for study and analysis. Her findings already testify to the rapid growth of feminist scholarship in communication and media studies.

She also observed that feminist work in the liberal-pluralist mode has concentrated "on the presence, absence, and circumstances of women in media," and has been typically coupled with the quest for "more women, particularly more nontraditional women, in communication content and institutions" (1987: 119). On the other hand, the contributions of critical (socialist) feminist scholarship have raised questions of power and ideology in the specific context of gender oppression and addressed, by and large, theoretical issues. Steeves predicted the emergence of two major strands of feminist theories, a "highly variable" socialist coalition of various Marxist feminist positions and "an unexplicated, implicit liberal position," the former in possession of a "more theoretically comprehensive perspective on women's oppression" (1987: 120), the latter still in need of reflecting on the "long-range theoretical and political value of their research" (1987: 121).

In her detailed review of feminist communication studies, which derive their theoretical foundations either from psychoanalysis or Cultural Studies, Steeves has also recognized the problem of accommodation by Marxism. She criticized the failure of "socialist feminist cultural studies" to address the complexity of theoretical issues, i.e., the integration of issues related to class and gender oppression, as well as the tendency of too much theory at the expense of empirical work (1987: 120).

Ann Kaplan, however, has suggested that the traditional liberal or leftist humanist position, which had been the theoretical source of feminist work, may have been rendered obsolete in the face of what Baudrillard has called a new "universe of communication" that relies on "connections, feedback, and interface; its processes are narcissistic and involve constant surface change." She proposed that such a change may affect the notion of gender as a major organizing category with "as-yet unclear (and not necessarily progressive) results" (1987: 247). Her conclusions about the potential of television that may lead the individual from self to image, from original to simulation, require a reconstitution of theoretical premises underlying feminist scholarship.

The growth of feminist communication and media studies had coincided with the rediscovery of alternative theories and methodologies of communication and media, in the context of seeking either cultural or ideological explanations of social phenomena. Such deliberations or paradigm dialogues provided initial support for bringing feminist theories to bear on an exploration of alternative perspectives on everyday life and introduced an interdisciplinary approach, since feminist communication scholarship also reflects and builds on the development of feminist perspectives in a variety of other academic fields, as well as on the activism of non-academic feminists. These dialogues resulted in a variety of consciousness-raising activities which located women in the field of communication studies, historically and in terms of contemporary scholarship, however, without initiating an attack on existing theoretical alternatives. The approaches can be identified as part of an existing liberal-pluralist tradition from which a feminist position developed that demanded visibility and equality. In this process women and their roles in society were rehabilitated and celebrated as significant contributors to the democratic cause and the advancement of society. It was an attempt to correct or amend history without challenging the premises of historical writing, that is, the ideological basis of communication and media studies.

Underlying these perspectives resides the problem of accommodation. Feminism must deal with the failure of Marxism to account for the oppression of women. Most recently, MacKinnon has described the Marxist response to feminism as it develops in one of three ways:

> equate and collapse, derive and subordinate, and substitute contradictions. The first equates sex with class, feminism with marxism, in order to collapse the former into the latter. The second derives an analysis of sex from an analysis of class, feminism from marxism, in order to subordinate sex to class, feminism to marxism. The third applies marxist method to sex or feminist method to class.

> (1989: 60–1)

Her discussion provokes a confrontation with the issue of theorizing under theoretical conditions that had prescribed the position of women in the concrete context of their history. MacKinnon provides an alternative synthesis of Marxism and feminism, revealing "a simultaneous critique of society that excludes women from its center and a critique of marxist theory that can see women only at its periphery" (1989: 80). It also offers a theoretical basis for a Marxist-feminist approach to communication and media studies.

At the end of the 1980s it seemed that women's studies continued to struggle "for legitimacy in most universities" (Press, 1989: 196), while the contribution of feminist theory and praxis to the field of communication and media studies has continuously increased, both in the quality and sophistication of its approach to questions of gender, and in its challenge of the unreflexive nature of traditional theoretical and empirical research positions of the field. As a result, there have been signs of an institutional manifestation of feminist scholarship in the form of publishing and organizing activities. Still, Kathryn Cirksena has argued that the "central body of knowledge which is the core of the discipline of communication research, and with which most communication researchers work, remains quite 'gender-blind'" (1989: 47). Her observations draw attention to the depth of a problem that includes critical and Cultural Studies. In fact, "genderedness" remains a major problem in many disciplines. Cirksena cited institutional factors, particularly the "active misogyny" of individuals and the "objectivist positivist" position of value-free research as contributing to the problem. In addition, she advocated a critique of classic communication research as an important step in a systematic treatment of "functionalist assumptions" about the role of men and women in society (1989: 48). Her comments suggest the importance of understanding the history of communication research as an expression of a male-dominated culture and the need to challenge the social-scientific assumptions related to the study of communication. For instance, it would be important to know not only about the contributions of a number of women whose careers developed in the shadow of Paul Lazarsfeld and his male colleagues, but also how issues of gender, the role of women in their private and public lives and their participation in communication were operationalized in the "milestones" research of the field.

Despite many unanswered questions, the mere presence of feminist theory has become a significant factor in any contemplation of the future of communication research and media studies in the United States, and there are additional signs that feminist theory may strengthen its position by leaving the epistemological straitjacket of mainstream communication research and becoming its permanent critique (Press, 1989: 189–99). These developments are also shaped by fears of cooptation through the deliberate institutionalization of feminist scholarship in communication and media studies as a special interest and its subsequent marginalization. Cathy Schwichtenberg has suggested that these are political issues which can be resolved only through a commitment to an interdisciplinary approach that builds on theoretical innovations and the active engagement in praxis, that is, in the analysis and critique of everyday life (1989: 203–4).

The problems of feminist scholarship in communication research arose throughout the literature of the 1980s in the form of existential struggles that involve the politics of the academy and its bureaucratic structures of learning and the nature of intellectual disputes; in this sense the problems of feminist scholars are the problems of marginal and frequently oppositional interests in communication research. However, the claims of feminist theories, including the possibility of a new discourse, the active pursuit of revelation through research, and the potential of a renewal of communication research, constitute major concerns for a self-reflexive intellectual endeavor like feminist communication studies, which must succeed against an established network of academic power that controls the reigning ideology and therefore the workplace.

In fact, the reception and assimilation of distinctly different and even oppositional theories and research practices has been an issue facing communication research in American universities for many years, raising questions about competition and accommodation within a rather limited field of academic inquiry. The arrival of feminist communication studies has certainly helped exasperate the situation. To paraphrase Schwichtenberg's view of British Cultural Studies, the greatest hope for a feminist approach to American communication studies lies in its recognition that working within the tensions of theoretical and practical (or political) demands and as part of an interdisciplinary alliance will allow and even encourage the confrontation of established truths and help sustain the challenge of dominant (mass) communication theories and methodologies.

Specifically, the advent of British Cultural Studies on the American academic scene has dramatized the problem of disciplinary boundaries and academic compartmentalization of knowledge, including the construction and administration of appropriate social research agendas. The potential of communication research and media studies is actually revealed through the strength of interdisciplinary work that threatens to reduce academic disciplines to participants in much less definable fields of intellectual endeavor and to executors of specific administrative or bureaucratic tasks, like journalism education. Thus, when Ernest Gombrich considered the study of culture some years ago, he concluded that the "so-called disciplines on which our academic organisation is founded are no more than techniques; they are means to an end but no more than that" (1969: 46).

The impact of Cultural Studies on the research literature of American communication studies constitutes a qualitative change since earlier encounters with Critical Theory or the subsequent exposure and critique of the field through the work of Smythe, Schiller, Gitlin, Ewen and others.

However, neither an accommodation by the cultural tradition of American communication research, nor the incorporation of traditional British media research, which had been favorably received and widely used in the analysis of political communication and the study of television effects by empirical research since the 1970s, can directly explain the prominence of Cultural Studies in the current literature of American communication. Instead, such popularity may rather have been the result of a growing disillusionment with contemporary (mass) communication research and its entrenchment in the traditional social sciences together with a rising radical critique of the liberal tradition in American thought. Indeed, the reception of such a critique may reflect the general conditions of a paradigm crisis affecting American social sciences.

The interrelatedness of "communication" and "society" has emerged as a fundamental position of Cultural Studies; its theoretical and practical consequences are a challenge to the dominant communication theory. For instance, in his discussion of economics, Richard Swedberg observed a few years ago that, based on the interventions of "neo-Marxism, 'second-wave' feminism, and Third World theory," concepts like "'economy' and 'society' are organically interconnected and cannot be analyzed as if they are essentially separate phenomena" (1986: 106). The demands of a totality-of-life perspective require different methods, too, and more recently the field has benefitted from a keen interest in the notions of culture and communication among other academic disciplines, which has resulted in an increased reception of the relevant intellectual discourse concerning communication and the media from outside the sphere of communication research.

The advent of Cultural Studies as an alternative discourse about communication and media also means that the type of communication research that is conceptually rooted in traditional models of (mass) communication research is under permanent siege. This problem is exacerbated by the atheoretical nature of the majority of communication studies, their continuing isolation from other disciplines that have been engaged in their own confrontation with Critical Theory and Cultural Studies and, possibly, a rejection of a Marxist critique of society and its devastating critique of the culture industry, which threatens the traditional relationship between media research and commerce and effectively precludes the accommodation of radical criticism.

Suggestions for compromises, however, presented in terms of cooperation or mergers of theoretical or methodological traditions, persevere (Gerbner, 1983: 355–62). They are offered as a "return to the bridge building between the social sciences and the humanities" or as a "cultural-empirical approach" (McQuail, 1984: 186), without specific references to the ideological problematic, that is, to conflicting theories and questions of accommodation. As a result, the paradigm struggle is effectively reduced to a paradigm dialogue.

Indeed, there is a noticeable tendency to search for an underlying intellectual consensus. In his discussion of developing sociological theories, Alvin Gouldner once referred to this process of discovering a common ground as an "Americanized version of Hegelianism, in which historical development presumably occurs not through polemic, struggle, and conflict, but through consensus" (1970: 17). But compromise can also mean a pluralism of critical approaches to the problems of media and communication, according to Halloran, who couched them in terms of methodological diversity, preferably as long as it excludes "an ideological approach" (1983: 272). This position is reminiscent of arguments in the 1970s that "radical sociology" can be "good sociology," if it is purged of an ideological bias (Becker and Horowitz, 1972: 48–66).

There are valid reasons to suspect that "good" communication research would operate on principles derived from the traditional epistemology of media studies which would also emphasize – to use the vocabulary of Becker and Horowitz – "meaningful descriptions" and "valid explanations" of social phenomena, while an accommodation of radical criticism would be accomplished under the label of "a full exploration of possibilities" within the range of a dominant, liberal-pluralist theory of society (1972: 50–1).

The presence of Cultural Studies is a radical development at a time when communication research suffers from a lack of creativity and intellectual leadership to advance its theoretical position and build on its past practice. In fact, communication research may feel threatened, perhaps for the first time, by the intervention of an integrative cultural approach to communication. The rise of feminist communication studies has strongly contributed to the climate of change. In the past, Marxist scholarship had been a marginal activity; now Cultural Studies promises to install a Marxist critique of communication and society as a theoretical contribution to the field and to reveal the dialectical character of (mass) communication research, which continues to be repressive in its support of the dominant social and economic system and liberating in its exposure of the power structure. The progress of Cultural Studies and its popularity in the American context may well depend upon its successful critique of the repressive elements in (mass) communication research.

In the meantime, the emergence of an alternative discourse in an atmosphere of participatory intellectual leadership thrives on a Gramscian understanding of intellectual work as involvement in the collective practice of producing and sharing knowledge. Thus, the diversity and quality of theoretical insights gained through retracing the hermeneutic tradition of European thought, and the impact of Western Marxism and feminism on contemporary social theory, have influenced these joint intellectual tasks of formulating theoretical propositions and research projects. In the past, the behavioral sciences have provided such guidance in the field of (mass) communication research on both sides of the Atlantic.

More important, perhaps, have been the political and economic conditions of societies that have directed the attention of social scientists to the realities of human misery and global disaster with the realization that generations of scholarship and research have been unable to affect the destiny of people. Consequently, there may have been a growing willingness to reconsider theoretical and methodological issues and to engage in critical reflections about the theoretical assumptions governing (mass) communication research.

The publication of the "Ferment in the Field" issue of the *Journal of Communication* (1983) was an indication of these uneasy times, in which ideological predispositions of researchers were acknowledged as crucial elements in the choice of research problems and methodologies (Smythe and Dinh, 1983: 117). Therefore, the future of alternative theories of culture and communication depends upon the vitality of a theoretical discourse that is linked to research practices designed to overcome the established and tested boundaries of mainstream (mass) communication research. Its success may depend upon a cooperative effort of critical research projects that are grounded in a feminist orientation and determined to move beyond a recycling of liberal-pluralist visions of society and the reinforcement of a degendered functionalism which dominated the early decades of sociological and philosophical inquiries into the nature of communication, the role of the media, and the making of a democratic society.

As a matter of fact, there is considerable power in the role of communication researchers who have been engaged in the creation and defense of theoretical positions. They maintain not only the prevailing traditional values, providing an ideological defense of particular class interests, but they are also indispensable in the struggle for alternative expressions. In recent years, the proponents of Critical Theory and Cultural Studies and, more recently, feminist scholarship have been deeply committed to the task of "breaking" with traditional notions of communication in society. They are in the process of redefining the realm of academic scholarship, of engaging in a pedagogical project through social research that deals with the daily existence of people and through a conscious intellectual engagement of the political structure of society. There is a continuing need for such involvement, as Trent Schroyer pointed out several years ago, because "the real process of enlightenment refers to the reinterpretation of their needs by the many people who are currently unable to do so. Thinking about ways in which communicative processes can be stimulated is crucial"; and he insisted that "critical theorists must construct models for the activation of communication about human requirements and the ways in which institutions can be changed to meet them" (1975: 248–9).

Throughout the last decade or so, the notion of the critical in communication research has shifted from various expressions of self-criticism in the context of traditional communication studies and within the consensual, patriarchic realm of theorizing that centered on ideas of objectivity and the moral power of a value-free science, to a critique of culture, which has emerged as a permanent discourse about relationships among individuals, media and society that is grounded in the cultural history of society and, of late, informed by the need to address issues of gender and ethnicity.

Talking about the prospects of Cultural Studies, Raymond Williams once said that if individuals are prepared to continue

> taking the best we can in intellectual work and going with it in this very open way to confront people for whom it is not a way of life, for whom it is not in any probability a job, but for whom it is a matter of their own intellectual interest, their own understanding of the pressures on them, pressures of every kind, from the most personal to the most broadly political,

there will be "a remarkable future indeed" (1989b: 162). Intellectual struggle is also a matter of justifying one's work before the future.

There is a danger, however, that the advent of Cultural Studies and the transformation of its original intent into specific strategies for elaborating on the conditions of contemporary American society has been engaged in retracing the boundaries of theorizing without moving beyond the obvious; and that the complexity and diversity of social formation, of textual representation, and of interpretation have been reduced to the litany of a polemical discourse that favors versions of existence that seem to exhaust themselves in states of subversion, intervention, or opposition. This involves the activities of an idealist cultural approach to communication studies that finds its populist base in the ideas of Pragmatism as well as those of a culturalist perspective that relies on a Marxist critique of society. After all, what is new is not the canonical reply to the question of being in this world, but the prospects of a future, the notion of utopian practices that lie imbedded in the dreams and aspirations of people which also constitute a terrain of hope. It seems that feminist scholarship has grasped these differences and in its critical, feminist/Marxist voice has begun to call for overcoming the space between the polemics of theorizing and the desires for change.

Chapter 6

On locating critical concerns
Communication research between Pragmatism and Marxism

> Critical thinking is the function neither of the isolated individual nor of a sum-total of individuals. Its subject is rather a definite individual in his real relation to other individuals and groups, in his conflict with a particular class, and, finally, in the resultant web of relationships with the social totality and with nature.
>
> Max Horkheimer

Throughout the recent history of the field, repeated demands for more theoretical considerations and the call for new theories to help explain communication and media phenomena in modern society have met with a variety of responses. Central to these discussions has been the notion of culture as a context for communication and media research both within the established boundaries of a traditional sociology of mass communication, and as a central concern of a Marxist challenge to the American idealism of classical communication and media studies. The preceding chapters have provided an opportunity to suggest the possibilities of a vision of theory, or an orientation, that relies on understanding the need for historicizing theory and theorizing history. The following is an attempt to summarize the conditions of the field.

The quest for a theoretical grounding of the search for specific solutions to a myriad of social and political problems has encouraged renewed attention to the philosophical traditions of American Pragmatism and its reformist demands. It has also resulted in a discovery of contemporary European Marxist thought as a potential and alternative source of theoretical insights about the nature of communication and media practices. Subsequently, considerations of culture have become a common concern of non-Marxist and Marxist scholarship alike.

Theories about the relationship of language, communication and culture typically extend into inquiries about the social and political nature of democracy, that is, the relationship between communication in society and the emergence of a democratic way of life. Modern social theorists from Dewey to Habermas, for instance, have maintained that the potential of democracy rests in the ability of societies to ensure participation through communication.

Thus, Dewey spoke of democracy as a significant social idea rooted in communication; he called it "primarily a mode of associated living, of conjoint communicated experience" (1954: 87). Habermas suggested the need for creating conditions of undistorted communication to establish the foundation for democratic practice, because "only in an emancipated society, whose members' autonomy and responsibility had been realized, would communication have developed into the non-authoritarian and universally practiced dialogue from which . . . our idea of true consensus [is] always implicitly derived" (1971: 314). In either case, communication constitutes a major element in structuring democracy; its definitions, however, provide an important difference between liberal-pluralist and Marxist understandings of democracy.

Both views on communication agree on the basic social function of communication, but diverge on questions of its application to a theory of society. While the idea of communication, beginning with Dewey's formulations, concentrates on the individual in association with others, emphasizing individualism and the primacy of communicative interests that are reflected in questions of rights of privacy and freedom of expression, Marxist notions of communication represent concerns about the collective aspects of existence, including the struggle against economic and political domination, stressing the importance of history and returning to the idea of totality.

Similarly, the idea of culture as the social context for the creation of meaning includes notions of communication systems (Leach, 1965), joining views of communication as participation (Dewey, 1966), or suggestions of communication as environments (McLuhan, 1964). Marxist understandings of communication, on the other hand, have focused on societal conditions for competence (Habermas, 1979) and political economy (Schiller, 1969), or were subsumed within a cultural notion of community and life processes (Williams, 1961).

However, the variety of theoretical positions in Pragmatist and Marxist writings, ranging from a narrow definition of communication as exercising influence over others to viewing communication as a cultural environment, is also grounded in varying understandings of "culture" as a potential theoretical turning-point. This is a particularly significant development in Marxist thought that has concentrated on the notion of cultural activity, its relation to other social activities, and the transformation of nature and society. As a result, cultural practices have become a central concern of communication studies in general.

For instance, where culture as an American social-scientific concern is less associated with the study of how people live together through communication (culture as a way of life) or with an analysis of specific intellectual or artistic activities (the demise of high culture and the rise of popular culture), but more with the study of real or potential effects on individuals or groups or with the power to manipulate or transform society, it offers narrow explanations of behavioral changes that are set in the ahistorical context of experimental inquiry and reflect the priorities of an administrative brand of communication research. In fact, an interest in the study of human behavior typically reduces the notion of culture to reflect the preoccupation of communication research with the analysis of effects. Similarly, Geertz once observed that the "dominant concept of culture in American social science identified culture with learned behavior" (1973: 249).

On the other hand, culture as an anthropological project in American scholarship has typically insisted upon coherence and totality since the writings of Malinowski (1944), Benedict (1961), or Douglas (1966) and, therefore, resembled the notion of social totality in Marxist theory. In fact, Archer has suggested that the "myth of cultural integration," which exhibited an aesthetic rather than an analytical orientation and which insisted on finding a coherence in culture, "surfaced intact in Functionalist thought" and "received monumental reinforcement by its adoption into Western humanistic Marxism," sharing the idea of coherence with the Parsonian normative system (1988: 3). The difference, however, lies in the dialectical, historically determined nature of totality, reflecting the dynamics of its parts and complexes.

Culture as a central Marxist concern, since the emergence of Western Marxism under the influence of Lukács and Gramsci, has become context and subject of contemporary critiques of capitalist societies. In fact, for Lukács, the crisis of capitalism was a crisis of culture, which could be overcome only with a transformation of the social structure, when "the inner and outer life of man is dominated by human and not by economic motives and impulses" (1973: 14). For Gramsci, the process of enlightenment included the unifying feature of culture and the rise of intellectuals as educators and leaders of a cultural hegemony that would unite people "in order to construct an intellectual-moral bloc which can make politically possible the intellectual progress of the mass and not only of small intellectual groups" (1971: 333).

Marcuse also provided a useful definition of culture in Marxist thought. He suggested in *Negations* (1968) that there is a

> concept of culture that can serve as an important instrument of social research because it expresses the implication of the mind in the historical process of society. It signifies the totality of social life in a given situation, in so far as both the areas of ideational reproduction (culture, in the narrower sense, the "spiritual world") and of material reproduction ("civilization") form a historically distinguishable and comprehensible unity.
>
> (1968: 94)

His formulation stresses the importance of culture as a point of departure (and return) for a critical analysis of bourgeois society, but it fails to recognize the need to overcome the preoccupation with the demise of high culture and to address issues related to modes of production and the reception of cultural products within an existing material culture.

Throughout the history of American social science research, and communication research in particular, there has been a quest for sustaining a critical approach to social institutions and ideas of development and progress as part of a progressive tradition that supported the public mission of social inquiry. Such critiques have led on occasion to a leveling of different critical perspectives, blurring competing ideologies and promoting a shift from class-related, economic concerns to issues of social cohesion.

Traditionally communication and media scholars have engaged in a theoretical discourse through their respective research agendas rather than through outright theoretical propositions. Subsequently and throughout the last decades, there have been few theoretical contributions to the periodical literature of the field. Instead, theory was revealed by doing, and doing was part of a collaboration in maintaining and strengthening the large and complex structure of society. Thus, a review of contemporary (mass) communication research in the United States reveals a firm commitment to a liberal-pluralist interpretation of the media and their relationship to society; such research emphasizes control (over minds or organizations) at the expense of raising questions about participants (audiences, or newsworkers and producers, for instance), their intent or purpose in the production and consumption of culture and their cultural environment, or more specifically, their social or economic positions *vis-à-vis* media ownership.

For example, press historians continue to demonstrate their fundamental belief in the political and economic system of the United States by producing work on issues of ownership, freedom of trade, and the adoption of media technologies that serves as evidence of the progressive nature of journalism and its dedication to safeguarding democracy. While their interpretations of historical "facts" strengthen prevailing ideas about media and their role in the development of a democratic system of government, there are no considerations of the historical consequences of capitalism and their effects upon theorizing about the relationship between communication, media and society. In fact,

> readers of press histories rarely get a sense of culture that is based on the experience of diversity, the economic realities of industrialization, and the social conditions of change.

Instead, history is presented in a top-down fashion as a series of

> interlocking technological inevitabilities about media institutions and their political or economic relationships to each other. It is the creation of authors, whose philosophical positions seem to reflect a firm belief in progress as the engine of democracy and technology as a means of looking at the future.
>
> (Hardt, 1990: 350)

Similarly, the study of newsworkers and their activities continues to occupy the literature of communication in ways that reinforce the ahistorical nature of social-scientific research. The historical role of newsworkers *vis-à-vis* media management and the creation of conditions of permanent change with the introduction of media technologies under ownership control, the issue of professionalization and the curtailment of freedom of expression, as well as the anti-labor attitudes of media owners, may offer alternative explanations for the contemporary status and working habits of newsworkers, the production of content matter, and may help provide a rationale for understanding audiences as consumers.

Instead, since the development of communication and media research in the United States, analyses of communication have typically grown out of studies of individual and group behavior or group processes, ranging from an interest in an individual's creation of knowledge, conduct and self-control to the role of media in the process of constructing and sharing social realities. In these contexts communication as an essential way of understanding the other as well as the self becomes an ordering mechanism and constitutes a process of control.

For instance, in discussing the "social foundations and functions of thought and communication," Mead argued for a principle of "communication involving participation in the other" as "basic to human organization." The result is a "taking the role of the other" which involves control of the self, self-criticism, and, in the final analysis, social control (1969: 253–4). Mead also confirmed the organizing principle of social communication by suggesting that the "development of communication is not simply a matter of abstract ideas, but a process of putting one's self in the place of the other person's attitude, communicating through significant symbols," serving as an "organizing process in the community" (1969: 327).

In addition, by extending this process to include the media, Mead saw journalism as a mechanism through which individuals "can enter into the attitude and experience of other persons" (1969: 257), providing a rationale for the structure of organized information systems. Consequently, media play a significant role in the formation and maintenance of democracy when they become facilitators of community structure and control. They also create new problems related to issues of presentation and representation of social and political realities, access, and public participation. This perspective on communication provided its own major argument for its centrality in the study of society, and, by implication, for the concentration of scholarly inquiry and the organization of communication studies within academic environments either in communication or mass communication programs.

Another major strand of theoretical considerations concerning culture and communication was introduced with Dewey's insistence upon the importance of inquiry as a mode of conduct and of knowledge as the basis for a self-correcting process in society that involves participation. Since communication is necessary for sharing in the process of inquiry, it also becomes the condition under which common attitudes and experiences will lead to the realization of mutual goals. These circumstances are reflected in Dewey's understanding of democracy in which the potential of social communication becomes the determinant of a political and economic structure that represents the spirit of community. Such a powerful vision allows for the diversity of ideas, but also suggests the importance of social control in the interest of the common good.

Dewey proceeded in the scientific spirit of his times to join the notion of democracy with the appeal of science. He suggested that "freedom of inquiry, toleration of diverse views, freedom of communication, the distribution of what is found out to every individual as the ultimate intellectual consumer, are involved in the democratic as in the scientific method" (1963: 102). Such a position not only legitimizes the place of science in society, but offers scientific credibility to the process of democracy. In the end, both science and democracy become the organizing principles of society.

Richard Rorty, as a contemporary exponent of the Pragmatist tradition, also stresses the importance of inquiry, conversation and the need to see knowledge as "coping with reality." He viewed the "social sciences as continuous with literature – as interpreting other people to us, and thus enlarging and deepening our sense of community." Consequently, "the lines between novels, newspaper articles and sociological research get blurred" (1982: 202–3). This is the vision of a shared culture that emerges from a liberal perspective that neglects to register the experience of the social and the reality of a controlled and structured or manipulated environment. Frank Lentricchia has observed that Rorty's vision of culture reduces the "conversation of culture" from the collective sound of voices to the private dialogues of autonomous individuals, promoting "the leisured vision of liberalism: the free pursuance of personal growth anchored in material security, as John Dewey, one of his philosophical favorites suggests" (1983: 140).

In fact, when communication and media practices have been

deemed viable objects of social-scientific investigation as instruments of social control, the result has been an emphasis on the study of effects and social deviance.

For example, Robert Park's work on the immigrant press (1922) was less an attempt to reconstruct the cultural diversity of this genre, or to document the contribution of immigrants to the formation of an American culture, but rather an exercise designed to deal with the social and political problems of assimilation and integration in American society. It was a politically motivated inquiry – particularly after the anti-war and pro-labor activities of radical ethnic groups before and after the First World War – to identify and describe the nature of culturally deviant group behavior. Similarly, histories of the American press since the latter part of the nineteenth century to the present day have consistently offered overwhelming evidence of the strength and homogeneity of English-language newspapers, demonstrating an almost total disregard for subcultural practices.

The problem of US media history is precisely its lack of commitment to a form of historical inquiry that acknowledges the importance of cultural diversity and the need to question the "truth" of observations about American media and society that are based upon previously unchallenged cycles of inquiry which continue to affect the production and status of contemporary social knowledge.

The contributions of social-scientific inquiry into the role of communication and the place of the media in modern society have consistently ignored the importance of history and concentrated upon identifying real or potential sources of social problems. Generally speaking, they have dealt with specific social or political conditions of the media as they might affect the structure of the democratic system. Even critical approaches have remained firmly committed to visions of pluralism and the potential of capitalism, despite the recent introduction of Marxist perspectives like the cultural critiques of the Frankfurt School and British Cultural Studies. It seems, instead, that an overwhelming number of studies has served to reinforce existing notions of society without questioning premises or conditions of existence that could significantly alter an understanding of contemporary democracy.

Lazarsfeld, for instance, whose own work reflects the need to yield to industry demands for this type of social research, admitted the problems of "administrative" research and pleaded for a "critical" approach as early as 1941, at least acknowledging the problems of social inquiry in a capitalist society. One must hasten to add, however, that his own work was hardly affected by his critical observations about the nature of research.

Over sixty-five years ago, Lippmann suggested that people were unable to grasp the complexity of the modern world (1922), and contemporary sociological findings provide increasing evidence of the failure to educate and prepare individuals for assuming their respective roles in society. Peters has stated that "Lippmann's vision of democracy rested on the capacity of the ordinary citizen to participate knowledgeably in public-governmental affairs. In his theoretical framework, democracy rose or fell with the intelligence of the masses" (1989: 212). Present-day understanding of communication and the quality of participation or sharing of experience continues to rest on the assumption that individuals are capable and willing to participate as "ultimate intellectual consumers" in society, presumably understanding and directing the democratic process.

Specifically, the vested interests of classical sociology have emphasized questions of individualism, rationality, freedom, and control of the marketplace, while a pragmatist tradition of culture has formulated ideas of community and advanced a pluralist notion of democracy that help confirm a shared belief in the path of progress. These ideas have kept their appeal as basic elements in any approach to the study of American society and offer contemporary guidelines for the development of cultural theories or models of communication and society.

The legacy of such visions of culture and society, as they emerged from theoretical and practical considerations of America's major source of intellectual activities – Pragmatism and the reform movement – is also the major challenge in the years to come. For communication and media scholars who adhere to the ideas of a pluralist society and believe in the pursuit of Dewey's ideal democracy, for instance, it is time to engage in a critical inquiry about the political, economic and cultural premises for participation, community or communication that goes beyond reasserting the importance of these concepts. Instead, it must address the need for a critique of existing (historical) knowledge and avoid reducing the new to what is already known.

In addition, the more recent works by Bloom (1987), Jacoby (1987) or Hirsch (1987) suggest most urgently that lingering ideas of the relationship between democracy and communication may have to be revised, since communicative competencies and the need to articulate social or political positions or to develop options are severely restricted for many individuals. The decline of education not only intensifies the problems of intellectuals in American society, but indicates the need to redefine notions of freedom and participation and to reassess the conditions for democratic practice. These developments are a serious challenge for the study of culture and the role of communication and media in the social and political struggle.

Currently, the ideological power and the political effects of a social science establishment in communication and media research and its industry support help strengthen the premises of a social theory that pits a belief in the ability of individuals to share in Dewey's dream of a democratic society against the economic and political realities of capitalism. A critical Cultural Studies perspective must take into account the fact that, although Dewey recognized the potential of communication in the realm of mediating between technocratic strategies and value orientations of participant groupings, his reliance upon the power of common sense ignored structural changes in society and the determination of culture by social and economic forces that redefined the public sphere, including the relationship between science and democracy. The result has been the emergence of what Miliband has called "elite pluralism," and the cooperation among various elites to form a dominant economic class (1969: 47–8) that operates and controls the media as well as communication and media research in its attempt to forge alliances and maintain class solidarity.

Prevailing (mass) communication research and media history, however, reflect a strong belief in the benefits of technology and the structure of the economic support system. They also reveal a proximity to the progressive ideas and pragmatic considerations of the dominant cultural elite in society. Consequently, there is reason to suspect that Rorty's modern-day Pragmatism appeals to mainstream media scholarship in the United States. Connolly has suggested that Rorty's "language tranquilizes and comforts his fellow Americans, first by celebrating the technocratic values, self-conceptions, and economic arrangements operative in . . . American institutions and, second by implying that once these endorsements have been offered there is not much more to be said" (1983: 131). Furthermore, Rorty's understanding of culture is separated from political power, as Lentricchia noted (1983: 141). Both observations are attractive to the type of communication and media research that continues to operate on the assumption that it is dealing with a pluralist society under free market conditions that benefit all participants. There will be a rather limited reception of alternative visions of communication or internal criticism of media institutions and their place in society that are based on an understanding of cultural conversations as collective practice under social and political conditions as long as the myth of a complete world reigns supreme.

Therefore, a rediscovery of Pragmatism as a potential theoretical structure that accommodates notions of culture, communication and democracy and provides a theory of social communication also offers a convenient explanation for the importance of the field, particularly when such a development fails to reassess original texts under the historical conditions of specific social, economic and political processes in contemporary society.

The direction of communication research in the United States may also have been determined by a clash between classical ideas about society as the site of the struggle of modernity and the rise of individualism and rationality, and the knowledge about new media technologies that were capable of manipulating democracy and redefining the meaning of modern society. For instance, when the potential of destroying or severely changing a traditional attachment to the rationality of a print-oriented culture converts communication research to a site of intellectual and emotional struggle, fostering an atmosphere of rejection, skepticism or disbelief, the result is a distorted vision of the social and political potential of the new media that prevents inquiries into innovative alternatives for creating favorable conditions for a participatory society. Although second-generation scholarship, generated by individuals brought up in an age of Cultural Studies when questions of culture and cultural practice may replace the classical sociology of the mass media, could provide a more realistic (personal or experiential) view of the media in the lives of people by reintroducing or restoring emancipatory powers to the individual, attachments to the past and political power of academic establishments are difficult to resist. In any event, the field of communication and media research in the United States has yet to confront its own history and to redefine its position in the context of a larger culture, taking into account the consequences of cooptation by the conditions of elite pluralism.

Marxist thought about communication and media in the United States, on the other hand, is indebted to a European tradition of social criticism that relies on structural conflicts or diverse cultural orientations, which have emerged from the historical changes in postwar Europe and the specific social and political conditions in Britain, France or Germany, for instance. When the ideas of Western Marxism reached the United States, particularly since the 1960s, communication and media scholarship that was receptive to these ideas seemed to ignore or turn away from the experience of social criticism and radical thought in the United States and a tradition that had grown out of a direct reaction to the social and economic problems of the working class.

The social history of the United States suggests that radical, socialist ideas have failed to inspire most Americans, including communication and media scientists, since notions of cooperation and community have retained their power as signifiers of contemporary culture. Searching for the reasons of such development, Schroyer asked, "Can it be that 'socialism' or its moral equivalent, is actually contained within the utopian concept of 'Americanism' itself?" (1985: 284). Indeed, the idea of Americanism as "substitute" socialism had been an intriguing possibility for Leon Samson, who observed that

> Mass as a substitute for class, as the abstract, attenuated, conceptualized, spiritualized, in a word, orientalized version – or rather inversion – of the Marxian by the Whitmanesque has served to lend to American life and thought a distinctive proletarian flavor, and at the very same time and by the very same token to dry up the bloodstream of proletarian thought and struggle at its very source.
>
> (1974: 435)

Nevertheless, the experience of the 1920s and 1930s provides a wide spectrum of radical dissent and the willingness to redress the ills of American capitalism, e.g., poverty and a loss of social identity. The need for reliable information and the distrust of government and the press as sources and resources of social communication led to the rise of a documentary spirit that included progressive ideas and Marxist critiques of society. Stott has discussed the production of evidence about the conditions of existence in a variety of styles and through various media, presenting the diversity and the emotional richness of participation and illustrating the potential of a radical critique (1973).

There are several reasonable explanations for the failure of communication research to build on this tradition: a lack of historical grounding and the identification of the field with the ahistorical nature of social science research; a temptation to conform to intellectual fads concerning the treatment of new ideas about the role of communication and culture; and a psychological detachment from the failures of the past that has led to an inability to relate to the experiences of American radicalism that emerged from real-life conditions, and to build upon such work with an understanding of the nature of historical knowledge and its explanatory power. In addition, there remains a tendency in contemporary critical communication scholarship to be caught up in itself, that is, in a contemplation of ideological differences as a self-serving, isolating academic exercise, while failing to consider the political consequences of Marxism and, therefore, missing opportunities for reconceptualizing media research or the writing of media history under real social and economic conditions.

In addition, contemporary critics of communication and media theories have tended to embrace an analytical perspective that reduced media to a "site" within a myriad of cultural practices. They have found support in an intellectual tradition of social criticism that operates in its own history and responds to its own concrete political conditions that do not prevail in the United States. In fact, European thought in its latest neo-Marxist form "continues to lead the way to the problems and the problematization of American mass culture" (Hardt, 1988: 108). It is introduced through interdisciplinary excursions into the realm of culture and communication that also threaten to infringe upon the traditional sphere of communication research.

For instance, when American literary criticism benefits from the work of Frederic Jameson, who brought "political questions back to the discipline" (Buhle, 1987: 271), the theoretical discourse in communication and media studies is, at best, marginally involved through the work of individuals whose interdisciplinary orientations produce insights into larger theoretical issues involving semiotics, structuralism, and the demise of modernism.

Indeed, the interdisciplinary consideration of communication, the acknowledgment of semiotics, the rediscovery of the importance of language as a philosophical concern, and an ever-widening search for the meaning of popular culture may signal an end to "mass communication research" *per se*. Instead, communication and media as a particular manifestation of social communication have evolved as effective and appropriate contexts for a study of society and the development of social theories from a variety of cultural, political and economic perspectives.

Throughout the history of ideas about the nature of society and the role of communication in the emergence of a modern culture, social thinkers have turned their attention to the problem of democracy. However, there are ideological differences in their efforts to produce a sense of democracy, based upon specific considerations of language, communication and community as prerequisite conditions for democratic practice. Thus, when Pragmatist and reformist writers define the social idea of democracy in terms of communication as a binding force in society, they rely on assumptions about the potential ability of individuals to participate in society and the quality of discourse that reflect an almost mythical belief in the spirit of community. Dewey's ideal of democracy is not only "a way of life," but an environment "which provides a moral standard for personal conduct" (1963: 130).

These writers also share an understanding of the role of experts in shaping social and political agendas in light of the identification of science with the goals of democracy. The liberal-pluralist analysis of communication in contemporary society relates problems of democracy to political and economic issues of freedom of inquiry and dissemination of information within a commodity culture. The result is a critique of specific conditions that tends to reinforce established social or political institutions and the ideology of the marketplace with its appeals to corrective rather than disruptive action. Consequently, "communication revolutions" in American cultural history typically refer to scientific progress and the technological benefits of expanding markets rather than to a liberation of communication from the interests of the dominant system.

On the other hand, Marxist considerations of communication focus on the social or cultural conditions of individuals as members of working-class or middle-class cultures. The problem of democracy and, indeed, of community, is its identification with the discourse of the market and its dependence on the language of consumption. As long as social harmony is defined in terms of the relationship between supply and demand, and individual happiness is measured by the gratification of a need to possess and to consume, communication is reduced to a process of acquiring a sense of existence. From a Marxist perspective, the idea of democracy is an emerging practice grounded in the ability of people to share their experiences through communication and under conditions of freedom from domination and manipulation by specific economic or political interests. Such a perspective recognizes the centrality of communication in the historical processes of alienation and emancipation, and regards the achievement of communicative competency as a prerequisite condition of democratic practice. Social communication and its institutionalization in cultural, economic and political contexts, that is, the participation of individuals, the creation of a public sphere, and the relationship between individuals and media, are the constituents of a Marxist discourse about the future of democracy.

And finally, there are other considerations that indicate a still different level of concern. The designation of culture – with its political and economic aspects – as the appropriate context for communication and media studies raises questions about the evolution of a Marxist perspective that emerges from a confrontation with the history of social criticism in the United States. They include the possibility of recognizing contemporary leftist social criticism as a continuation of an earlier tradition, the need to reconcile the ambitions of intellectuals with the importance of political practice, and the problem of defining the relationship between intellectual and social responsibility.

It is ironic that the preoccupation of American intellectuals with an analysis of popular cultures has created explanations about contemporary society that remain inaccessible to people and therefore tend to lose their political potential. The reduction to jargon and theologies seems an inescapable consequence of real or imagined organizational power.

Buhle, for example, noted the failure of recent critiques of traditional social science practice, suggesting that the

> tardy growth of cultural studies . . . seems to have yielded a theology of its own, as impenetrable to the uninitiated as the most exotic religious text and as precious to the initiates. This latter development has not been either democratic or particularly fruitful in any broader theoretical terms
>
> (1987: 272)

In either case, intellectual responsibility is discharged as an exercise in power over developing and sharing instrumental knowledge. Consequently, charges of intellectual elitism may further help isolate theoretical discourse from common, everyday existence and those who feel committed to the implementation of political alternatives.

Nevertheless, American cultural studies as envisioned by Carey, for example, or as executed by those working in a Marxist tradition, combines into a persistent and powerful, if not persuasive, reminder of the need to participate in the intellectual debates that are dominating the cultural and political discourse. The literature of communication theory and research in the United States has been void of any sustained participation in these debates that seem to have pushed the field (since the 1970s) into undesirable intellectual isolation.

The limitations of the field as a social-scientific endeavor were recently confirmed by So, who concluded that communication as a subfield, or as a field with lesser status than other social-scientific disciplines, operates with an "'in-born' constraint" and may be limited in its development (1988: 253). While the reasons for such a condition may involve the strength of other disciplines, particularly psychology and sociology, the lack of a vigorous exchange of ideas across disciplinary boundaries may also prove disastrous for the field. The results are already evident with a shifting emphasis to the scholarship in literary criticism, comparative literature, feminist studies and other linguistic or ethnic interests as sources of Cultural Studies and loci of a contemporary discourse about media and communication.

The significance of interdisciplinary work and collaborative activities was addressed several years ago by Lucien Goldmann, who suggested that

> Those who will want to defend the humanist tradition, as well as the development of personal character and of the real intellectual level, must recognize that today the different aspects of the human problematic are more inseparable than ever before. Thus they gain nothing by acting in their own domain alone, because their action will be ineffective if it is not integrated into an overall struggle.
>
> (1976: 50)

Although recent contributions in major communication journals, like *Critical Studies in Mass Communication* or *Journal of Communication*, are evidence of a new sensitivity toward incorporating debates on culture and communication as legitimate concerns of communication and media scholarship, editors of scholarly journals and national organizations should encourage interdisciplinary inquiries by redefining their mission as professional gatekeepers of their fields. With new journals entering the arena of Cultural Studies, and critical assessments of classical mass communication sociology becoming a professional ritual of sorts, traditional outlets for (mass) communication scholarship are challenged to reflect theoretical debates and methodological controversies to protect their claims as premier journals in the field.

Such conclusions shift the problematic of cultural concerns to the role of intellectuals, their allegiance to the interests of specific groups or classes in contemporary society, and their educational responsibilities; they also raise questions of legitimation and emphasize the importance of a moral grounding of critical discourse.

Under the leadership of American Pragmatism, social theorists had focused upon the importance of culture and the idea that communication as a life process leads to democratic practice. This conclusion constituted the beginning of a critical position in social science theory and research within a liberal-pluralist tradition. When the Frankfurt School offered a comprehensive modernist view of the cultural and political crisis of Western society, its Critical Theory found a modest and eclectic response among communication and media scholars in the United States. The success of British Cultural Studies at this time has been a reminder that a cultural approach to the problems of communication and media has remained a consistent and recognized theme in the literature of the field.

There can be no doubt that the problems of communication, including the operation of the media, are imbedded in the history of a culture. For this reason, there is also an affinity with those communication studies in the United States which have had a strong cultural tradition. After all, the idea of culture and society in the context of communication and media research in the United States is defined through its assimilation of nineteenth-century European social thought into American practice; that is to say, by the effects of Pragmatism on the development of academic disciplines and their particular social concerns. Thus, the evolutionary concept of society with its own social dynamic, the emphasis upon social forces, and the recognition that individuals may need the assistance and protection of the state in their encounters with the modern world, were not only characteristics of the German historical school or of nineteenth-century European socialism, they also described the theoretical thrust of American political economy after the turn of this century. Pragmatism added a dynamic vision of the new world to this perspective and provided the social context for the study of media and communication.

Consequently, (mass) communication studies rose to academic prominence and political importance with the recognition of commercial and political propaganda as essential aspects of mass persuasion *vis-à-vis* an increasing need for the mediation of knowledge in complex urban societies. But the cultural approach of the field also shared the basic tenets of the social sciences of the time, namely the belief in a world that is knowable through the application of scientific techniques that stressed the plurality and equality of facts, through the belief in the objectivity of expert observations and the power of empirical explanations. "Mass" communication was treated as a series of specific, isolated social phenomena, which resulted in a narrow understanding of communication and culture and in a conduct of media studies that lacked historicity.

This approach to communication and culture in the United States depended upon a firm belief in a utopian model of society. It was based upon a vision of consensual participation as democratic practice and an understanding of the exercise of political and economic power as acts of progressive intervention in the advancement of people.

Radical dissent, including Marxist criticism of American society, remained outside the mainstream of communication research. When it arose, it belonged to the literature of social criticism rooted in rhetorical studies, literature, political economy and sociology, in particular, from where it was unable to engage the field in an extensive and prolonged debate concerning the foundations of social theory and the false optimism of social inquiries into the role and function of communication and media.

At the same time, the enthusiasm for an alternative explanation of communication in society, if sustained, cannot rest upon the good will toward Cultural Studies and a calculated indifference toward the dominant interpretation of the social structure. Instead, a commitment to a critical approach, in the sense of a Marxist critique of society, will lead to a number of significant changes in the definition of society, social problems and the media, as well as in the organization and execution of research projects. They are changes rooted in radical ideas, uncompromising in their demands for rethinking the theoretical basis of (mass) communication studies and innovative in their creation of appropriate methodologies. Thus, Cultural Studies, not unlike radical sociology of the late 1960s and early 1970s, "finds itself providing the facts, theories, and understandings that a radical politics requires for its implementation" (Becker and Horowitz, 1972: 54). It also reflects the emancipatory power of a social theory that is grounded in the potential of individuals to rise beyond their social and economic conditions. Since the traditional literature of communication theory and research restricts the imagination by its refusal to engage in critical reflections on human ideals as normative (or unscientific) issues and by its denial of the historical process in the presentation of communication phenomena, it must be replaced by an emancipatory social theory, which locates the inquiry about communication in the realm of the ideological and explains the role of communication and the place of the media through an examination of the cultural process. The arrival of a feminist critique, both in Cultural Studies, where feminism played a major role, and in the American social studies environment, including media studies, offers such an opportunity. This is particularly true when feminists begin to question the received critical social theories, ranging from Critical Theory to Cultural Studies and poststructuralist arguments. Such a challenge is a reminder of the role of skepticism in the confrontation with new ideas and is not restricted to a feminist position. Thus, when Robin West concludes that skepticism "towards particular claims of objective truth, a particular account of the self, and any particular account of gender, sexuality, biology or what is or is not natural, is absolutely necessary to a healthy and modern feminism," her statement applies to the theoretical and practical approaches to understanding and coping with everyday life (1989: 96–7).

The result of rethinking communication theory and practice in these ways will be a reconceptualization of disciplinary and administrative boundaries, which has theoretical as well as political implications for the definition of a field, in which culture as a way of life will become the framework for an interpretation of communication in society.

Similarly, Robert Sklar argued over fifteen years ago that American Studies, by turning to the works of Roland Barthes, E.P. Thompson, Eric Hobsbawm, Antonio Gramsci, Theodor Adorno, Walter Benjamin, Raymond Williams and George Lukács, would discover "an untapped powerful resource for the essential task of linking the forms of consciousness and expression with the forms of social organization" (1975: 260–1).

But the "discovery" of Cultural Studies through the exposure to a specific type of media studies in Britain, and the current preoccupation with "critical" research should not obscure the fact that there is no history of a systematic acknowledgment of Marxist scholarship by traditional communication research in the United States. Indeed, its success still rests on the old question of how socialism as a "foreign" idea fits the peculiar nature of American society, particularly after the experiences of American radicalism since the 1920s, which Christopher Lasch has characterized as "sectarianism, marginality, and alienation from American life" (1969: 40), and of what happens when Marxism becomes Americanized.

Subsequently, the reception of individual Marxist scholars throughout various periods by mainstream communication research has remained questionable, and their influence upon the development of the field has continued to be negligible. In general, communication studies have followed the path of American social science in the rejection of a critical Marxist approach to questions of media and society. In light of these experiences and the history of social criticism and radical critique in the field, the Cultural Studies perspective remains a temporary phenomenon, while the notion of "critical" research will be defined by and identified with "liberal" communication scholarship and its own critical position *vis-à-vis* society.

Indeed, there is always a chance for the return of the "critical" as an accommodation of liberal dissent, while Marxist thought retreats again into the shadow of the dominant ideology. In any case, British Cultural Studies as a cultural phenomenon holds its own interpretation; its language and practice are contained in the specific historical moment, which may be accessible to American communication research, but it cannot be appropriated, adapted or coopted without losing its meaning.

The dilemma of American communication studies continues to lie in its failure to comprehend and overcome the limitations of its own intellectual history, not only by failing to address the theoretical and methodological problems of an established academic discipline, but also by failing to recognize the potential of radical thought.

Notes and references

1 ON DEFINING THE ISSUES: COMMUNICATION, HISTORY AND THEORY

References

Anderson, Perry (1983). *In the Tracks of Historical Materialism*. London: Verso.

Berger, Peter L. and Thomas Luckmann (1966). *The Social Construction of Reality: A Treatise in the Sociology of Knowledge*. New York: Doubleday.

Brown, Roger L. (1970). "Approaches to the Historical Development of Mass Media Studies," in Jeremy Tunstall, ed. *Media Sociology*. Urbana: University of Illinois Press, 41–57.

Chaffee, Steven and John L. Hochheimer (1985). "The Beginnings of Political Communication Research in the United States: Origins of the Limited Effects Model," in Everett M. Rogers and Francis Balle, eds *The Media Revolution in America and Western Europe*. Norwood, NJ: Ablex, 267–96.

Craig, Robert T. (1989). "Communication as a Practical Discipline," in Brenda Dervin, Lawrence Grossberg, Barbara J. O'Keefe, Ellen Wartella, eds *Rethinking Communication*, Volume 1: *Paradigm Issues*. Newbury Park, CA: Sage, 97–122.

DeFleur, Melvin L. and Sandra Ball-Rokeach (1989). *Theories of Mass Communication*. New York: Longman.

Delia, Jesse G. (1987). "Communication Research: A History," in Charles E. Berger and Steve H. Chaffee, eds *Handbook of Communication Science*. Newbury Park, CA: Sage, 20–98.

Dervin, Brenda, Lawrence Grossberg, Barbara J. O'Keefe, Ellen Wartella, eds (1989). *Rethinking Communication*. 2 Volumes: *Paradigm Issues* and *Paradigm Exemplars*. Newbury Park, CA: Sage.

Dilthey, Wilhelm (1962). *Pattern and Meaning in History: Thoughts on History and Society*, edited and introduced by H. P. Rickman. New York: Harper & Row.

Fox-Genovese, Elizabeth (1989). "Literary Criticism and the Politics of the New Historicism," in H. Aram Veeser, ed. *The New Historicism*. New York: Routledge, 213–24.

Fox-Genovese, Elizabeth and Eugene D. Genovese (1976–7). "The Political Crisis of Social History: A Marxian Perspective," in *Journal of Social History* 10 (2), 205–19.

Gerbner, George (1962). "On Defining Communication: Still Another View," in *Journal of Communication* 16 (2), 99–103.

Giddens, Anthony (1989). "The Orthodox Consensus and the Emerging Synthesis," in Brenda Dervin, Lawrence Grossberg, Barbara J. O'Keefe, Ellen Wartella, eds *Rethinking Communication*, Volume 1: *Paradigm Issues*. Newbury Park, CA: Sage, 63–5.

——(1981). *A Contemporary Critique of Historical Materialism*, Volume 1: *Power, Property and the State*. Berkeley: University of California Press.

——(1979). *Central Problems in Social Theory: Action, Structure and Contradiction in Social Analysis*. Berkeley: University of California Press.

Gouldner, Alvin W. (1979). *The Future of Intellectuals and the Rise of the New Class*. New York: Continuum.

——(1970). *The Coming Crisis of Western Sociology*. New York: Basic Books.

Hawthorn, Geoffrey (1976). *Enlightenment and Despair: A History of Sociology*. Cambridge: Cambridge University Press.

Heidegger, Martin (1961). *An Introduction to Metaphysics*. Garden City, NY: Doubleday Anchor Books.

Henretta, James A. (1979). "Social History as Lived and Written," in *American Historical Review* 84 (5), 1293–322.

Heyer, Paul (1988). *Communications and History: Theories of Media, Knowledge, and Civilization*. New York: Greenwood Press.

Hobsbawm, Eric J. (1971). "From Social History to the History of Society," in *Daedalus* 100 (1), 20–43.

Horkheimer, Max (1972). *Critical Theory: Selected Essays*. New York: Herder and Herder.

Jones, Gareth Stedman (1972). "History: The Poverty of Empiricism," in Robin Blackburn, ed. *Ideology in Social Science: Readings in Critical Social Theory*. New York: Pantheon Books, 96–115.

Journal of Communication (1983) 33 (3). "Ferment in the Field."

Katz, Elihu (1987). "Communication Research Since Lazarsfeld," in *Public Opinion Quarterly* 51 Supplement, 25–45.

Kline, Gerald F. (1972). "Theory in Mass Communication Research," in Gerald F. Kline and Phil Tichenor, eds *Current Perspectives in Mass Communication Research*. Beverly Hills, CA: Sage, 17–40.

Lang, Kurt (1979). "The Critical Functions of Empirical Communication Research: Observations on German–American Influences," in *Media, Culture and Society* 1, 83–96.

McQuail, Denis (1987). *Mass Communication Theory: An Introduction*. Beverly Hills, CA: Sage.

Marvin, Carolyn (1989). "Experts, Black Boxes, and Artifacts: New

Allegories for the History of the Electronic Media," in Brenda Dervin, Lawrence Grossberg, Barbara J. O'Keefe, Ellen Wartella, eds *Rethinking Communication*, Volume 2: *Paradigm Exemplars*. Newbury Park, CA: Sage, 188–98.

Marx, Karl and Friedrich Engels (1947). *The German Ideology*, Parts I and III. New York: International Publishers.

Meltzer, Bernard N., John W. Petras and Larry T. Reynolds (1975). *Symbolic Interactionism: Genesis, Varieties and Criticism*. London: Routledge & Kegan Paul.

Mills, C. Wright (1959). *The Sociological Imagination*. New York: Oxford University Press.

Morrison, David (1978). "The Beginnings of Modern Mass Communication Research," in *European Journal of Sociology* 19 (2) 347–59.

Parsons, Talcott (1964). "Evolutionary Universals in Society," in *American Sociological Review* 29 (3), 339–57.

Robinson, Gertrude J. (1988). "'Here be Dragons': Problems in Charting the US History of Communication Studies," in *Communication* 10, 97–119.

Runciman, Walter G. (1983). *A Treatise on Social Theory: The Problem of Social Reality*, Volume I. Cambridge: Cambridge University Press.

Schutz, Alfred (1962). *Collected Papers*, Volume 1. The Hague: Nijhoff.

Shaskolsky, Leon (1970). "The Development of Sociological Theory in America – a Sociology of Knowledge Interpretation," in Larry T. Reynolds and Janice M. Reynolds, eds *The Sociology of Sociology*. New York: McKay, 6–30.

Stearns, Peter N. (1985). "Social History and History: A Progress Report," in *Journal of Social History* 19 (Winter), 319–34.

Thomas, Sari (1989). "Functionalism Revised and Applied to Mass Communication Study," in Brenda Dervin, Lawrence Grossberg, Barbara J. O'Keefe, Ellen Wartella, eds *Rethinking Communication*, Volume 2: *Paradigm Exemplars*. Newbury Park, CA: Sage, 376–96.

Todorov, Tzvetan (1984). *Mikhail Bakhtin: The Dialogical Principle*. Minneapolis: University of Minnesota Press.

Veeser, H. Aram, ed. (1989). *The New Historicism*. New York: Routledge.

Wartella, Ellen and Byron Reeves (1985). "Historical Trends in Research on Children and the Media: 1900–1960," in *Journal of Communication* 35 (2), 118–33.

White, David Manning (1964). "Mass Communication Research: A View in Perspective," in Lewis A. Dexter and David M. White, *People, Society and Mass Communications*. New York: Free Press, 521–46.

Williams, Raymond (1981). *Human Communication and its History*. London: Thames & Hudson.

——(1977). *Marxism and Literature*. New York: Oxford University Press.

Wright, Charles R. (1975). *Mass Communication: A Sociological Perspective*. New York: Random House.

2 ON DISCOVERING COMMUNICATION: PRAGMATISM AND THE PURSUIT OF SOCIAL CRITICISM

References

Aaron, Daniel (1965). *Writers on the Left*. New York: Avon Books.

Albig, William (1957). "Two Decades of Opinion Study: 1936–1956," in *Public Opinion Quarterly* 21 (1), 15–22.

Apel, Karl-Otto (1973). *Transformation der Philosophie*, Volume II: *Das Apriori der Kommunikationsgemeinschaft*. Frankfurt: Suhrkamp.

Beard, Charles A. (1935). "The Social Sciences in the United States," in *Zeitschrift für Sozialforschung* 4 (1), 61–5.

——(1914). *Contemporary American History, 1877–1913*. New York: Macmillan.

Bellamy, Edward (1888). *Looking Backward*, edited by John L. Thomas. Cambridge, MA: Harvard University Press, 1967.

Bernstein, Richard J. (1971). *Praxis and Action: Contemporary Philosophies of Human Activity*. Philadelphia: University of Pennsylvania Press.

——(1967). *John Dewey*. New York: Washington Square Press.

Brown, Lee (1974). *The Reluctant Reformation: On Criticizing the Press in America*. New York: McKay.

Buhle, Paul (1987). *Marxism in the United States: Remapping the History of the American Left*. London: Verso.

Commager, Henry Steele, ed. (1967). *Lester Ward and the Welfare State*. Indianapolis: Bobbs-Merrill.

Commission on Freedom of the Press (1947). *A Free and Responsible Press*. Chicago: University of Chicago Press.

Cooley, Charles Horton (1918). *Social Process*. New York: Charles Scribner's Sons.

——(1909). *Social Organization: A Study of the Larger Mind*. New York: Charles Scribner's Sons.

——(1902). *Human Nature and the Social Order*. New York: Charles Scribner's Sons.

Dewey, John (1939). *Freedom and Culture*. New York: Capricorn Books.

——(1935). *Liberalism and Social Action*. New York: Capricorn Books.

——(1934). *Art as Experience*. New York: Putman's Sons.

——(1931). *Philosophy and Civilization*. New York: Minton, Balch & Co.

——(1930). *Individualism Old and New*. New York: Minton, Balch & Co.

——(1929). *The Quest for Certainty*. New York: Minton, Balch & Co.

——(1927). *The Public and Its Problems*. Chicago: Swallow Press.

——(1925). *Experience and Nature*. Chicago: Open Court Publishing Co.

——(1917). *Creative Intelligence: Essays in the Pragmatic Attitude*. New York: Henry Holt & Co.

——(1916). *Democracy and Education*. New York: Macmillan.

Duncan, Hugh Dalziel (1969). *Symbols and Social Theory*. New York: Oxford University Press.

Fenton, Frances (1910–11). "The Influence of Newspaper Presentations upon the Growth of Crime and other Anti-Social Activity," in *American Journal of Sociology* 16 (3), 342–71, and 16 (4), 538–64.

Freeden, Michael (1978). *The New Liberalism: An Ideology of Social Reform*. Oxford: Clarendon Press.

Gallie, W. B. (1966). *Peirce and Pragmatism*. New York: Dover.

George, Henry (n.d.) *Progress and Poverty*. New York: Modern Library.

Gouldner, Alvin W. (1976). *The Dialectic of Ideology and Technology: The Origins, Grammar, and Future of Ideology*. New York: The Seabury Press.

Habermas, Jürgen (1979). *Communication and the Evolution of Society*. Boston: Beacon Press.

Hardt, Hanno (1987). "Communication and Economic Thought: Cultural Imagination in German and American Scholarship," in *Communication* 10, 141–63.

——(1979). *Social Theories of the Press: Early German and American Perspectives*. Beverly Hills, CA: Sage.

Haskell, Thomas (1977). *The Emergence of Professional Social Science*. Urbana: University of Illinois Press.

Heidegger, Martin (1971). *Poetry, Language, Thought*. New York: Harper & Row.

Horowitz, Irving Louis (1964). "The Intellectual Genesis of C. Wright Mills," in C. Wright Mills, *Sociology and Pragmatism: The Higher Learning in America*. New York: Oxford University Press, 11–31.

James, Henry, ed. (1920). *The Letters of William James*, Volume 2. Boston: The Atlantic Monthly Press.

James, William (1970a). "What Pragmatism Means," in H. S. Thayer, ed. *Pragmatism: The Classic Writings*. New York: Mentor Books, 209–26.

——(1970b). "An Interview – Pragmatism – What It Is," in H. S. Thayer, ed. *Pragmatism: The Classic Writings*. New York: Mentor Books, 131–4.

——(1970c). "The Will to Believe," in H. S. Thayer, ed. *Pragmatism: The Classic Writings*. New York: Mentor Books, 186–208.

——(1963). *Pragmatism and Four Essays from the Meaning of Truth*. Cleveland: Meridian Books.

——(1909). *The Meaning of Truth*. New York: Longmans, Green & Co.

Lippmann, Walter (1922). *Public Opinion*. New York: Harcourt, Brace.

——(1920). *Liberty and the News*. New York: Macmillan.

Lloyd, Henry Demarest (1894). *Wealth Against Commonwealth*. New York: Harper & Brothers.

McIntyre, Jerilyn S. (1987). "Repositioning A Landmark: The Hutchins Commission on Freedom of the Press," in *Critical Studies in Mass Communication* 4 (2), 136–60.

Matthews, Fred H. (1977). *Quest for an American Sociology: Robert E. Park and the Chicago School*. Montreal: McGill-Queens University Press.

Mead, George Herbert (1967). *Mind, Self and Society*. Chicago: University of Chicago Press.

——(1964). *On Social Psychology*, edited by Anselm Strauss. Chicago: University of Chicago Press.

——(1936). *Movements of Thought in the Nineteenth Century*. Chicago: University of Chicago Press.

——(1907). "Review of Jane Addams's *The Newer Ideals of Peace*," in *American Journal of Sociology* 13 (1), 121–8.

Mills, C. Wright (1964). *Sociology and Pragmatism: The Higher Learning in America*. New York: Oxford University Press.

——(1943). "The Professional Ideology of Social Pathologists," in *American Journal of Sociology* 49 (2), 165–80.

Niebuhr, Reinhold (1932). *Moral Man and Immoral Society*. New York: Charles Scribner's Sons.

Novack, George Edward (1975). *Pragmatism versus Marxism: An Appraisal of John Dewey's Philosophy*. New York: Pathfinder Press.

Oberschall, Anthony, ed. (1972). *The Establishment of Empirical Sociology*. New York: Harper & Row.

Ogburn, William F. (1964). "Trends in Social Science," in Otis Dudley Duncan, ed. *William F. Ogburn on Culture and Social Change*. Chicago: University of Chicago Press, 207–20.

Park, Robert (1967). "Foreign Language Press and Social Progress," in Ralph H. Turner, ed. *Robert E. Park on Social Control and Collective Behavior*. Chicago: University of Chicago Press, 133–44.

——(1938). "Reflections on Communication and Culture," in *American Journal of Sociology*, 44 (2), 187–205.

——(1923). "The Natural History of the Newspaper," in *American Journal of Sociology* 29 (3), 273–89.

Patten, Simon Nelson (1924). *Essays in Economic Theory*, edited by Rexford G. Tugwell. New York: Alfred A. Knopf.

Peirce, Charles Sanders (1935). *Collected Papers of Charles Sanders Peirce*, Volume 6, edited by Charles Hartshorne and Paul Weiss. Cambridge, MA: Harvard University Press.

——(1934). *Collected Papers of Charles Sanders Peirce*, Volume 5, edited by Charles Hartshorne and Paul Weiss. Cambridge, MA: Harvard University Press.

——(1931). *Collected Papers of Charles Sanders Peirce*, Volume 1, edited by Charles Hartshorne and Paul Weiss. Cambridge, MA: Harvard University Press.

Perry, Ralph Barton (1948). *The Thought and Character of William James*. Cambridge, MA: Harvard University Press.

——(1935). *The Thought and Character of William James*. Boston: Little, Brown.

——(1916). *Present Philosophical Tendencies*. New York: Longmans, Green & Co.

Peters, John Durham (1989). "Satan and Savior: Mass Communication in Progressive Thought," in *Critical Studies in Mass Communication* 6, 247–63.

Quandt, Jean B. (1970). *From the Small Town to the Great Community*. New Brunswick: Rutgers University Press.

Riesman, David (1953). *Thorstein Veblen: A Critical Interpretation*. New York: Seabury Press.

Ross, Edward A. (1938). *Principles of Sociology*. New York: D. Appleton-Century.

——(1918). "Social Decadence," in *American Journal of Sociology* 23 (5), 620–32.

——(1910). "The Suppression of Important News," in *Atlantic Monthly* (March), 303–11.

——(1907). *Sin and Society: An Analysis of Latter-Day Iniquity*. New York: Houghton, Mifflin.

——(1901). *Social Control*. New York: Macmillan.

Samson, Leon (1933). *Toward a United Front: A Philosophy for American Workers*. New York: Farrar & Rinehart.

Schroyer, Trent (1975). "The Re-politicization of the Relations of Production: An Interpretation of Jürgen Habermas' Analytic Theory of Late Capitalist Development," in *New German Critique* 5 (Spring), 107–28.

Seldes, George (1938). *Lords of the Press*. New York: Julian Messner.

Shalin, Dmitri N. (1988). "G. H. Mead, Socialism, and the Progressive Agenda," in *American Journal of Sociology* 93 (4), 913–51.

Sinclair, Upton (1919). *The Brass Check: A Study of American Journalism*. Published by the author.

Small, Albion (1912). "General Sociology," in *American Journal of Sociology* 18 (2), 200–14.

——(1910). *The Meaning of Social Science*. Chicago: University of Chicago Press.

Small, Albion and George Vincent (1894). *An Introduction to the Study of Society*. New York: American Book.

Summer, W. G. (1906). *Folkways: A Study of the Sociological Importance of Usage, Manners, Customs, and Morals*. Boston: Ginn.

Thayer, H. S. (1973). *Meaning and Action: A Study of American Pragmatism*. Indianapolis: Bobbs-Merrill.

Thomas, John L. (1983). *Alternative America: Henry George, Edward Bellamy, Henry Demarest Lloyd and the Adversary Tradition*. Cambridge, MA: Harvard University Press.

Veblen, Thorstein (1899). *The Theory of the Leisure Class: An Economic Study of Institutions*. New York: Macmillan.

Villard, Oswald Garrison (1923). *Some Newspapers and Newspaper-Men*. New York: Alfred A. Knopf.

Vincent, George (1905). "A Laboratory Experiment in Journalism," in *American Journal of Sociology* 11 (3), 297–311.

White, Morton (1949). *Social Thought in America: The Revolt against Formalism*. New York: Viking Press.

Whitehead, Alfred North (1968). *Modes of Thought*. New York: The Free Press.

Yarros, Victor S. (1916). "A Neglected Opportunity and Duty in Journalism," in *American Journal of Sociology* 22 (2), 203–11.

——(1899). "The Press and Public Opinion," in *American Journal of Sociology* 5 (3), 372–82.

3 ON IGNORING HISTORY: MASS COMMUNICATION RESEARCH AND THE CRITIQUE OF SOCIETY

Notes

(The following listings reflect the selection of authors included in these initial collections of readings (see p.91); they are reproduced in the order of their appearance in the respective books; information in parentheses refers to university or business affiliations of the individuals as provided by the editors of the volumes.)

1 The contributors included (in the order of their presentations): Fred S. Siebert (Illinois), Charles V. Kinter (Shaw, Isham & Co.), Raymond B. Nixon (Emory), Carl Hovland (Yale), Edgar Dale (Ohio State), Leo Lowenthal (Columbia), Ralph O. Nafziger (Minnesota), Elmo C. Wilson (International Public Opinion Research, Inc.), Hugh M. Belville, Jr. (NBC), John E. Ivey, Jr. (North Carolina Institute for Research in Social Science), Clyde Hart (National Opinion Research Center), Bernard Berelson (Chicago), Paul Lazarsfeld (Columbia), Ralph D. Casey (Minnesota), Robert J. Blakely (Des Moines *Register and Tribune*).

2 The contributors included in alphabetical order: James M. Clarke (Editor-in-Charge, Readability Laboratory), Joseph M. Goldsen (Nejelski & Co., Inc.), Lennox Grey (Columbia), Wendell Johnson (Iowa), Harold D. Lasswell (Yale), Paul F. Lazarsfeld (Columbia), Robert D. Leigh (Chicago), Irving Lorge (Columbia), Margaret Mead (American Museum of Natural History), Robert K. Merton (Columbia), Leo Nejelski (Nejelski & Co., Inc.), Whitney J. Oates (Princeton), Charles A. Siepmann (New York University).

3 The contributors included in the order of their presentation: Robert E. Park (Chicago), Terry Ramsaye (*Motion Picture Almanac/Motion Picture Herald*), Llewellyn White (Commission on Freedom of the Press), Robert D. Leigh (Commission on Freedom of the Press), Harold D. Lasswell (Yale), Edward P. Cheyney (Pennsylvania), Fred S. Siebert (Illinois), Ralph D. Casey (Minnesota), Raymond B. Nixon (Emory), Robert A. Brady (Berkeley), Neil H. Borden (Harvard), Charles V. Kinter (Shaw, Isham & Co.), Wendell Johnson (Iowa), Daniel Katz (Michigan), Margaret Mead (American Museum of Natural History), Hadley Cantril (Princeton), Gordon W. Allport (Harvard), Frank Luther Mott (Missouri), Martha Wolfenstein (Walden School, New York), Nathan Leites (UNESCO), Kenneth Baker (NAB), Rudolf Arnheim (Columbia), Patricke Johns-Heine (Wisconsin), Hans H. Gerth (Wisconsin), Rudolf Flesch (Columbia), Alfred McClung Lee, Elizabeth Briant Lee (authors, *The Fine Art of Propaganda*), Paul Lazarsfeld (Columbia), Patricia Kendall (Columbia), David M. White

(Boston), H. M. Belville, Jr. (NBC), Lester Asheim (Chicago), Walter Lippmann (author, *Public Opinion*), Douglas Waples (Chicago), Bernard Berelson (Chicago), Franklin R. Bradshaw (Chicago), Robert Merton (Columbia), Hazel Gaudet (Columbia), John Dollard (Yale), Louis Wirth (Chicago).

4 The contributors included in the order of their presentations (without their institutional affiliations): Paul A. Palmer, George Carslake Thompson, A. Lawrence Lowell, Harold D. Lasswell, Herbert Blumer, Daniel Katz, Walter Lippmann, Arthur W. Kornhauser, Hadley Cantril, Bruno Bettelheim, Morris Janowitz, Paul F. Lazarsfeld, Bernard Berelson, Hazel Gaudet, A. V. Dicey, Frank V. Cantwell, John C. Ranney, Charles H. Cooley, George Herbert Mead, Edward Sapir, Robert E. Park, Carl Hovland, Raymond Nixon, Llewellyn White, Donald Horton, Zechariah Chafee, R. H. Coase, Ernst Kris, Nathan Leites, Leo Lowenthal, Lester Asheim, T. W. Adorno, Helen M. Hughes, David Riesman, Reuel Denney, Douglas Waples, Herta Herzog, Robert Angell, Hans Speier, W. W. Charters, Edward Shils, W. Lloyd Warner, William Henry, Arthur A. Lumsdaine, Fred D. Sheffield.

5 The contributors included in the order of their presentations: Bernard Berelson (Ford Foundation), Katherine M. Wolfe (Columbia), Marjorie Fiske (Columbia), Herta Herzog (McCann-Erickson), Douglas Waples (Chicago), Franklyn R. Bradshaw (Chicago), Paul F. Lazarsfeld (Columbia), Patricia Kendall (Columbia), David M. White (Boston), Joseph T. Klapper (United States Information Agency), David Krech (California), Richard S. Crutchfield (Swarthmore), Leonard Doob (Yale), Gordon Allport (Harvard), Leo Postman (Indiana), Alexander H. Leighton (Cornell), Morris Edward Opler (Lucknow, India), Bruce L. Smith (Michigan State), Ralph K. White (United States Information Agency), William Buchanan, Hadley Cantril (Princeton), Eugene L. Hartley (Brokley College), Ruth E. Hartley (City College of New York), Clyde Hart (Chicago), Charles E. Osgood (Illinois), Percy H. Tannenbaum (Illinois), Carl I. Hovland (Yale), Arthur A. Lumsdaine (Chanute Laboratory, United States Air Force), Fred D. Sheffield (Yale), Walter Weiss (Boston), Herbert Blumer (Chicago), Eliot Freidson (Illinois), Matilda White Riley (American Sociological Society), John W. Riley, Jr. (Rutgers), Stanley K. Bigman (United States Information Agency), Robert K. Merton (Columbia), W. Phillips Davison (Rand Corporation), Alexander L. George (Rand Corporation), Hans Speier (Rand Corporation), Charles Y. Glock (Columbia), Daniel Lerner (MIT), Ernst Kris, Nathan Leites (UNESCO), Edward A. Shils (Chicago), Morris Janowitz (Michigan), Harold D. Lasswell (Yale), Philip Selznick (Rand Corporation).

6 The contributors included (in the order of their presentation): Alexis De Tocqueville, Walt Whitman, Jose Ortega y Gassett, Leo Lowenthal, Dwight MacDonald, Gilbert Seldes, Clement Greenberg, Frank Luther Mott, Bernard Berelson, Alan Dutscher, Cecil Hemley, Edmund Wilson, George Orwell, Charles J. Rolo, Christopher La

Farge, Leo Bogart, Robert Warshow, Lyle W. Shannon, Arthur J. Brodbeck, Patricke Johns-Heine, Hans H. Gerth, Patricia J. Salter, Siegfried Kracauer, Hortense Powdermaker, Martha Wolfenstein, Nathan Leites, Frederick Elkin, Herbert J. Gans, Eric Larrabee, David Riesman, Rolf B. Meyersohn, Gunther Anders, Henry Rabassiere, Murray Hausknecht, Kurt Lang, S. I. Hayakawa, Morroe Berger, Irving Crespi, Henry Popkin, Marshall McLuhan, Robert S. Albert, R. Alan Seeger, Paul F. Lazarsfeld, Robert K. Merton, T. W. Adorno, Irving Howe, Ernest van den Haag, Leslie A. Fiedler, Melvin Tumin.

7 The contributors included (in alphabetical order): Hannah Arendt (author), James Baldwin (author), Daniel Bell (Columbia), Arthur Berger (Brandeis), Alan Willard Brown (Metropolitan Educational TV Association), H. William Fitelson (attorney), Charles Frankel (Columbia), Nathan Glazer (sociologist), Ernest van den Haag (NYU), Oscar Handlin (Harvard), Patrick Hazard (Pennsylvania), Sidney Hook (NYU), Gerald Holton (Harvard), H. Stuart Hughes (Harvard), Stanley Edgar Hyman (Bennington College), Norman Jacobs (NYU), Randall Jarrell (North Carolina), Irving Kristol (editor), Paul Lazarsfeld (Columbia), Leo Lionni (*Fortune*), Leo Lowenthal (Berkeley), William Phillips (*Partisan Review*), Bernard Rosenberg (CCNY), Leo Rosten (*Look* magazine), Robert Saudek (TV producer), Arthur Schlesinger, Jr. (Harvard), Gilbert Seldes (Pennsylvania), Edward Shils (Chicago), Frank Stanton (CBS), James Johnson Sweeney (Solomon R. Guggenheim Museum), Melvin Tumin (Princeton).

References

Adorno, Theodor W. (1976). "Sociology and Empirical Research," in Theodor W. Adorno *et al.*, eds *The Positivist Dispute in German Sociology*. New York: Harper & Row, 68–86.

Albig, William (1957). "Two Decades of Opinion Study: 1936–1956," in *Public Opinion Quarterly* 21 (1), 15–22.

Bauer, Raymond (1959). "Comments," in *Public Opinion Quarterly* 23 (1), 14–17.

Berelson, Bernard (1959). "The State of Communication Research," in *Public Opinion Quarterly* 23 (1) (Spring), 1–5.

——(1952). *Content Analysis in Communication Research*. Glencoe, IL: Free Press.

Berelson, Bernard and Morris Janowitz, eds (1950). *Reader in Public Opinion and Communication*. Glencoe, IL: Free Press.

Bittner, John R. (1985). *Broadcasting and Telecommunication: An Introduction*. Englewood Cliffs, NJ: Prentice-Hall.

Blumer, Herbert (1939). "Collective Behavior," in Robert E. Park, ed. *An Outline of the Principles of Sociology*. New York: Barnes & Noble, 221–80.

Borchers, Detlef (1988). "Paul Lazarsfeld: A Marxist on Leave," in *Communication* 10 (2), 211–22.

Bryson, Lyman, ed. (1948). *The Communication of Ideas: A Series of Addresses*. New York: Harper & Row.

Cantril, Hadley (1941). *The Psychology of Social Movements*. New York: Wiley.

Cartier, Jacqueline (1988). "Wilbur Schramm: The Beginnings of American Communication Theory: A History of Ideas." Unpublished dissertation, University of Iowa.

DeFleur, Melvin L. and Sandra Ball-Rokeach (1989). *Theories of Mass Communication*, fifth edition. New York: Longman.

Eulau, Heinz (1969). "The Maddening Methods of Harold D. Lasswell: Some Philosophical Underpinnings," in Arnold A. Rogow, ed. *Politics, Personality, and Social Science in the Twentieth Century: Essays in Honor of Harold D. Lasswell*. Chicago: University of Chicago Press.

Festinger, Leon A. (1957). *A Theory of Cognitive Dissonance*. Evanston, IL: Row & Peterson.

Gans, Herbert J. (1972). "The Famine in American Mass Communication Research," in *American Journal of Sociology* 77 (4), 697–705.

Gerbner, George (1967). "Mass Media and Human Communication Theory," in Frank E. X. Dance, ed. *Human Communication Theory: Original Essays*. New York: Holt, Rinehart & Winston, 40–60.

——(1964). "On Content Analysis and Critical Research in Mass Communication," in Lewis Anthony Dexter and David Manning White, *People, Society and Mass Communication*. New York: Free Press of Glencoe, 476–500.

——(1958). "On Content Analysis and Critical Research in Mass Communication," in *Audio Visual Communication Review* 6 (2), 85–108.

——(1956). "Toward a General Model of Communication," in *Audio Visual Communication Review* 4 (3), 171–99.

Gitlin, Todd (1981). "Media Sociology: The Dominant Paradigm," in G. Cleveland Wilhoit and Harold de Bock, eds *Mass Communication Review Yearbook*, Volume 2. Beverly Hills, CA: Sage, 73–121; reprinted from *Theory and Society* 6 (2) (1978), 205–53.

Harris, Marvin (1979). *Cultural Materialism: The Struggle for a Science of Culture*. New York: Random House.

Heider, Fritz (1946). "Attitudes and Cognitive Information," in *Journal of Psychology* 21 (1), 107–12.

Horkheimer, Max (1941). "Introduction," in *Studies in Philosophy and Social Science* 9 (1), 1.

Horkheimer, Max and Theodor W. Adorno (1972). *Dialectics of Enlightenment*. New York: Herder & Herder.

Hovland, Carl I., Arthur A. Lumsdaine and Fred Sheffield (1949). *Experiments in Mass Communication*. Princeton: Princeton University Press.

Jacobs, Norman, ed. (1961). *Culture for the Millions? Mass Media in Modern Society*. New York: D. Van Nostrand; originally published in 1960 without the Lazarsfeld preface as a special issue, "Mass Culture and Mass Society," in *Daedalus* 89 (2).

Jameson, Frederic R. (1982). "The Symbolic Inference; or, Kenneth Burke and Ideological Analysis," in Hayden White and Margaret Brose, eds *Representing Kenneth Burke*. Baltimore, MD: Johns Hopkins University Press, 68–91.

Janowitz, Morris (1968). "Communication, Mass: The Study of Mass Communication," in David L. Sills, ed. *International Encyclopedia of the Social Sciences*, Volume 3. New York: Macmillan and Free Press, 41–53.

Johnson, F. Craig and George R. Klare (1961). "General Models of Communication Research: A Survey of the Developments of a Decade," in *Journal of Communication* 11 (1), 13–26.

Klapper, Joseph T. (1960) *The Effects of Mass Communication*. New York: Free Press.

——(1949). *The Effects of Mass Media: A Report to the Director of the Public Library Inquiry*. New York: Bureau of Applied Social Research, Columbia University. Mimeographed.

Kornhauser, William (1959). *The Politics of Mass Society*. New York: Free Press.

Lasswell, Harold D. (1972). "Communications Research and Public Policy," in *Public Opinion Quarterly* 36, 301–10.

——(1948). "The Structure and Function of Communication in Society," in Lyman Bryson, ed. *The Communication of Ideas*. New York: Harper & Row, 37–51.

——(1935). *World Politics and Personal Insecurity*. New York: McGraw-Hill.

Lasswell, Harold D., Nathan Leites *et al.* (1949). *Language of Politics: Studies in Quantitative Semantics*. New York: George W. Stewart.

Lazarsfeld, Paul F. (1969). "An Episode in the History of Social Research: A Memoir," in Donald Fleming and Bernard Bailyn, eds *The Intellectual Migration: Europe and America, 1930–1960*. Cambridge, MA: Harvard University Press, 270–337.

——(1948). "Role of Criticism in Management of Mass Communications," in Wilbur Schramm, ed. *Communications in Modern Society*. Urbana: University of Illinois Press, 187–203.

——(1941a). "Remarks on Administrative and Critical Communications Research," in *Studies in Philosophy and Social Science* 9 (1), 2–16.

——(1941b). "Some Notes on the Relationship Between Radio and the Press," in *Journalism Quarterly* 18 (1), 10–13.

——(1940). "Introduction by the Guest Editor," in *Journal of Applied Psychology* 24 (6), 661–5.

——(1939). "Radio Research and Applied Psychology," in *Journal of Applied Psychology* 23 (1), 1–7.

——(1938). Unpublished letter, undated, response to Theodor Adorno's manuscript, "Memorandum." Music in Radio, Princeton Radio Research Project, June 26, 1938.

Lazarsfeld, Paul F., Hadley Cantril and Frank N. Stanton (1939). "Current Radio Research in Universities: Princeton," in *Journal of Applied Psychology* 23 (1), 201–4.

Lazarsfeld, Paul F. and Henry Field (1946). *The People Look at Radio*. Chapel Hill: University of North Carolina Press.

Lazarsfeld, Paul F. and Patricia L. Kendall (1948). *Radio Listening in*

America: The People Look at Radio – Again. New York: Prentice-Hall.

Lazarsfeld, Paul F. and Robert K. Merton (1957). "Mass Communication, Popular Taste and Organized Social Action," in Bernard Rosenberg and David M. White, eds *Mass Culture: The Popular Arts in America.* Glencoe, IL: Free Press, 457–73.

Lazarsfeld, Paul F. and Frank N. Stanton, eds (1949). *Communications Research, 1948–49.* New York: Harper Brothers.

——(1944). *Radio Research, 1942–43.* New York: Duell, Sloan & Pearce.

Lazarsfeld, Paul F., Frank N. Stanton, John Niles, Arthur Kornhauser and Samuel Stouffer (1938). "What Happens to the Listener?" in C. S. Marsh, ed. *Educational Broadcasting 1937.* Chicago: University of Chicago Press, 227–57.

Lentricchia, Frank (1982). "Reading History with Kenneth Burke," in Hayden White and Margaret Brose, eds *Representing Kenneth Burke.* Baltimore, MD: Johns Hopkins University Press, 119–49.

Linton, Ralph (1945). *The Cultural Background of Personality.* New York: Appleton-Century-Crofts.

Lippmann, Walter (1922). *Public Opinion.* New York: Harcourt, Brace.

Lowery, Shearon A. and Melvin L. DeFleur (1988). *Milestones in Mass Communication Research*, second edition. New York: Longman.

McLuskie, Ed (1988). "Silence from the Start: Paul Lazarsfeld's Appropriation and Suppression of Critical Theory for Communication and Social Research." Unpublished paper. Boise, ID: Boise State University.

——(1977). "Integration of Critical Theory with North American Communication Study: Barriers and Prospects." Unpublished paper. ICA convention, Berlin, West Germany.

——(1975). "A Critical Epistemology of Paul Lazarsfeld's Administrative Communication Inquiry." Unpublished dissertation, University of Iowa.

McQuail, Denis and Sven Windahl (1981). *Communication Models for the Study of Mass Communications.* New York: Longman.

Matthews, Fred H. (1977). *Quest for an American Sociology: Robert E. Park and the Chicago School.* Montreal: McGill-Queens University Press.

Merton, Robert (1957). *Social Theory and Social Structure.* New York: Free Press.

Mills, C. Wright (1970). *The Sociological Imagination.* Harmondsworth: Penguin Books.

Morrison, David E. (1988). "The Transference of Experience and the Impact of Ideas: Paul Lazarsfeld and Mass Communication Research," in *Communication* 10 (2), 185–209.

——(1978). "Kultur and Culture: The Case of Theodor W. Adorno and Paul F. Lazarsfeld," in *Social Research* 45 (2), 331–55.

Newcomb, Theodore M. (1953). "An Approach to the Study of Communicative Acts," in *Psychological Review* 60 (6), 393–404.

Park, Robert (1923). "The Natural History of the Newspaper," in *American Journal of Sociology* 29 (3), 273–89.

Parsons, Talcott and Edward A. Shils, eds (1951). *Toward a General Theory of Action: Theoretical Foundations of the Social Sciences*. New York: Harper Torchbooks.

Peters, John (1989). "Democracy and American Mass Communication Theory: Dewey, Lippmann, Lazarsfeld," in *Communication* 11, 199–220.

Riesman, David (1959). "Comments," in *Public Opinion Quarterly* 23 (1), 10–13.

Robinson, Gertrude J. (1988). "Paul F. Lazarsfeld & Robert K. Merton: The Columbia School's Contributions to US Communication Studies." Unpublished paper. Montreal: McGill University.

Rose, Gillian (1978). *The Melancholy Science: An Introduction to the Thought of Theodor W. Adorno*. New York: Columbia University Press.

Rosenberg, Bernard and David Manning White (1957). *Mass Culture: The Popular Arts in America*. Glencoe, IL: The Free Press.

Sapir, Edward (1930). "Communication," in Edwin R. A. Seligman, ed. *Encyclopedia of the Social Sciences*, Volume 4. New York: Macmillan, 78–80.

Schramm, Wilbur (1983). "The Unique Perspective of Communication: A Retrospective View," in *Journal of Communication* 33 (3), 6–17.

——ed. (1963). *The Science of Human Communication: New Directions and New Findings in Communication Research*. New York: Basic Books.

——(1959). "Comments," in *Public Opinion Quarterly* 23 (1), 6–9.

——(1957). *Responsibility in Mass Communication*. New York: Harper & Brothers.

——(1954). "How Communication Works," in Wilbur Schramm, ed. *The Process and Effects of Mass Communication*. Urbana: University of Illinois Press, 3–26.

——ed. (1954). *The Process and Effects of Mass Communication*. Urbana: University of Illinois Press.

——ed. (1949). *Mass Communications*. Urbana: University of Illinois Press.

——ed. (1948). *Communications in Modern Society*. Urbana: University of Illinois Press.

Schramm, Wilbur and Donald F. Roberts, eds (1971). *The Process and Effects of Mass Communication*, revised edition. Urbana: University of Illinois Press.

Shannon, Claude and Warren Weaver (1949). *The Mathematical Theory of Communication*. Urbana: University of Illinois Press.

Sherif, Musafer (1936). *The Psychology of Social Norms*. New York: Harper & Row.

Shils, Edward (1961). "Mass Society and Its Culture," in Norman Jacobs, ed. *Culture for the Millions? Mass Media in Modern Society*. Boston: Beacon Press, 1–27.

Siepmann, Charles A. (1950). *Radio, Television and Society*. New York: Oxford University Press.

Sills, David L. (1979). "Lazarsfeld, Paul F.," in David L. Sills, ed. *International Encyclopedia of the Social Sciences: Biographical Supplement*. New York: Free Press, 411–27.

Sklar, Robert (1975). "The Problem of an American Studies Philosophy: A Bibliography of New Directions," in *American Quarterly* 27 (3), 245–62.

Smith, Dennis (1988). *The Chicago School: A Liberal Critique of Capitalism*. New York: St Martin's Press.

Smythe, Dallas W. (1969). "Preface," in Herbert I. Schiller, *Mass Communications and American Empire*. New York: Augustus M. Kelley, vii–viii.

——(1954). "Some Observations on Communications Theory," in *Audio Visual Communication Review* 2 (1), 24–37.

Sproule, J. Michael (1987). "Propaganda Studies in American Social Science: The Rise and Fall of the Critical Paradigm," *Quarterly Journal of Speech* 73 (1), 60–87.

Westley, Bruce and Malcolm S. MacLean (1957). "A Conceptual Model for Mass Communication Research," in *Journalism Quarterly* 34 (1), 31–8.

Willey, Malcolm M. and Stuart A. Rice (1933). "The Agencies of Communication," in *Recent Social Trends in the United States*, edited by the Presidential Committee on Social Trends, Volume 1. New York: McGraw-Hill, 167–217.

Wirth, Louis (1948). "Consensus and Mass Communication," in *American Sociological Review* 13 (1), 1–15.

4 ON INTRODUCING IDEOLOGY: CRITICAL THEORY AND THE CRITIQUE OF CULTURE

Note

A major historical treatment of Critical Theory is provided by Martin Jay (1973), *The Dialectical Imagination: A History of the Frankfurt School and the Institute of Social Research, 1923–1950*. Boston: Little, Brown.

Recent literature on Critical Theory, which should be of particular interest to communication scholarship, includes the following monographs in chronological order:

John O'Neill, ed. (1976), *On Critical Theory*. New York: Seabury Press; Phil Slater (1977), *Origin and Significance of the Frankfurt School: A Marxist Perspective*. London: Routledge & Kegan Paul; Zoltan Tar (1977), *The Frankfurt School: The Critical Theories of Max Horkheimer and Theodor W. Adorno*. New York: Wiley; Susan Buck-Morss (1977), *The Origin of Negative Dialectics: Theodor W. Adorno, Walter Benjamin and the Frankfurt Institute*. New York: Free Press; Andrew Arato and Eike Gebhardt, eds (1978), *The Essential Frankfurt School Reader*. New York: Urizen Books; Thomas McCarthy (1978), *The Critical Theory of Jürgen Habermas*. Cambridge, MA:

MIT Press; Paul Connerton (1980), *The Tragedy of Enlightenment: An Essay on the Frankfurt School*. New York: Cambridge University Press; David Held (1980), *Introduction to Critical Theory: Horkheimer to Habermas*. Berkeley: University of California Press; George Friedman (1981), *The Political Philosophy of the Frankfurt School*. Ithaca, NY: Cornell University Press; Raymond Geuss (1981), *The Idea of a Critical Theory: Habermas and the Frankfurt School*. New York: Cambridge University Press; Eugene Lunn (1982), *Marxism and Modernism: An Historical Study of Lukács, Brecht, Benjamin and Adorno*. Berkeley: University of California Press; Richard Wolin (1982), *Walter Benjamin: An Aesthetic of Redemption*. New York: Columbia University Press; John Thompson and David Held, eds (1982), *Habermas: Critical Debates*. Cambridge, MA: MIT Press; Helmut Dubiel (1985), *Theory and Politics: The Development of Critical Theory*. Cambridge, MA: MIT Press; John Forester, ed. (1985), *Critical Theory and Public Life*. Cambridge, MA: MIT Press; Hazard Adams and Leroy Searle, eds (1986), *Critical Theory since 1965*. Tallahassee: Florida State University Press; Seyla Benhabib (1986), *Critique, Norm and Utopia: A Study of the Foundations of Critical Theory*. New York: Columbia University Press; David Ingram (1987), *Habermas and the Dialectic of Reason*. New Haven: Yale University Press; Tom Rockmore (1989), *Habermas on Historical Materialism*. Bloomington: Indiana University Press.

Also, an indispensable source for an ongoing discussion of issues in Critical Theory and culture is the *New German Critique*.

References

Adorno, Theodor W. (1981). *Prism*. Cambridge, MA: MIT Press.

——(1969). "Scientific Experiences of a European Scholar in America," in Donald Fleming and Bernard Bailyn, eds *The Intellectual Migration. Europe and America, 1930–1960*. Cambridge, MA: Harvard University Press, 338–70.

——(1954). "Television and the Patterns of Mass Culture," in *The Quarterly of Film, Radio and Television* 8 (3), 215–35.

Adorno, Theodor, Else Frenkel-Brunswik, D. J. Levinson and R. N. Sanford (1950), *The Authoritarian Personality*. New York: Norton.

Arato, Andrew and Eike Gebhardt, eds (1982). *The Essential Frankfurt School Reader*. New York: Continuum.

Berelson, Bernard (1959). "The State of Communication Research," in *Public Opinion Quarterly* 23 (1), 1–6.

——(1952). *Content Analysis in Communication Research*. Glencoe, IL: Free Press.

Bernstein, Richard J., ed. (1985). *Habermas and Modernity*. Cambridge, MA: Polity Press.

——(1971). *Praxis and Action: Contemporary Philosophies of Human Activity*. Philadelphia: University of Pennsylvania Press.

Burke, Kenneth (1950). *A Rhetoric of Motives*. New York: Prentice-Hall.

——(1945). *A Grammar of Motives*. New York: Prentice-Hall.

——(1937). *Attitudes toward History*, Volume 2. New York: New Republic.

——(1935). *Permanence and Change: An Anatomy of Purpose*. New York: New Republic.

Carey, James W. (1982). "The Mass Media and Critical Theory: An American View," in Michael Burgoon, ed. *Communication Yearbook 6*. Beverly Hills, CA: Sage, 18–33.

——(1979). "Mass Communication Research and Cultural Studies: An American View," in James Curran, Michael Gurevitch and Janet Woollacott, eds *Mass Communication and Society*. Beverly Hills, CA: Sage, 409–25.

Cartier, Jacqueline (1988). "Wilbur Schramm: The Beginnings of American Communication Theory. A History of Ideas." Unpublished dissertation, University of Iowa.

Casanova Gonzáles, Pablo (1964). "C. Wright Mills: An American Conscience," in Irving Louis Horowitz, ed. *The New Sociology: Essays in Social Science and Social Theory in Honor of C. Wright Mills*. New York: Oxford University Press, 66–75.

Clecak, Peter (1973). *Radical Paradoxes: Dilemmas of the American Left, 1945–1970*. New York: Harper & Row.

Davison, W. Phillips and Frederick T. C. Yu, eds (1974). *Mass Communication Research: Major Issues and Future Directions*. New York: Praeger.

Dewey, John (1960). *Quest for Certainty: A Study in the Relation of Knowledge and Action*. New York: Capricorn Books.

Duncan, Hugh Dalziel (1968). *Symbols in Society*. New York: Oxford University Press.

——(1967a). "Discussion," in Lee Thayer, ed. *Communication: Theory and Research*. Springfield, IL: Charles C. Thomas, 223–7.

——(1967b). "The Search for a Social Theory of Communication in American Sociology," in Frank E. X. Dance, ed. *Human Communication Theory: Original Essays*. New York: Holt, Rinehart & Winston, 236–63.

——(1962). *Communication and the Social Order*. London: Oxford University Press.

——(1953). *Language and Literature in Society: A Sociological Essay on Theory and Method in the Interpretation of Linguistic Symbols*. New York: Bedminster Press.

——(1951). Review of *A Rhetoric of Motives*, in *American Journal of Sociology* 56 (6), 592–4.

Frankfurt Institute for Social Research (1972). *Aspects of Sociology*. Boston: Beacon Press.

Gerbner, George (1983). "The Importance of Being Critical – In One's Own Fashion," in *Journal of Communication* 33 (3), 355–62.

——(1958). "On Content Analysis and Critical Research in Mass Communication," in *Audio Visual Communication Review* 6 (2), 85–108.

Goodman, Paul and Percival Goodman (1960). *Communitas: Means of Livelihood and Ways of Life*. New York: Vintage.

Gouldner, Alvin W. (1981). "Alvin Ward Gouldner – July 20, 1920 – December 15, 1980," in *Transaction: Social Science and Modern Society* 18 (3), 82–3.

——(1976). *The Dialectic of Ideology and Technology: The Origins, Grammar, and Future of Ideology*. New York: Seabury Press.

——(1970). *The Coming Crisis of Western Sociology*. New York: Basic Books.

Gusfield, Joseph R. (1989). *Kenneth Burke: On Symbols and Society*. Chicago: University of Chicago Press.

Habermas, Jürgen (1985). "Questions and counterquestions," in Richard J. Bernstein, ed. *Habermas and Modernity*. Cambridge, MA: Polity Press, 192–216.

——(1984a). *The Theory of Communicative Action*, Volume 1: *Reason and the Rationalization of Society*. Boston: Beacon Press.

——(1984b). *Vorstudien und Ergänzungen zur Theorie des kommunikativen Handelns*. Frankfurt: Suhrkamp.

——(1981). *Theorie des kommunikativen Handelns*. 2 Volumes. Frankfurt: Suhrkamp.

——(1979). *Communication and the Evolution of Society*. Boston: Beacon Press.

——(1971). *Knowledge and Human Interests*. Boston: Beacon Press.

Haight, Timothy R. (1983). "The Critical Researcher's Dilemma," in *Journal of Communication* 33 (3), 226–36.

Hallin, Daniel C. (1985). "The American News Media: A Critical Theory Perspective," in John Forester, ed. *Critical Theory and Public Life*. Cambridge, MA: MIT Press, 122–46.

Hardt, Hanno (1991). "The Conscience of Society: Leo Lowenthal and Communication Research," in *Journal of Communication*, in press.

Hartshorne, Thomas L. (1968). *The Distorted Image: Changing Conceptions of the American Character since Turner*. Cleveland: Case Western Reserve University Press.

Horkheimer, Max (1989). *Critical Theory: Selected Essays*. New York: Continuum.

——(1947). *Eclipse of Reason*. New York: Oxford University Press.

——(1941b). "Notes on Institute Activities," in *Studies in Philosophy and Social Science* 9 (1), 121–3.

Horkheimer, Max and Theodor W. Adorno (1972). *Dialectic of Enlightenment*. New York: Herder & Herder.

Horowitz, Irving Louis (1964). "An Introduction to the New Sociology," in Irving Louis Horowitz, ed. *The New Sociology: Essays in Social Science and Social Theory in Honor of C. Wright Mills*. New York: Oxford University Press, 3–48.

James, William (1967). *The Meaning of Truth*. Ann Arbor: University of Michigan Modern Library.

Jameson, Frederic R. (1982). "The Symbolic Inference; or, Kenneth Burke and Ideological Analysis," in Hayden White and Margaret Brose, eds *Representing Kenneth Burke*. Baltimore, MD: Johns Hopkins University Press, 68–91.

Jay, Martin (1985). *Permanent Exiles: Essays on the Intellectual Migration from Germany to America*. New York: Columbia University Press.

——(1984). *Adorno*. Cambridge, MA: Harvard University Press.

——(1973). *The Dialectical Imagination: A History of the Frankfurt School and the Institute of Social Research, 1923–1950*. Boston: Little, Brown.

——(1972). "The Frankfurt School's Critique of Marxist Humanism," in *Social Research* 39 (2), 285–305.

Journal of Communication (1983) 33 (3). "Ferment in the Field."

Kolakowski, Leszek (1978). *Main Currents of Marxism: The Breakdown*, Volume 3. Oxford: Clarendon Press.

Kracauer, Siegfried (1952–3). "The Challenge of Quantitative Content Analysis," in *Public Opinion Quarterly* 16 (4), 631–42.

Lang, Kurt (1979). "The Critical Function of Empirical Communication Research: Observations on German–American Influences," in *Media, Culture and Society* 1 (1), 83–96.

Lanigan, Richard L. (1988). "Is Erving Goffman a Phenomenologist?" in *Critical Studies in Mass Communication* 5 (4), 335–45.

Lasswell, Harold D. (1935). *World Politics and Personal Insecurity*. New York: McGraw-Hill.

——(1927). *Propaganda Technique in the World War*. New York: Peter Smith.

Lazarsfeld, Paul F. (1969). "An Episode in the History of Social Research: A Memoir," in Donald Fleming and Bernard Bailyn, eds *The Intellectual Migration: Europe and America, 1930–1960*. Cambridge, MA: Harvard University Press, 270–337.

——(1941). "Remarks on Administrative and Critical Communications Research," in *Studies in Philosophy and Social Science* 9 (1), 2–16.

Lentricchia, Frank (1982). "Reading History with Kenneth Burke," in Hayden White and Margaret Brose, eds *Representing Kenneth Burke*. Baltimore, MD: Johns Hopkins University Press, 119–49.

Lerner, Daniel (1979). "Lasswell, Harold," in David L. Sills, ed. *International Encyclopedia of the Social Sciences: Biographical Supplement*. New York: Free Press, 405–11.

Lerner, Daniel and Lyle M. Nelson, eds (1977). *Communication Research – a Half-Century Appraisal*. Honolulu: University of Hawaii Press.

Lippmann, Walter (1925). *The Phantom Public*. New York: Harcourt, Brace.

——(1922). *Public Opinion*. New York: Harcourt, Brace.

Lowenthal, Leo, ed. (1989). *Critical Theory and Frankfurt Theorists: Lectures–Correspondence–Conversations*. New Brunswick, NJ: Transaction.

——(1987). "Berkeley," in Martin Jay, ed. *An Unmastered Past: The Autobiographical Reflections of Leo Lowenthal*. Berkeley, University of California Press, 139–59.

——(1984). *Literature and Mass Culture: Communication in Society*, Volume 1. New Brunswick: Transaction.

——(1967). "Communication and Humanitas," in Floyd W. Matson and

Ashley Montagu, eds *The Human Dialogue: Perspectives on Communication*. New York: Free Press, 335–45.

——(1961). *Literature, Popular Culture, and Society*. Englewood Cliffs, NJ: Spectrum Books.

——(1948). "The Sociology of Literature," in Wilbur Schramm, ed. *Communication in Modern Society*. Urbana: University of Illinois Press, 82–100.

——(1944). "Biographies in Popular Magazines," in Paul F. Lazarsfeld and Frank N. Stanton, eds *Radio Research, 1942–43*. New York: Duell, Sloan & Pierce, 507–48.

Lowenthal, Leo and Norbert Guterman (1949). *Prophets of Deceit: A Study of the Techniques of the American Agitator*. New York: Harper.

Lukács, Georg (1971). *History and Class Consciousness*. Cambridge, MA: MIT Press.

——(1923). *Geschichte und Klassenbewuβtsein* [History and Class Consciousness]. Berlin: Malik Verlag.

——(1916). "Die Theorie des Romans" [Theory of the Novel], *Zeitschrift für Ästhetik und allgemeine Kunstwissenschaft* II, 225–71, 390–431.

Marcuse, Herbert (1978). *The Aesthetic Dimension: Toward a Critique of Marxist Aesthetics*. Boston: Beacon Press.

——(1968). *Negations: Essays in Critical Theory*. Boston: Beacon Press.

——(1964). *One-Dimensional Man: Studies in the Ideology of Advanced Industrial Society*. Boston: Beacon Press.

——(1955). *Eros and Civilization: A Philosophical Inquiry into Freud*. Boston: Beacon Press.

Merton, Robert (1957). *Social Theory and Social Structure*. New York: Free Press.

Mills, C. Wright (1959). *The Sociological Imagination*. New York: Oxford University Press.

——(1956). *The Power Elite*. New York: Oxford University Press.

——(1951). *White Collar: The American Middle Classes*. New York: Oxford University Press.

——(1948). *The New Men of Power: American Labor Leaders*. New York: Harcourt, Brace.

Mosco, Vincent (1983). "Critical Research and the Role of Labor," in *Journal of Communication* 33 (3), 237–48.

Novack, George (1975). *Pragmatism versus Marxism: An Appraisal of John Dewey's Philosophy*. New York: Pathfinder Press.

Packard, Vance O. (1957). *The Hidden Persuaders*. New York: McKay.

Potter, David M. (1954). *People of Plenty: Economic Abundance and the American Character*. Chicago: University of Chicago Press.

Riesman, David (1961). *The Lonely Crowd: A Study of the Changing American Character*. New Haven: Yale University Press.

——(1959). "The State of Communication Research: Comments," in *Public Opinion Quarterly* 23 (1), 10–13.

Rogers, Everett M. (1986). *Communication Technology: The New Media in Society*. New York: Free Press.

Rogers, Everett M. and Francis Balle, eds (1985). *The Media Revolution in America and Western Europe*. Norwood, NJ: Ablex.

Rorty, Richard (1985). "Habermas and Lyotard on Postmodernity," in Richard J. Bernstein, ed. *Habermas and Modernity*. Cambridge, MA: Polity Press, 161–75.

Rosten, Leo (1969). "Harold Lasswell: A Memoir," in Arnold A. Rogow, ed. *Politics, Personality, and Social Science in the Twentieth Century*. Chicago: University of Chicago Press, 1–13.

Schiller, Herbert I. (1989). *Culture, Inc.: The Corporate Takeover of Public Expression*. New York: Oxford University Press.

——(1984). *Information and the Crisis Economy*. Norwood, NJ: Ablex.

——(1983). "Critical Research in the Information Age," in *Journal of Communication* 33 (3), 249–57.

——(1981). *Who Knows: Information in the Age of the Fortune 500*. Norwood, NJ: Ablex.

——(1976). *Communication and Cultural Domination*. White Plains, NY: International Arts and Sciences Press.

——(1973). *The Mind Managers*. Boston: Beacon Press.

——(1969). *Mass Communications and American Empire*. New York: Augustus M. Kelley.

Schroyer, Trent (1975a). *The Critique of Domination: The Origins and Development of Critical Theory*. Boston: Beacon Press.

——(1975b). "The Re-politicization of the Relations of Production: An Interpretation of Jürgen Habermas' Analytic Theory of Late Capitalist Development," in *New German Critique* 5, 107–28.

Shalin, Dmitri N. (1986). "Pragmatism and Social Interactionism," in *American Sociological Review* 51 (1), 9–29.

Shils, Edward (1972). *The Intellectuals and the Powers*. Chicago: University of Chicago Press.

Slack, Jennifer Daryl and Martin Allor (1983). "The Political and Epistemological Constituents of Critical Communication Research," in *Journal of Communication* 33 (3), 208–18.

Smith, Bruce Lannes (1969). "The Mystifying Intellectual History of Harold D. Lasswell," in Arnold A. Rogow, ed. *Politics, Personality and Social Science in the Twentieth Century*. Chicago: University of Chicago Press, 41–105.

Smythe, Dallas W. (1981). *Dependency Road: Communications, Capitalism, Consciousness, and Canada*. Norwood, NJ: Ablex.

Smythe, Dallas W. and Tran Van Dinh (1983). "On Critical and Administrative Research: A New Critical Analysis," in *Journal of Communication* 33 (3), 117–27.

Sproule, J. Michael (1987). "Propaganda Studies in American Social Science: The Rise and Fall of the Critical Paradigm," in *Quarterly Journal of Speech* 73 (1), 60–78.

Stevenson, Robert L. (1983). "A Critical Look at Critical Analysis," in *Journal of Communication* 33 (3), 262–9.

Voskeritchian, Taline D. (1981). "Communication as Drama: The Dramaturgical Idea in the Work of Kenneth Burke, Hugh Duncan and Erving Goffman." Unpublished dissertation, University of Iowa.

Whyte, William H. (1957). *The Organization Man*. New York: Doubleday.

5 ON UNDERSTANDING HEGEMONY: CULTURAL STUDIES AND THE RECOVERY OF THE CRITICAL

Notes

1 The following sources (in chronological order) are particularly useful for a perspective on British Cultural Studies:

Michael Green (1974), "Raymond Williams and Cultural Studies," in *Working Papers in Cultural Studies* 6, 31–48; Colin Sparks (1977), "The Evolution of Cultural Studies . . .," in *Screen Education* 22, 16–30; Larry Grossberg (1977), "Cultural Interpretation and Mass Communication," in *Communication Research* 4, 339–60; Stuart Hall (1979), "Culture, the Media and the 'Ideological Effect'," in James Curran, Michael Gurevitch and Janet Woollacott, eds *Mass Communication and Society*. Beverly Hills, CA: Sage, 315–48; Stuart Hall (1980), "Cultural Studies: Two Paradigms," in *Media, Culture and Society* 2, 57–72; Stuart Hall (1980), "Cultural Studies and the Center: Some Problematics and Problems," and "Introduction to Media Studies at the Centre," in Stuart Hall, Dorothy Hobson, Andrew Lowe and Paul Willis, eds *Culture, Media, Language*. London: Hutchinson & Co., 15–47, 117–21; Raymond Williams (1980), *Problems in Materialism and Culture*. London: Verso; Stuart Hall (1980), "Encoding/decoding," in Stuart Hall, Dorothy Hobson, Andrew Lowe and Paul Willis, eds *Culture, Media, Language*. London: Hutchinson & Co., 128–38; Stuart Hall (1982), "The Rediscovery of 'Ideology': Return of the Repressed in Media Studies," in Michael Gurevitch, Tony Bennett, James Curran and Janet Woollacott, eds *Culture, Society and the Media*. London: Methuen, 56–90; Larry Grossberg (1983), "Cultural Studies Revisited and Revised," in Mary S. Mander, ed. *Communications in Transition*. New York: Praeger, 39–70; Richard Johnson (1983), "What is Cultural Studies Anyway?" Stencilled occasional paper, General Series: SP No. 74, Centre for Contemporary Cultural Studies, University of Birmingham, September 1983; Larry Grossberg (1986), "History, Politics and Postmodernism: Stuart Hall and Cultural Studies," in *Journal of Communication Inquiry* 10 (2), 61–77; Richard Johnson (1987), "What is Cultural Studies Anyway?" in *Social Text* 16 (6), 38–80; John Fiske (1987), "British Cultural Studies and Television," in Robert C. Allen, ed. *Channels of Discourse: Television and Contemporary Criticism*. Chapel Hill: University of North Carolina, 254–90; Colin Sparks (1987), "The Strengths and Limits of the 'Cultural' Approach to Communication," Paper, Communication and Culture Colloquium, Dubrovnik, Yugoslavia, September 1987; Colin Sparks (1990), "Experience, Ideology, and Articulation: Stuart Hall and the Development of Culture," in *Journal of Communication Inquiry* 13 (2), 79–87; Jan Gorak (1988), *The Alien Mind of Raymond Williams*. Columbia: University of Missouri Press; Graeme Turner (1990), *British Cultural Studies: An Introduction*. Boston: Unwin Hyman.

The influence of Cultural Studies upon cultural and historical studies in the United States has been documented in a special issue of *The Radical History Review* 19 (Winter 1978/79), entitled: "Marxism and History: The British Contribution." More recently, the *Journal of Communication Inquiry* 10 (2) (Summer 1986) devoted a special issue to Stuart Hall which contains a working bibliography of Hall's publications. A complete bibliography of Raymond Williams can be found in Alan O'Connor (1989). *Raymond Williams: Writings, Culture, Politics.* London: Basil Blackwell.

2 The theoretical contributions to the literature of feminist studies which are particularly relevant in the context of communication and media studies in the United States include (in chronological order):

Maryann Yodelis Smith (1982), "Research Retrospective: Feminism and the Media," in *Communication Research* 9 (1), 145–60; Janice A. Radway (1986), "Identifying Ideological Seams: Mass Culture, Analytical Method, and Political Practice," in *Communication* 9 (1), 93–123; Paula A. Treichler and Ellen Wartella (1986), "Interventions: Feminist Theory and Communication Studies," in *Communication* 9 (1), 1–18; Lana F. Rakow (1986), "Rethinking Gender Research in Communication," in *Journal of Communication* 36 (4), 11–26; Lana F. Rakow (1986), "Feminist Approaches to Popular Culture: Giving Patriarchy its Due," in *Communication* 9 (1), 19–42; Lana F. Rakow (1987), "Looking to the Future: Five Questions for Gender Research," in *Women's Studies in Communication* 10, 79–86; H. Leslie Steeves (1987), "Feminist Theories and Media Studies," in *Critical Studies in Mass Communication* 4 (2), 95–135; Brenda Dervin (1987), "The Potential Contribution of Feminist Scholarship to the Field of Communication," in *Journal of Communication* 37 (4), 107–20; Kathryn Cirksena (1987), "Politics and Difference: Radical Feminist Epistemological Premises for Communication Studies," in *Journal of Communication Inquiry,* 11 (1), 19–28; Carole Spitzack and Kathryn Carter (1987), "Women in Communication Studies, A Typology for Revision," in *Quarterly Journal of Speech,* 73 (4), 401–23; E. Ann Kaplan (1987), "Feminist Criticism and Television," in Robert C. Allen, ed. *Channels of Discourse: Television and Contemporary Criticism.* Chapel Hill: University of North Carolina Press, 211–53; H. Leslie Steeves (1988), "What Distinguishes Feminist Scholarship in Communication Studies?" in *Women's Studies in Communication* 11 (1), 12–17; Kathryn Cirksena (1989), "Women's Liberation from Spirals of Science: The Need for Feminist Studies in Mass Communication Research," in Ramona Rush and Donna Allen, eds *Communication at the Crossroads: The Gender Gap Connection.* Norwood, NJ: Ablex, 46–58; Elizabeth Long (1989), "Feminism and Cultural Studies," *Critical Studies in Mass Communication* 6 (4), 427–35; Andrea Press (1989), "The Ongoing Feminist Revolution," *Critical Studies in Mass Communication* 6 (2), 196–202; Cathy Schwichtenberg (1989), "Feminist Cultural Studies," *Critical Studies in Mass Communication* 6 (2), 202–8; Lana F. Rakow (1989), "Feminist

Studies: The Next Stage," *Critical Studies in Mass Communication* 6 (2), 209–15.

References

Althusser, Louis (1971). *Lenin and Philosophy and other Essays*. London: New Left Books.

Anderson, Perry (1965). "The Left in the Fifties," in *New Left Review* 29 (January–February), 3–18.

Becker, Howard S. and Irving Louis Horowitz (1972). "Radical Politics and Sociological Research: Observations on Methodology and Ideology," in *American Journal of Sociology* 78 (1), 48–66.

Benjamin, Walter (1969). "The Work of Art in the Age of Mechanical Reproduction," in Hannah Arendt, ed. *Illuminations*. New York: Schocken Books, 217–51.

Bennett, Tony, Colin Mercer and Janet Woollacott, eds (1986). *Popular Culture and Social Relations*. Milton Keynes: Open University Press.

Bennett, Tony, Graham Martin, Colin Mercer and Janet Woollacott, eds (1981). "Editors' Introduction," in *Culture, Ideology and Social Process: A Reader*. London: Open University Press, 9–15.

Bernstein, Richard J. (1971). *Praxis and Action: Contemporary Philosophies of Human Activity*. Philadelphia: University of Pennsylvania Press.

Brantlinger, Patrick (1983). *Bread and Circuses: Theories of Mass Culture as Social Decay*. Ithaca, NY: Cornell University Press.

Carey, James W. (1989). *Communication as Culture: Essays on Media and Society*. Boston: Unwin Hyman.

——(1985). "Overcoming Resistance to Cultural Studies," in Mark R. Levy, ed. *Mass Communication Review Yearbook* 5. Beverly Hills, CA: Sage, 27–40; also in Carey (1989), 89–112.

——(1983). "The Origins of the Radical Discourse on Cultural Studies in the United States," in *Journal of Communication* 33 (3), 311–13.

——(1982). "The Mass Media and Critical Theory: An American View," in Michael Burgoon, ed. *Communication Yearbook* 6. Beverly Hills, CA: Sage, 18–33.

——(1977). "Mass Communication Research and Cultural Studies: An American View," in James Curran, Michael Gurevitch and Janet Woollacott, eds *Mass Communication and Society*. Beverly Hills, CA: Sage, 409–25; the article appeared revised in Carey (1989), 37–68.

——(1975). "A Cultural Approach to Communication," in *Communication* 2 (2), 1–22; the article appeared in Carey (1989), 13–36.

——(1974). "The Problem of History," in *Journalism History* 1 (1), 3–5, 27.

Cassirer, Ernst (1944). *An Essay on Man: An Introduction to a Philosophy of Human Culture*. New Haven: Yale University Press.

Cirksena, Kathryn (1989). "Women's Liberation from Spirals of Silence: The Need for Feminist Studies in Mass Communication: Research," in

Ramona Rush and Donna Allen, eds *Communication at the Crossroads: The Gender Gap Connection*. Norwood, NJ: Ablex, 46–58.

Creedon, Pamela, ed. (1989). *Women in Mass Communication: Challenging Gender Values*. Newbury Park, CA: Sage.

Curran, James, Michael Gurevitch and Janet Woollacott (1982). "The Study of the Media: Theoretical Approaches," in Michael Gurevitch, Tony Bennett, James Curran and Janet Woollacott, eds *Culture, Society and the Media*. London: Methuen, 11–29.

——eds (1977). *Mass Communication and Society*. London: Edward Arnold/Open University Press.

Dervin, Brenda (1987). "The Potential Contribution of Feminist Scholarship to the Field of Communication," in *Journal of Communication* 37 (4), 107–20.

Fiske, John (1987). "British Cultural Studies and Television," in Robert C. Allen, ed. *Channels of Discourse: Television and Contemporary Criticism*. Chapel Hill: University of North Carolina Press, 254–90.

Fraser, Nancy (1989). *Unruly Practices: Power, Discourse, and Gender in Contemporary Social Theory*. Minneapolis: University of Minnesota Press.

Geertz, Clifford (1973). *The Interpretation of Cultures: Selected Essays*. New York: Basic Books.

Gerbner, George (1983). "The Importance of Being Critical – In One's Own Fashion," in *Journal of Communication* 33 (3), 355–62.

Gombrich, Ernest H. (1969). *In Search of Cultural History*. Oxford: Oxford University Press.

Gouldner, Alvin W. (1970). *The Coming Crisis of Western Sociology*. New York: Basic Books.

Gramsci, Antonio (1971). *Selections from the Prison Notebooks of Antonio Gramsci*, edited and translated by Quintin Hoare and Geoffrey Nowell Smith. New York: International Publishers.

Grossberg, Lawrence (1989). "The Circulation of Cultural Studies," in *Critical Studies in Mass Communication* 6 (4), 413–20.

——(1984). "Strategies of Marxist Cultural Interpretation," in *Critical Studies in Mass Communication* 1 (4), 392–421.

Habermas, Jürgen (1971). *Knowledge and Human Interests*. Boston: Beacon Press.

Hall, Stuart (1986). "The Problem of Ideology – Marxism without Guarantees," in *Journal of Communication Inquiry* 10 (2), 28–44.

——(1985). "Signification, Representation, Ideology: Althusser and the Post-Structuralist Debates," in *Critical Studies in Mass Communication* 2 (2), 91–114.

——(1982). "The Rediscovery of 'Ideology': Return of the Repressed in Media Studies," in Michael Gurevitch, Tony Bennett, James Curran and Janet Woollacott, eds *Culture, Society and the Media*. London: Methuen, 56–90.

——(1980a). "Cultural Studies and the Centre: Some Problematics and Problems," in Stuart Hall, Dorothy Hobson, Andrew Lowe and Paul Willis, eds *Culture, Media, Language*. London: Hutchinson & Co., 15–47.

——(1980b). "Introduction to Media Studies at the Centre," in Stuart Hall, Dorothy Hobson, Andrew Lowe and Paul Willis, eds *Culture, Media, Language.* London: Hutchinson & Co., 117–21.

——(1979). "Culture, the Media and the 'Ideological Effect'," in James Curran, Michael Gurevitch and Janet Woollacott, eds *Mass Communication and Society.* Beverly Hills, CA: Sage, 315–48.

Halloran, James D. (1983). "A Case for Critical Eclecticism," in *Journal of Communication* 33 (3), 270–8.

Hardt, Hanno (1989). "The Foreign-Language Press in American Press History," in *Journal of Communication* 38 (2), 114–31.

Hoggart, Richard (1990). *A Sort of Clowning.* London: Chatto.

——(1973). *Speaking to Each Other,* Volume 1: *About Society.* Harmondsworth: Penguin Books.

——(1957, 1970). *The Uses of Literacy: Aspects of Working-Class Life with Special Reference to Publications and Entertainments.* New York: Oxford University Press.

Johnson, Richard (1983). "What is Cultural Studies Anyway?" Stencilled Occasional Paper. General Series: SP No. 74. Birmingham: Centre for Contemporary Cultural Studies.

——(1981). "Against Absolutism," in Raphael Samuel, ed. *People's History and Socialist Theory.* London: Routledge & Kegan Paul, 386–96.

Journal of Communication (1983) 33 (3). "Ferment in the Field."

Kaplan, E. Ann (1987). "Feminist Criticism and Television," in Robert C. Allen, ed. *Channels of Discourse: Television and Contemporary Criticism.* Chapel Hill: University of North Carolina Press, 211–53.

Katz, Elihu, Jay G. Blumler and Michael Gurevitch (1974). "Utilization of Mass Communication by the Individual," in Jay G. Blumler and Elihu Katz, eds *The Uses of Mass Communications.* Beverly Hills, CA: Sage, 19–32.

Laing, Stuart (1986). *Representations of Working-Class Life 1957–1964.* London: Macmillan.

McCombs, Maxwell E. and Donald L. Shaw (1976). "Structuring the 'Unseen Environment'," in *Journal of Communication* 26 (2), 18–22.

——(1972). "The Agenda-Setting Function of Mass Media," in *Public Opinion Quarterly* 36 (2), 76–87.

MacKinnon, Catherine A. (1989). *Toward a Feminist Theory of the State.* Cambridge, MA: Harvard University Press.

McQuail, Denis (1984). "With the Benefit of Hindsight: Reflections on Uses and Gratification Research," in *Critical Studies in Mass Communication* 1 (2), 177–93.

Marwick, Arthur (1962). *The Explosion of British Society, 1914–62.* London: Pan Books.

Meehan, Eileen (1986). "Between Political Economy and Cultural Studies: Towards a Refinement of American Critical Communication Research," in *Journal of Communication Inquiry* 10 (3), 86–94.

Merleau-Ponty, Maurice (1962). *Phenomenology of Perception.* London: Routledge & Kegan Paul.

Miliband, Ralph (1969). *The State in Capitalist Society.* London: Weidenfeld & Nicolson.

Nelson, Cary and Lawrence Grossberg, eds (1989). *Marxism and the Interpretation of Cultures*. Urbana: University of Illinois Press.

O'Connor, Alan (1989a). *Raymond Williams: Writing, Culture, Politics*. London: Blackwell.

——(1989b). "The Problem of American Cultural Studies," in *Critical Studies in Mass Communication* 6 (4), 405–13.

Palmer, Bryan D. (1981). *The Making of E. P. Thompson: Marxism, Humanism, and History*. Toronto: New Hogtown Press.

Pickering, Michael and David Chaney (1986). "Democracy and Communication: *Mass Observation* 1937–1943," in *Journal of Communication* 36 (1), 41–56.

Press, Andrea (1989). "The Ongoing Feminist Revolution," in *Critical Studies in Mass Communication* 6 (2), 196–202.

Rakow, Lana F. (1989). "Feminist Studies: The Next Stage," in *Critical Studies in Mass Communication* 6 (2), 209–13.

Ramazanoglu, Caroline (1989). *Feminism and the Contradictions of Oppression*. London: Routledge.

Samuel, Raphael, ed. (1981). *People's History and Socialist Theory*. London: Routledge & Kegan Paul.

Schroyer, Trent (1975). *The Critique of Domination: The Origins and Development of Critical Theory*. Boston: Beacon Press.

Schwichtenberg, Cathy (1989). "Feminist Cultural Studies," in *Critical Studies in Mass Communication* 6 (2), 202–8.

Shaw, Eugene F. (1979). "Agenda-Setting and Mass Communication Theory," in *Gazette* 25 (2), 96–105.

Sholle, David J. (1988). "Critical Studies: From the Theory of Ideology to Power/Knowledge," in *Critical Studies in Mass Communication* 5 (1), 16–41.

Smythe Dallas W. and Tran Van Dinh (1983). "On Critical and Administrative Research: A New Critical Analysis," in *Journal of Communication* 33 (3), 117–27.

Sparks, Colin (1990). "Experience, Ideology, and Articulation: Stuart Hall and the Development of Culture," in *Journal of Communication Inquiry* 13 (2), 79–87.

——(1987). "British Cultural Studies." Unpublished paper, Colloquium on Culture and Communication, Dubrovnik, Yugoslavia.

——(1977). "The Evolution of Cultural Studies . . .," in *Screen Education* 22 (Spring), 16–30.

Stearns, Peter N. (1982). "Toward a Wider Vision: Trends in Social History," in Michael Kammen, ed. *The Past Before Us: Contemporary Historical Writing in the United States*. Ithaca, NY: Cornell University Press.

Steeves, H. Leslie (1987). "Feminist Theories and Media Studies," in *Critical Studies in Mass Communication* 4 (2), 95–135.

Swedberg, Richard (1986). "The Critique of the 'Economy and Society' Perspective During the Paradigm Crisis: From the United States to Sweden," in *Acta Sociologica* 29 (2), 91–112.

Swingewood, Alan (1977). *The Myth of Mass Culture*. Atlantic Highlands, NJ: Humanities Press.

Thompson, E. P. (1981). "The Politics of Theory," in Raphael Samuel, ed. *People's History and Socialist Theory*. London: Routledge & Kegan Paul, 396–408.

——(1976). "E. P. Thompson," in Henry Abelove *et al.*, eds *Visions of History*. New York: Pantheon, 5–25.

——(1963). *The Making of the English Working Class*. London: Gollancz.

Williams, Raymond (1989a). *Resources of Hope: Culture, Democracy, Socialism*, edited by Robin Gable. London: Verso.

——(1989b). *The Politics of Modernism: Against the New Conformists*, edited and introduced by Tony Pinkney. London: Verso.

——(1980a). "Base and Superstructure in Marxist Cultural Theory," in *Problems in Materialism and Culture: Selected Essays*. London: Verso, 31–49.

——(1980b). "Means of Communication as Means of Production," in *Problems in Materialism and Culture*. London: Verso, 50–66.

——(1979). *Politics and Letters: Interviews with New Left Review*. London: Verso.

——(1977). *Marxism and Literature*. New York: Oxford University Press.

——(1974). "Communications as Cultural Science," in *Journal of Communication* 24 (3), 17–25.

——(1962). *Communications*. Harmondsworth: Penguin Books.

——(1961). *The Long Revolution*. London: Chatto & Windus.

——(1958). *Culture and Society: 1780–1950*. London: Chatto & Windus.

Wolin, Richard (1982). *Walter Benjamin: An Aesthetic of Redemption*. New York: Columbia University Press.

6 ON LOCATING CRITICAL CONCERNS: COMMUNICATION RESEARCH BETWEEN PRAGMATISM AND MARXISM

References

Archer, Margaret S. (1988). *Culture and Agency: The Place of Culture in Social Theory*. New York: Cambridge University Press.

Becker, Howard S. and Irving Louis Horowitz (1972). "Radical Politics and Sociological Research: Observations on Methodology and Ideology," in *American Journal of Sociology* 78 (1), 48–66.

Benedict, Ruth (1961). *Patterns of Culture*. London: Routledge & Kegan Paul.

Bloom, Alan D. (1987). *The Closing of the American Mind*. New York: Simon & Schuster.

Buhle, Paul (1987). *Marxism in the USA: Remapping the History of the American Left*. London: Verso.

Carey, James W. (1989). *Communication As Culture: Essays on Media and Society*. Boston: Unwin Hyman.

Connolly, William E. (1983). "Mirror of America," in *Raritan* 3 (1), 124–35.

Dewey, John (1966). *Democracy and Education*. New York: Free Press.

——(1963). *Freedom and Culture*. New York: Capricorn Books.

——(1954). *The Public and its Problems*. Chicago: Swallow Press.

Douglas, Mary (1966). *Purity and Danger*. London: Routledge & Kegan Paul.

Geertz, Clifford (1973). *The Interpretation of Cultures*. New York: Basic Books.

Goldmann, Lucien (1976). *Cultural Creation in Modern Society*. Oxford: Blackwell.

Gramsci, Antonio (1971). *Selections from the Prison Notebooks of Antonio Gramsci*, edited by Quintin Hoare and Geoffrey Nowell Smith. New York: International Publishers.

Habermas, Jürgen (1979). *Communication and the Evolution of Society*. Boston: Beacon Press.

——(1971). *Knowledge and Human Interests*. Boston: Beacon Press.

Hardt, Hanno (1990). "Newsworkers, Technology and Journalism History," in *Critical Studies in Mass Communications* 7, 346–65.

——(1988). "Marxist Cultures: A Review Essay," in *Journal of Communication Inquiry* 12 (1), 104–10.

Hirsch, Eric D., Jr. (1987). *Cultural Literacy*. New York: Houghton Mifflin.

Jacoby, Russell (1987). *The Last Intellectuals: American Culture in the Age of Academe*. New York: Basic Books.

Journal of Communication (1983) 33 (3), "Ferment in the Field."

Lasch, Christopher (1969). *The Agony of the American Left*. New York: Alfred A. Knopf.

Lazarsfeld, Paul (1941). "Remarks on Administrative and Critical Communications Research," in *Studies in Philosophy and Social Science* 9 (1), 2–16.

Leach, Edmund R. (1965). "Culture and Social Cohesion: An Anthropologist's View," in G. Horton, ed. *Science and Culture: A Study of Cohesive and Conjunctive Forces*. Boston: Beacon Press, 24–38.

Lentricchia, Frank (1983). "Rorty's Cultural Conversation," in *Raritan* 3 (1), 136–41.

Lippmann, Walter (1922). *Public Opinion*. New York: Harcourt, Brace.

Lukács, Georg (1973). *Marxism and Human Liberation: Essays on History, Culture and Revolution by Georg Lukács*, edited by E. San Juan, Jr. New York: Dell.

McLuhan, Marshall (1964). *Understanding Media: The Extensions of Man*. New York: McGraw-Hill.

Malinowski, Bronislaw K. (1944). *A Scientific Theory of Culture*. Chapel Hill: University of North Carolina Press.

Marcuse, Herbert (1968). *Negations: Essays in Critical Theory*. Boston: Beacon Press.

Mead, George Herbert (1969). *Mind, Self, and Society: From the Standpoint of a Social Behaviorist*. Chicago: University of Chicago Press.

Miliband, Ralph (1969). *The State in Capitalist Society: An Analysis of the Western System of Power*. New York: Basic Books.

Park, Robert E. (1922). *The Immigrant Press and Its Control*. New York: Harper & Brothers.

Peters, John (1989). "Democracy and American Mass Communication Theory: Dewey, Lippmann, Lazarsfeld," in *Communication* 11, 199–220.

Rorty, Richard (1982). *Consequences of Pragmatism: Essays 1972–1980*. Minneapolis: University of Minnesota Press.

Samson, Leon (1974). "Americanism as Surrogate Socialism," in John M. Laslett and Seymor Martin Lipset, eds *Failure of a Dream? Essays in the History of American Socialism*. New York: Doubleday, 426–42.

Schiller, Herbert (1969). *Mass Communication and American Empire*. New York: Augustus Kelley.

Schroyer, Trent (1985). "Corruption of Freedom in America," in John Forester, ed. *Critical Theory and Public Life*. Cambridge, MA: MIT Press, 283–316.

Sklar, Robert (1975). "The Problem of an American Studies Philosophy: A Bibliography of New Directions," in *American Quarterly* 27 (3), 245–62.

So, C. Y. K. (1988). "Citation Patterns of Core Communication Journals: An Assessment of the Developmental Status of Communication," in *Human Communication Research* 15 (2), 236–55.

Stott, William (1973). *Documentary Expression and Thirties America*. New York: Oxford University Press.

West, Robin (1989). "Feminism, Critical Social Theory and Law," in *Feminism in the Law: Theory, Practice and Criticism*. The University of Chicago Legal Forum, 59–97.

Williams, Raymond (1961). *The Long Revolution*. New York: Columbia University Press.

Index